Filming *Hour of the Wolf*: Max von Sydow, Liv Ullmann, Bergman and Gertrud Fridh

BERGMAN ON BERGMAN

interviews with Ingmar Bergman by
Stig Björkman
Torsten Manns
Jonas Sima

translated from the Swedish by
Paul Britten Austin

Simon and Schuster
New York

Foreword

Our first meeting with Ingmar Bergman for this book of interviews was held at the Råsunda Film Studios, Solna, in January 1968. We had already spoken to Bergman of our project.

To see whether we could collaborate on it we gathered in Bergman's old room at Råsunda to talk to him about the film *The Hour of the Wolf*, just then due for release. The interview was later published in our magazine *Chaplin* and in similar foreign journals.

After this first tentative interview we agreed to try to produce this book. The main interview started just after midsummer the same year. Altogether we were to have twelve appointments with Bergman to interview him up to the meeting of February 1969. In April 1970 we met Bergman again for yet another interview, partly so that the book could be brought up to date with his two films released in 1969/70, and partly because Bergman himself wanted an opportunity to give an account of his changing view of films and his own new working methods.

Each interview lasted on an average four hours. Altogether we spoke with Bergman about his films for rather more than fifty hours. About half our conversations were tape-recorded. This book is based exclusively on this interview material.

We who are talking with Ingmar Bergman are:
Stig Björkman, b. 1938, architect, editor of *Chaplin*, film critic, film director.
Torsten Manns, b. 1923, translator, editor of *Chaplin*, film critic.
Jonas Sima, b. 1937, journalist, editor of *Chaplin*, film critic, film-maker.

Stockholm, Sweden, 1 May 1970

Solna, 25 June 1968

STIG BJÖRKMAN: Can you tell us something about the genesis of your interest in films and theatre?

INGMAR BERGMAN: It's all so deeply buried in my childhood I can hardly remember. I know the first film I ever saw—it must have been some time in 1924, when I was six or so, at the Sture Cinema in Stockholm—was *Black Beauty*. About a stallion. I still recall a sequence with a fire. It was burning, I remember that vividly. And I remember too how it excited me, and how afterwards we bought the book of *Black Beauty* and how I learned the chapter on the fire by heart—at that time I still hadn't learned to read.

JONAS SIMA: It's said you used to go to film shows with your elder brother.

IB: Yes, at the Östermalm Grammar School. But that was later. On Saturday evenings at six o'clock.

JS: What did you see on those occasions?

IB: Films suitable for schoolchildren. But what fascinated me most I remember was the projector up in the gallery, and the chap who operated it. And how envious I was of him! I was often at my grandmother's in Uppsala, I remember, where I made the acquaintance of a man who was projectionist at the Castle Cinema—I thought of him as someone who went up to heaven every evening. We struck up a friendship and whenever my grandmother let me go to the movies I'd go to the Castle Cinema and stand watching the film from the projection room and save my money.

s b : How old were you then?

i b : About ten or eleven, I suppose. The chap brewed coffee on the rail at the back of the auditorium and used to cuddle me a bit, I remember, but circumspectly: so I don't think anything untoward happened. Anyway, I remember thinking there was something not quite nice about him and so gradually I stopped going there.

In our family we had a well-to-do aunt who always gave us magnificent Christmas presents. She was so much part of the family that we even included her in our prayers at bedtime. At Christmas the basket with all the presents stood under the stairs, and gradually grew fuller and fuller. I suppose I must have been about nine or ten years old at the time. Suddenly Aunt Anna's Christmas presents were lying there too, and among them a parcel with 'Forsner's' on it. So of course I instantly knew it contained a projector. For a couple of years I'd been consumed with a passionate longing to own one, but had been considered too small for such a present.

j s : 'Forsner's'. Were they a well-known dealer?

i b : Yes, a Stockholm photographic firm, in Hamngatan. I was incredibly excited. Because my father was a clergyman we never got our presents on Christmas Eve, like other Swedish children do. We got them on Christmas Day. To survive so long was almost more than I could manage. Well, you can imagine my disappointment when it turned out to be my older brother—he's four years older than myself—who got the projector—and I was given a teddy bear. It was one of my life's bitterest disappointments. After all, my brother wasn't a scrap interested in cinematography. But both of us had masses of lead soldiers. So on Boxing Day I bought the projector off him for half my army and he beat me hollow in every war ever afterwards. But I'd got the projector, anyway.

As long as I live I'll never forget what it looked like, or how it was constructed. Have you seen one of those little machines? Well, it was just a tall tin box, black, with a simple system of lenses and a paraffin lamp and a chimney sticking out of the top. A little smoke would come out of the chimney. One of its functions was to run circular film strips—two or three metres long. Another was to project slides. These could be inserted into the lens system: coloured slides—German, done in poker-work, with Red Riding Hood and Snow White. Then there were films you could buy, the old inflammable sort. The image was as small as could be, the only source of light being a paraffin lamp.

I can still remember every detail of those first films. It was a magical experience. My very first film was a brownish colour and was called *Frau Holle*.

TORSTEN MANNS : That fairytale figure who shakes out feathers all over the place so that the whole image looks as if it is covered with snow?

IB: Exactly! In that film Frau Holle didn't put in the least appearance. There was a girl in national costume who lay sleeping in a meadow. Then she woke and got up and danced around and disappeared off to the right; or if you looked into the lens upside down, she vanished to the left. This repeated itself as long as you went on turning the handle. And that's all there was in the film.

Afterwards I discovered I could go down to Claestorpsboden—a toyshop opposite The Artists' Bar restaurant, in Smålandsgatan, it was already there when I was a kid—and buy films for 5 öre a metre. They had both long reels and short ones. For a number of years I used to go there to buy my films. By and by I discovered I could stick films together with glue. At the chemist's I bought something called acetic ester, which smelt like python and produced, I suppose, the same poisonous effects as paint-thinner.

Then I made up a plot for the scraps of film I'd gradually collected, and as I wound off the reels I would narrate what was going on. I made a sort of container, a sort of film spool, out of Meccano. It could take about 50 to 75 metres of film. And there I sat inside a cupboard with that paraffin lamp, winding and winding my film. (Just imagine what would have happened if it had caught fire! We lived in a big wooden house.) Afterwards this cinema of mine was electrified and a 75-watt bulb was obtained, and fixed with a bulb-holder in such a way that I got a proper image and could see it from six feet away. Gradually I saved up enough money to buy myself a larger projector, which cost the enormous sum of 65 kronor—say $13.00 or £5.50p.

Then I began playing with a theatre—a toy theatre. I've never acted myself—well, once maybe. But mostly it was a toy theatre, with puppets.

JS: Was that a present, too?

IB: No, I'd built it myself. It all started in the most primitive way under the table in the playroom, with the table cloth as curtain. Afterwards, during the years before I took my matriculation exam, I built various puppet and marionette theatres with revolving stages, traps that rose and fell, and all sorts of refinements.

TM: And that brings us up to when?

IB: I took my matric in 1937, so this is the 1924–1937 period.

TM: But the toy theatre—that came . . .?

IB: That came at the age of eleven or twelve.

But to go back to that projector of mine. After a while I bought myself a box camera for Sw.cr. 6:50—say $1.75 or 50p. I made, or rather arranged, films for my box camera; then made a cinema out of cardboard with a screen, on which I glued up the photos I'd taken. I made whole series of feature films and ran them through on that screen and made believe it was a cinema.

JS: And you had an audience?

IB: Yes. Mostly it was my sister who was exposed to all this.

The farce in *The Devil's Wanton*

s b : Do you still possess any of these films?

i b : No, they're all gone.

j s : So you didn't collect all the kids of the district to come and watch your shows?

i b : No, I was far too shy. Now and again, when I put on a show in my theatre, my mother would come and watch. Otherwise there was no audience. When I was about sixteen or seventeen, I staged somewhat larger-scale productions.

s b : What sort of plays did you put on? Were they based on books you had read?

i b : I took them from the whole of world drama. I put on Strindberg's *Lucky Per's Travels* and *Master Olof*—Strindberg featured prominently in the repertoire—and even Maeterlinck's *Blue Bird*. But chiefly they had to be spectacular plays that gave plenty of scope for stage machinery and lighting.

j s : You say you bought films. Did you get Chaplin's films, for instance?

i b : No, they weren't to be had. In fact you couldn't get complete films of any sort, only scraps of newsreels, old feature films and suchlike—all disjointed.

In those days reduction prints simply didn't exist. After I had matriculated I sold the whole lot to a cousin—I was always short of cash—and they got scattered. I don't know where they've gone to. Sometimes I'm sorry about this. It would be fun to see them again. But that little farce in *The Devil's Wanton** is a reconstruction of one little scrap of film I bought at Claestorpsboden.

JS: One has the impression it was a Pathé production.

IB: Yes, it must be an old Pathé, I fancy. It was all about a man who comes into a room where there's a ghost. Suddenly a skull pops out from behind the venetian blinds and the devil jumps out of a chest, and finally a murderer comes in and chases him. Then a policeman chases the murderer, and they all chase each other round and round. But there was never any end to it.

JS: The people you used for your reconstructed version—were they from the ballet?

IB: No, they were three variety artistes, three Italians called Bragazzi, who'd been more or less snowed up here in Sweden.

SB: When you used to put on these plays, did you make the figures for each production, the scenery and so on?

IB: I have a sister, as I've said. She's four years younger than me, and was deeply involved in all that.

JS: During your college years, did you often go to the movies?

IB: I was crazy about movies, yes. Sometimes I still get spasms of it. Particularly when I'm working on a film myself.

JS: Doesn't it distract you?

IB: Not in the least. Formerly, in the beginning, it did, tremendously. I'd go to the cinema in the evening and compare it with what I was doing myself.

SB: Even if one is sure one is making films in one's own way, one still tends to relate what one sees to what one is doing. Individual scenes, particular images which have captured one's interest, can exert an influence?

IB: If I'm busy on some film of my own and I see a film by Vilgot Sjöman or Fellini, for instance, I judge what I see on the basis of what I'm doing. But any direct comparison—no. I keep them in rigid watertight compartments, I think. Sometimes something experienced very intensely in a film can make one's own work seem meaningless for a moment or so. But I get this sort of feeling much more strongly when looking at TV. Then all this business of feature films can suddenly seem quite out of date. Something that could be

* Also known as *Prison*.

dispensed with. Mostly, I suppose, it's a moral dilemma. The dramas we *fabricate* can never approach the drama of TV in suggestive force, immediacy, or their ability to stimulate the imagination.

J S : In other words, you watch TV?

I B : Yes, a great deal.

S B : Do you watch feature films too, on TV?

I B : Yes.

S B : And what's your opinion of that?

I B : I'm no bookworm. Never have been, never will be. But of everything to do with pictures and images I'm omnivorous. All that affects me intensely, closely. Whatever is visible or audible—image and sound—that's what affects me most.

S B : As a schoolboy did you have any film idols?

I B : My childhood and youth during the twenties and early thirties, in the environment where I was growing up, the sort of school I went to, the whole style of life, meant I was walking about half-asleep. As yet nothing had stirred my intellect or woken it up. Emotionally I was confused. I was being brought up in an environment which, in relation to the world I was later to be thrown out into, was utterly naïve. So any stirrings of intellectual hunger were completely unconscious, and I was utterly exposed to any strong influence that might come along. I went to a private school. Much of the time I was ill or absent. And a good deal of it I was up in Dalarna* with my grandmother. The home atmosphere was god-fearing. Everything was fifty years behind the times. I had no mentor, no teacher, no one to take me by the hand and lead me out of it. My schoolmates were just as dumb, just as debile, just as flabby, just as drifting as I was. There was absolutely nothing in our milieu which could wake us up or stimulate us. Outwardly it was a protected world. Inwardly, it was grossly insecure.

T M : By and by something came along which ...?

I B : Yes. I got into high school, as it was called in those days, in 1938. And that was when a faint breeze began to blow, though as breezes go it was a pretty stuffy and fusty one ...

J S : In many ways as an artist you seem, naturally enough, to show close affinities with our Swedish writers and artists of the forties.† Yet you didn't belong to any group. Was there some connection, perhaps, between the

* Rural province in Central Sweden.

† The *'fyrtiotal'*, a period marked by introverted and metaphysical ideas, much influenced by T. S. Eliot and Kafka.

Wild Strawberries: 'A Protected World'

isolation of your parents' home, the lack of social contact you experienced at school and among your schoolmates, and this relative isolation from your own generation and the 'fortyist' groups?

IB: In those days there were watertight bulkheads between people in the theatre, in films, and in literature. Now and again some author would slip through, scribble a script, and get paid for it. This scorn for films and theatre, I suppose, had its roots in the universities; and it rubbed off in high degree on to the literature of the forties—particularly here in Sweden. The theatrical profession repaid this scorn in kind by despising all literary bigwigs and academics. The standing criticism I was subjected to—a criticism so tediously repeated it might have been copied on tracing paper—was that 'Ingmar Bergman is a bad author, but he's an excellent film director and stage producer; and *when* is he going to pack in writing his own scripts, and *when* is he going to begin filming the visions of his contemporaries?' In all quarters my plays were regarded with maximum suspicion.

SB: Did you feel any solidarity with the social, cultural, and philosophical currents of the mid-forties?

IB: Then came existentialism—Sartre and Camus. Above all, Sartre. Camus came later, with a sort of refined existentialism. I came into contact with it in the theatre, among other things in connection with my production of *Caligula* with Anders Ek at the Gothenburg City Theatre in 1946. But its inner political and social contexts largely left me cold.

JS: My thumbnail sketch of your relation to your own generation and the society of the forties is based maybe on a notion that you came to be identified much less than other artists during those years with what was then called the new social awareness. This is a long-standing view among your critics and among Bergman experts, and so perhaps that's why you experience this description...

IB: That I wasn't interested in politics or social matters, that's dead right. I was utterly indifferent. After the war and the discovery of the concentration camps, and with the collapse of political collaboration between the Russians and the Americans, I just contracted out. My involvement became religious. I went in for a psychological, religious line.

JS: Your revolt against the conventions of a bourgeois society—above all against the bourgeois family—is a major theme in all your early productions. Theoretically one might ask why this anti-bourgeois revolt didn't lead to a more socially radical attitude; not least when one thinks of the 'fortyist' writers' close affiliations with socialism and radicalism?

IB: In our day we didn't think of 'fortyism' as a single unified movement, as you, writing history, do today. At that time 'fortyism' consisted of a collection of disparate literary personalities. I was friendly with Lars Ahlin,* and to some extent I associated with Stig Dagerman† and Lars Göransson.

JS: But both Ahlin and Dagerman were deeply conscious of political matters.

IB: Of course. But on the political level we had very little contact with each other. Besides, I wasn't in Stockholm. And that, in this context, was crucial. First I was down in Hälsingborg. Then I moved to Gothenburg. So I lost contact with the literary figures of my generation, most of whom lived and worked in Stockholm.

SB: In *Music in Darkness* ‡ Bengt Eklund, who plays the hero, has been attributed a sort of left-wing socialist involvement.

IB: I had no political passions of any sort. For the most part I was working like a galley-slave to get enough money to support two families. I didn't bother my head about anything except putting on plays and making films.

JS: Do you feel this type of question to be accusatory? The sort of criticism levelled at you, for instance, after *The Virgin Spring*?

* Novelist and short-story writer.   † Novelist and anarchist political writer.
‡ Also known as *Night is My Future*.

'Fortyist' figures: Doris Svedlund in *The Devil's Wanton* and ...

IB: Not in the least! I see its relevance. But the salvation–damnation issue, for me, was never political. It was religious. For me, in those days, the great question was: Does God exist? Or doesn't God exist? Can we, by an attitude of faith, attain to a sense of community and a better world? Or, if God doesn't exist, what do we do then? What does our world look like then? In none of this was there the least political colour. My revolt against bourgeois society was a revolt-against-the-father. I was a peripheral fellow, regarded with deep suspicion from every quarter and no little subjected to material humiliations.

TM: And that's something which seems to have applied to actors too, though today they can't be said to suffer from it here in Sweden. Don't you find it rather strange that a whole group of people—and artists, after all, are quite a big group—didn't somehow try to react against, or reply to, such a view of themselves ...?

IB: The situation in those days was radically different. When I arrived in Gothenburg after the war, the actors at the Municipal Theatre fell into distinct groups: old ex-Nazis, Jews, and anti-Nazis. Politically speaking there was dynamite in that company: but Torsten Hammarén, the head of the theatre, held it together in his iron grasp. And he had an effective means of twisting their arms, don't forget that! In those days there was a good deal of

... Stig Järrel in *Frenzy*

unemployment among actors here in Sweden. And they were underpaid. Contracts only ran for eight months at a time, and for four months of the year no one gave a damn, or needed to, what an actor did with himself. He was expected to be grateful for having a job at all. If it hadn't been for this economic factor it would have been impossible to keep the company—with its strong personalities and violent internal dissensions—together at all.

Apart from the Gothenburg Municipal Theatre there was only the Royal Dramatic Theatre in Stockholm, the Malmö City Theatre, which had just started up, and the city theatre in Hälsingborg. Except for the State Touring Theatre,* for what it was then worth, there was nothing else. So it was understandable if actors were apathetic: despair usually breeds apathy.

J S : But don't you think this very situation provided a breeding-ground for the profession's future growth? It's true, actors as a profession made their break-through here in Sweden in the thirties. But it hasn't been until today that their union has grown powerful and become accepted. Was it perhaps some sort of romantic attitude to their own profession that made it so difficult to unite actors as a group?

* *Riksteatern*, a State-subsidized touring company, which brings drama to outlying parts of the country.

IB: An actor says: 'I've a good part, why should I go on strike for that idiot over there, who hasn't even got any talent?' It's quite another matter to unite people who turn the same bolt on a moving belt. But when it comes to actors you won't find two who see their own profession in the same light.

SB: Maybe many actors feel they are in a unique situation?

IB: It's embedded in their whole psyche. That's what has made it so hard to get actors to be aware of themselves as a profession. When I was appointed head of the Royal Dramatic Theatre, one of the older actors, a very prominent one, said: 'We've got a new boss. So what? I don't give a damn who oppresses me, providing I get good roles.' Gradually actors have come to enjoy a better position, and as they've done so their interest in their professional status has grown. We must never forget that people who are badly off, splintered into little groups where some are better off and some worse, never find it easy to unite.

SB: Do you feel that actors—whether stage or film actors—have a wish, or a need, to submit to an authoritarian will, a producer/director? And that maybe it is this that has retarded their political and social awareness?

IB: You're really asking me two separate questions. First let me answer the one where I'm most sure of myself. An actor exposes himself. He exposes his voice. He exposes his body. He exposes his soul to the public, from a stage, before a camera, or a microphone. In the moment of self-exposure he feels a strong need to have an eye or an ear on him all the time, correcting and controlling; just as a dancer has his mirror, or the musician a tape recorder. It's a perfectly legitimate need, which we must understand and gratify.

But anyone who irresponsibly exploits this need in order to indoctrinate actors is guilty of a dangerous fraud, if you see what I mean. The actor's lack of political and social interest is rooted in the fact that he is his own instrument, in his being in so high degree enclosed within his own world, within himself.

SB: The other day one of the actors at the Royal Dramatic Theatre said something strange: actors, he thought, shouldn't get involved in politics. Only in the theatre.

IB: Actors are no different from other people. At the same time I think all this hysteria about actors being 'socially involved' is a load of nonsense. An actor should feel free to be whatever he wants to be, to do whatever he is capable of doing. I'm opposed to all forms of indoctrination by intimidation. It's wrong.

JS: Concerning Bergman and political involvement, Jörn Donner has formulated the matter very elegantly, I think. Let me quote from his *The Personal Vision of Ingmar Bergman*:* 'His way of setting in question and testing all social conventions makes Bergman, precisely because he concen-

* Bloomington, University of Indiana Press, 1962.

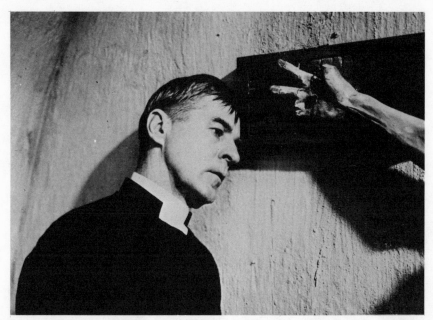

Winter Light: Gunnar Björnstrand

trates on their moral value, a poet for our time.' You describe and interpret a situation of chaos and insecurity in our western culture. That's why Donner regards you as a poet who intuitively stands on the same level as the age. How do you react to such a description? Are you satisfied with such a social alibi from a critic who, when all is said and done, has accused you—is perhaps still accusing you—of the opposite?

I B : Certain things I express with passion. Other things I'm indifferent to. I won't be pushed about or let myself be dragged this way or that. I refuse absolutely to adapt myself to a formula or a system, or to concern myself with anything that doesn't interest me, because from that moment I know I'd be making a bad job of it.

S B : You give an account of your experience of the world. But you don't make films programmatically?

I B : No, never tied to any ideology. I can't. For me nothing of that exists.

J S : Yet at the same time you're rigorously faithful to your own basic view of things. People like to see the films you've made as constituting a single whole.

I B : My basic view of things is—not to have any basic view of things. From having been exceedingly dogmatic, my views on life have gradually dissolved. They don't exist any longer.

JS: I'd like to hark back to Jörn Donner's statement: that you're a poet who stands intuitively on the same level as the age. Suddenly here you are saying 'I'm someone who hasn't any opinions.' Well, let's turn the problem upside down and say—to put it rather pompously—that you're still standing on the same level as the age, but that what you're now speaking of is itself one of the dilemmas of the age.

IB: I'm a radar set. I pick up one thing or another and reflect it back in mirrored form, all jumbled up with memories, dreams, and ideas. A longing and a will to form.

JS: In today's society is it really possible to have no ideology? However difficult it may be, surely one is obliged to adopt *some* political attitude?

IB: I've a strong impression our world is about to go under. Our political systems are deeply compromised and have no further uses. Our social behaviour patterns—interior and exterior—have proved a fiasco. The tragic thing is, we neither can nor want to, nor have the strength to alter course. It's too late for revolutions, and deep down inside ourselves we no longer even believe in their positive effects. Just around the corner an insect world is waiting for us—and one day it's going to roll in over our ultra-individualized existence. Otherwise I'm a respectable social democrat.

TM: You have said how much you've been influenced and fascinated by Strindberg. But your view of women is quite different from his. After all, you're *in favour of* women. Strindberg's a misogynist . . .

IB: Strindberg's way of experiencing women is ambivalent. While he's an obsessive worshipper of women, he also persecutes them obsessively. He does both things at once. His psyche is fifty percent woman and fifty percent man. You can see this most clearly in *Miss Julie*, where the man and the woman never stop swapping masks. As for my so-called view of women, there's nothing particularly methodical about it, as Marianne Höök,* for instance, has tried to make out in her Bergman book. In all dramatists certain basic types appear, and then are disguised in various ways, which makes it easy to recognize these basic types if one is so inclined. But I draw no special distinction between male and female. I've no decided view of women. I enjoy working with women, but—as I told your colleague Lars-Olof Löthwall in an interview—that's simply because I'm a man.

JS: It seems to me you almost always describe woman—to put it in the simplest terms—as a sexual creature with a very strong capacity for survival; and then depict the intellectual woman, the modern emancipated female, as cold and frigid and neurotic. Take, for example, Cecilia in *So Close to Life*,†

* Marianne Höök: *Ingmar Bergman*, Stockholm, 1962.
† Also known as *Brink of Life*.

Harriet Andersson in *Now About These Women*   Ingrid Thulin in *Wild Strawberries*

and Ester in *The Silence*, both, significantly enough, played by the same actress, Ingrid Thulin. To me they seem unhappy precisely because they take a modern view of womanhood.

IB: The fact is, I plead innocent to Cecilia, inasmuch as she was Ulla Isaksson's creation. But Ester—I'll accept responsibility for her. Ester in *The Silence* could just as well have been a man. In fact, in my original draft, she *was* a man. Ester and Anna were man and woman. So you can't find anything there about the emancipated woman being in any way more neurotic or frigid or wrong-headed, or anything of that sort.

JS: So, you've no reservations against the modern, socially conscious woman?

IB: On the contrary. After all, I associate daily with professional women in my job, and really I don't regard them as damaged or neurotic. Surely the slow and complex process of liberation we are watching today can only be regarded as something admirable and heartening?

JS: Do you think your films contain female figures who constitute something of a direct comment on the current discussion about the woman question, the life-rôles of the sexes?

IB: No, none.

JS: But surely you will admit that certain views of the life-rôles of the sexes are to be found in your earlier work? An adorable melting girl should look like an adorable melting girl?

IB: Yes, I think there were such views. But we must distinguish between how I see things today and how I saw them quite a while back—ten or fifteen years ago.

SB: In this context Nelly, in *To Joy*, is surely a highly charged figure?

IB: Yes, terribly.

TM: And then—as Jonas says—you have flowery figures and soft, rounded ones. Anna in *The Silence*.

JS: In her book, Marianne Höök makes use of a model in discussing your female rôles. She operates with three types of woman: 'the Venus triumphant'—Eva Dahlbeck—while Diana is represented by Anita Björk, and Ingrid Thulin stands for Hebe.

IB: For people who write books the main thing is often to be able to get hold of a point of view. They assert that things are like this or that: then they force their square pegs into round holes. There may possibly be something in what Marianne Höök says. I just think it's all totally uninteresting.

TM: In that case it's also totally uninteresting to ask you where Liv Ullmann can be squeezed into the system?

IB: Yes, totally uninteresting. I'm enormously fascinated by her. I find her an immensely suggestive actress. She has a long stage career behind her. I've worked with her in the theatre. I see various rôles mirrored in her face. It's a face which can lend itself to an immense number of different rôles. And then, in private life, she rather appeals to me—but that's another matter.

SB: These 'models' which Marianne Höök has described—one might say they have provided the basis for your portraits in *Now About These Women*, a film in which you really gave the public and the critics all they wanted in the way of female types.

IB: That film is an outburst of really bad temper. I looked at it again a few weeks ago. I hadn't seen it since the fiasco, so I thought it would be amusing to take another look at it. And I thought to myself when I saw it: 'that was a bloody nasty film'. At the same time I realized how it ought to have been made. Well, that's to say, I'd realized that some time before. But let's leave that.

SB: I don't know that we should. I think it's a film which has been both misunderstood and too little appreciated.

IB: Yes, I think so too. But as far as I know it was a catastrophe wherever it went.

SB: In France and Britain, at least, it got a positive reception from the critics . . .

IB: Really? I didn't know that. I just put it back into the cupboard. I regarded it as a product that had turned rancid. But can't we talk about this when we get to it? When I made that film I was tired and fed up. And it shows. It's a nasty, hurt sort of film. It's based on a real incident. My then wife—who is a pianist—had a teacher, an Italian, who was married to a prominent German violinist—he died a few years ago—who used to tour the world with her, staying in châteaux and manor houses. He was a little, fat, boss-eyed man who had something remarkably demonic about him, and she had to play traffic-cop to all his women. He suffered from some sort of satyr complex, had to have one woman after another. And the women were crazy about him—all the time, everywhere.

That's where the story begins—I thought it was an amusing idea for a film. They were staying with some wealthy old ladies, one of whom had once launched him on his career in his youth and kept him and brought him up— an utterly lower-class, utterly uneducated, utterly amoral man, but a fantastic musician.

Then one day—long after the film was finished—my wife's teacher showed me an album with photos of their wild life. And there—it sounds silly, telling it now, but I can't resist it—there, suddenly, was the photograph of how the film *ought* to have been made! It shows the violinist, a château, and the steps leading up to the château. Obviously it's evening. The sunlight is falling from a low angle. The musician, together with some equally celebrated geniuses, presumably after a good dinner, is standing on the steps outside the château. The plaster is flaking off one of the walls, and the steps are all weed-grown. In the background, set at an angle across one corner, can be seen an old tumble-down pavilion, and at the bottom right is a statue, which also looks as if all the doves of the last fifty years have been using it as a shithouse. In the background are a couple of glass doors. Behind the glass doors a glimpse of the faces of four or five women, one an old witch—looked at through a magnifying glass it's the most vicious face one can possibly imagine! Well, there they stand, those old robbers with pot-bellies and misty spectacles, slightly unshaven and in their crumpled summer suits, all a bit spotty and unbuttoned. And everything's just decay and drunkenness and laziness and summer evening and a dense stench of sweat and lechery—and yet, over this madly comic world, some sort of endless peace and calm.

That's how the film should have been made! That's the world Cornelius ought to have got into. That's how I should have made *Now About These Women*. Walls ought to have come tumbling down. Beds should have collapsed. And all these people should have been staggering about, as it were. As it is, the whole thing's glossy, sophisticated, swift, hard, and poisonous. And

Inga Landgré and Marianne Löfgren in *Crisis*

they're all too aesthetic—while really everything should have been dreadfully unaesthetic, dreadfully slow, dreadfully indifferent, dreadfully tumbledown. And in all this mess there should have been just this one heavenly clear ray of sunshine—when the violinist puts his hand to his instrument.

TM: Let's go back to *Crisis*, your début as a film director, in 1945. You tried to evoke an authentic small-town milieu.

IB: No, Torsten, the film's lousy, through and through. Carl-Anders Dymling* came down to see me at Hälsingborg—I was artistic director of the theatre there, 1944 I think it was. He'd just bought a Danish play called *Moderdyret* or something of that sort. It was an out-and-out bit of whoredom for the public—and no one could ever have called it anything else. He wanted to make a film of it. But everyone he'd asked had backed down. He said to me: 'If you make *Moderdyret*, you can make a film.' I replied: 'I'll make any rubbish you like, providing I can make a film.' For that was what I was longing to do above all—more than anything else I was longing to be allowed to make films. Dymling replied: 'Well, it's decided, then.' And so I was to make my first film! I went almost crazy with joy. There's one sequence in it which went well, and that's the bit in the beauty salon. About 200 metres.

* Then managing director of Svensk Filmindustri AB.

T M : You mean where Marianne Löfgren's head is 'chopped off'?

I B : The whole of that sequence has a sort of suggestive quality about it. Suddenly the film jells.

S B : Don't you think the actors are good, either?

I B : No. Nothing's good.

S B : I'd like to put a technical question—about your scripts. How do you usually write them? Do you gather material for your films in note form, jot down ideas and scenes as they come to you, and then work them up later into scripts? Or do you usually write them straight off the cuff?

I B : For a long time I go about with one or two ideas in my head, gathering material, making notes, and so on. Since I've always been busy with so many things, I've had to be methodical about the way I divide up my working time. I know a time will come when I shall be able to say: 'Now I've got six or eight weeks, when I can write my script.' So it's all planned well in advance. Then all I have to do is to sit down and make a start. After which the writing of the script goes on in a very, very methodical, very disciplined, very pedantic fashion.

S B : So you work more or less like someone in an office, from nine to five?

I B : Half-past nine to three; and then I don't do anything else. This is all I have to do. The arrangement suits me, I like it. If I'm to improvise, I must have made thorough preparations. If I'm not prepared I can't improvise.

J S : How do you stand vis-à-vis the romantic and naturalistic tradition in Swedish art and literature?

I B : That's something I can't possibly sort out now. It's so deeply interwoven with my own experience. Where it's to be found and how much it has influenced me—no, it's all so deeply integrated. I can't sort that out today.

J S : Strindberg's *The Son of a Servant* seems to have played a certain part during your rebellious years . . .

I B : Strindberg's aggressions—and my own—that's what made the deepest impression on me. As for Strindberg's humour, I didn't even notice it. *The People of Hemsö*,* for instance, left me pretty well cold. What I felt most strongly were the big angry pieces, *Svarta Fanor* (*Black Banners*), etc. As for *The Red Room*,† well, I knew its opening chapter virtually by heart.

J S : Did you read plays in those days, too?

I B : Yes, and even earlier. But Strindberg has followed me all my life. Sometimes I've felt deeply attracted to him, sometimes repelled.

* *The People of Hemsö* (1887). Trans. Elizabeth Harley-Schubert. Jonathan Cape, 1959.

† *The Red Room* (1879). Trans. Elizabeth Sprigge. J. M. Dent & Sons (Everyman's Library), 1967.

23

JS: Did you feel there was something similar between Strindberg's artistic temperament and your own?

IB: No. It was just that he expressed things which I'd experienced and which I couldn't find words for. I was stuffed with inhibitions—that's something we mustn't forget in this connection. I had difficulty in speaking, sometimes I even stammered a little, as I still do at times to this day. I also found it hard to express myself in writing—a tremendous resistance. I couldn't draw. I couldn't sing. I played a little, but wasn't much of a hand at any musical instrument, either——I found it hard to read the music. I couldn't dance. I was shut in in every way.

JS: Your adolescence was unusually troublesome?

IB: Yes, you can certainly say that. About as near to a madhouse as anything could be.

JS: Sometimes it is said that you've been influenced by the Swedish writers of the 1910–20 period—Hjalmar Söderberg* and Hjalmar Bergman†?

IB: Yes, but Hjalmar Bergman came later.

JS: Did you read much as a youngster?

IB: Yes, much more than I do now. In those days I had much more time for it. From a literary point of view, though, I must say my reading-matter was pretty well indiscriminate. I hadn't much literary judgment, and read pretty well anything. I only began to have some discrimination when I started at university; and for that I have to thank the education of my fellow-students.

TM: And you had no mentor at that time, either?

IB: No. But Martin Lamm‡ and his lectures were absolutely crucial. What I'm trying to say—though somehow I find it difficult to formulate—is that the boy who tried to start up some sort of a confused artistic activity at the end of the thirties lacked any sort of bearings and was really made up of nothing but one big emotional tumult, with aggressions flying out in all directions. Intellectually he was virtually in a blackout; immature and undeveloped. Yes, that's more or less the picture I'd like to draw of myself at the age of eighteen to twenty; and I don't think it's just a retrospective rationalization, either. On the contrary, it's something I now realize almost with a feeling of terror. All this other aspect of the matter—my masters in films, in theatre, my idols, my view of life—all that sort of thing only came very slowly; and very very late.

For instance: during the five years I was in Gothenburg and Torsten Hammarén was head of the theatre there. But it simply never dawned on me

---

* Hj. Söderberg (1869–1941): *Doctor Glas*. Trans. Paul Britten Austin, 1963. Chatto & Windus and Atlantic Monthly Press, 1964.

† Hj. Bergman (1883–1931).

‡ Martin Lamm, professor of Swedish literature.

to regard him as my teacher; I fought him all the way. Sometimes I hated him. But I sat in on his rehearsals. When he was showing the actors how to play farce, for instance—and he knew more about how to produce farce, this remarkable man, than any Swede who ever lived—I could never really understand why I was sitting there at all; and when he interrupted my rehearsals and talked to the actors over my head, then I'd rush out of the door in a rage, firmly determined never to come back again. For half an hour I'd sit and sulk in the w.c. Then I'd go in again, hear him altering my instructions and realize I was learning something from this, however heavy-handed his methods were. It was the same with Lorens Marmstedt—at the time I never realized he was teaching me anything. Does all this interest you? If so, we'll talk about it a little.

TM: Yes, of course.

IB: When I was making *Crisis*, Victor Sjöström was the only living person who could even talk to me or I had the least respect for. All through that dreadfully unhappy period he was kind to me. After he'd seen the day's rushes he'd come in and have a chat. If the entire production wasn't cancelled— Sjöström was artistic director out here at Råsunda in those days—it was almost entirely his doing. At that moment Ingmar Bergman's to-be-or-not-to-be as a film director really hung by a thread! But Sjöström chatted with me in the mornings and was decent to me. At the same time he was enormously good for me in a way I didn't appreciate then. He gave me the benefit of his own immense experience. I felt safe with him.

But then along came Lorens Marmstedt and looked at my rushes in a sort of cold fury and called me an incompetent bloody amateur—swore we'd have to scrub the whole production—that he'd have to call in Hasse Ekman to make the film instead—that he must find some form for it, yet keep it all wide open—and if I thought I was some sort of a Marcel Carné, and Birger Malmsten was a Jean Gabin, then I was bloody well mistaken, and we were a couple of idiots living in a dreamland of wishful thinking. When we were filming, he said, we weren't filming at all, we were just 'soul-shaking'. 'Bloody soul-shakers,' he called us, acting out our private lives in public, a bunch of traitors; no, worse, charlatans, who were throwing away his money. He couldn't stand the sight of me. I was pretentious and nasty—the lot!

Well, I didn't mince my words, either. I told him he was nothing but a vulgar, conceited playboy. He ought to stick to his confounded vices, I said, and not meddle with artistic matters he didn't know the first thing about. That's how we carried on! But one thing he did teach me—apart from being the first person ever to invest in me by letting me make *The Devil's Wanton*, my first script—and taught me thoroughly, and I'm eternally grateful to him for it. He taught me to look coldly and objectively at my own rushes. I hate the word 're-run', but when one looks at one's own takes one is hoping with all one's heart that they'll be good; that the pictures will have something; that all one has thought and dreamed up will have become manifest in them. And all the other people, too, sitting there looking at your rushes with you, from cameraman to script-girl, you know they, too, are all hoping and dreaming the same thing: that what we're going to see will be good, well-made, well-acted, beautiful, effective pictures. Lorens taught me to be objective, to observe coldly, to ask myself whether I've realized my intentions—or whether I haven't. This is a lesson I've applied ever since, down to the last detail, and one I've tried to pass on to my colleagues.

Looking at our own rushes we have to act as if we were our own critics—but completely objective and unneurotic critics, without any crises of conscience. The material goes rushing by, and all that matters is to decide what's good and what's bad. Only on these terms can one go ahead. And the same applies in the cutting room, and when the film is first run. I think it was Faulkner who coined the expression 'kill your darlings'. These two rules, for me, are basic.

TM : And did your relationship to Victor Sjöström and Lorens Marmstedt stay that way?

IB : No; with Victor Sjöström it was different. His films have meant a tremendous lot to me, particularly *The Phantom Carriage* (1921) and *Ingeborg Holm* (1913).

TM : When did you see them?

IB : It must have been when I joined SF in 1941, and began looking through the whole archive of silents. I'd seen *The Phantom Carriage* before, and it had made a strong impression. I'd first seen it when I was about sixteen. There are scenes in *Sons of Ingmar* and *Karin Ingmarsdotter* which with their precision, their lack of sentimentality, their genuineness and clarity, still make the same educative impression of being honest artistic products. It's there Victor Sjöström has meant most to me. But Lorens Marmstedt still means a great deal to me today. He was stimulating. He egged me on. He was irritable, enthusiastic. When we'd got as far as making *The Devil's Wanton*, which we had to shoot in eighteen days on a budget of 150,000 Sw.cr. ($30,000, £10,000), he offered his support and backed us up and encouraged us—it was magnificent. So I'm really deeply in his debt.

SB : Just after you had made your international breakthrough there was a lot of speculation about whether you would be making films outside Sweden. There was a persistent rumour going the rounds that what was in question was something by Camus—obviously some American offer. Were there any serious plans for that? I don't remember which book it was.

IB : I think it was *The Downfall*. Things had even gone so far that Camus and I had conversed by letter. I was to go and see him and we'd make the script together. It wasn't to have been a major production—the film had been suggested by Hecht-Lancaster, a small but ambitious firm. And the budget was small. But then Camus was killed in that car accident, and nothing came

of it. Though I don't think I'd have managed it anyway. I th
been a poor film.

JS: But you were keen to do it?

IB: Chiefly because it would have been marvellous to have met Camus.

JS: You haven't mentioned Kafka among your literary influences.

IB: No, but it's obvious.

JS: Like other artists, I suppose you don't like questions aimed at tracking down influences?

IB: No, I don't, not at all! My view is, I'm the sum total of everything I've read, seen, heard, and experienced. I don't believe that an artist has his roots in the air. I regard myself as a little brick in a big building, dependent on what is on either side of me, under me, and behind me.

JS: That's extremely interesting, not least in relation to what you said about the experiences of your youth being so confused, almost chaotic; now you give the impression of being very clear and straightforward about your intellectual experiences.

IB: Anyone who gradually discovers there's something artistic about himself, something tumultuous and unclear, that he's an intellectually suspect hodge-podge, becomes somewhat guarded. It's like the day one realizes one is getting a pot belly and methodically starts getting rid of it. In my job it's a torment not to be physically nimble. To have to drag a great heavy body around with one is dreadfully unpleasant physically.

I've often thought how Hitchcock must suffer from it. Much of Hitchcock's limitations, I think, but also his greatness within them, are to be found in his heavy body. His way of always working in the studio, using a static camera, not moving about, he has erected it all into a system, using long scenes where he won't have to give himself the trouble of having to move about.

JS: What a theory! It fits Orson Welles, too. He likes to work in a studio, too.

SB: Yes, but no one could call his films immobile. He lets his camera rush through his sets.

IB: Yes, but it can also go by contraries. Suddenly this heavy man finds he has an instrument capable of flying. He can't fly, but his instrument can! For my part, anyway, I feel a need to be not only physically nimble but also to try to keep my resources, the ones I still haven't sorted out, in some sort of good order. It's a fight against chaos. If you're chaotic your artistry is restricted. You can't survey things properly. You fall victim to a lot of dubious impulses, each pulling in a different direction.

SB: Perhaps we can return to what we were saying about the way you construct your scripts? In which case let's take your second film, *It Rains on Our Love*. Why did you choose to use a narrator to tell the story?

A Ship to India: Gertrud Fridh and Holger Löwenadler

IB: I didn't write the script. It was Herbert Grevenius.

JS: Based on a play by Oskar Braathen?

IB: *Decent People* or some such name, it had, in Norwegian. Anyway, that Braathen fellow's a good writer. He had written some good Norwegian folk-plays, though I didn't realize it at the time. I got hold of his MS at a late stage and the only thing I wrote into the play is the trial at the end. All the rest of the script was by Grevenius.

SB: When you were making your first films, with ready-made scripts, did they let you change them? Did you want to? And if so, how?

IB: Yes, they let me change them within certain limits—after discussions between Lorens and Herbert and myself. *Ship to India** was given me ready-made, too. A play I had to turn into a film. I remember Lorens calling me down to the Riviera, where he was playing roulette. He gave me a lesson both in roulette and script-writing.

SB: The story of *It Rains on Our Love* is told in a manner reminiscent of an old broadsheet.

IB: As was intended.

* Also known as *The Land of Desire*.

28

Woman Without a Face: Gunn Wållgren and Alf Kjellin

J S : It shows a heavy influence from the *film noir*.

I B : Yes. At that time the *film noir* directors were my gods. One who meant a lot to me was Michael Curtiz. I remember how Lars-Eric Kjellgren and I— we'd started together at SF and were close friends—saw Curtiz's films, the same films, over and over again, evening after evening, to find out how he did it. It was extremely good for us. Curtiz knew how to tell a story quite clearly, simply, and straightforwardly, as Raoul Walsh did.

J S : Then came *Woman Without a Face*, in 1947.

I B : Yes, but I didn't make it.

T M : Is there much of yourself in it?

I B : Yes, it's my script.

J S : Would you have liked to make it instead of Gustaf Molander?

I B : Yes, but I was flattered and grateful. Besides, I got some money for it.

J S : What do you think that film would have been like if you had directed it?

I B : Cruder, I suppose; because it bristles with aggressions. Maybe I would have chosen other actors, if they had let me. But the people at SF had their heads screwed on. If I'd made it, God knows how it would have turned out!

TM: Isn't Molander's work extremely sophisticated?

IB: It is.

TM: Which clashes with the script?

IB: But it was well-made, really worth looking at. I don't remember much about *Woman Without a Face*, though.

TM: The character of Ruth Köhler—would you like to tell us something about it?

IB: Well, she was based on personal experiences, which I wrote out of my system. In those days I was living artistically from hand to mouth, taking things that had happened—anything, just to get something out.

JS: Is Ruth Köhler—one of the books about you says so—more or less a portrait from life?

IB: Yes. Not more or less, either, but in high degree. But Gustaf tidied it up very cleverly, to make it acceptable to the audiences of those days. It was a box-office success.

TM: Do you think he has romanticized the relationship between Gunn Wållgren and Alf Kjellin?

IB: Certainly.

TM: Frenchified it?

IB: Without question. But, unlike many other people, I've tremendous respect for Gustaf Molander. I've learned a lot from him, and he was always generous and friendly and helpful; a real colleague, in the best sense of the word. He never adopted a dog-in-the-manger attitude about what he knew. He shared it around.

TM: You weren't in on the shooting?

IB: No, not at all.

JS: You wrote the script for *Ship to India* and directed it from a play by Martin Söderhjelm, in 1947?

IB: That's right.

SB: Two motifs appear in it, which you developed afterwards: the father complex and authoritarianism, for one . . .

IB: But that was in the play already, though I stressed it.

SB: And then the play-within-the-play, which you so often use in your films:

I'm thinking of the visit to the variety show. These plays become little intermezzi . . .

I B : Quite.

S B : Were they in the play, too, or were they your additions?

I B : The variety show wasn't in the play, it came into existence step by step. But that sort of thing has always fascinated me. Hesse's 'Magical Theatre', I suppose. *Ship to India* was on TV a year or so ago. But I didn't dare to see it.

J S : That was the first time I'd seen the film. I like seeing old films like that on television. They've got such a special atmosphere, and they suit TV admirably. Drinking whisky and looking at nostalgic old films from the forties . . .

T M : Old films from the forties! You talk as if it was fifty years ago!

J S : One can look at a Stroheim film from the twenties and feel it has more in common with us today . . .

I B : Listen, boys, don't let's forget—Jonas, you once made a joke of it (you see I don't forget things. I don't bear grudges, but I've got a long memory!)— I said once that 'The first artistically ambitious Swedish film was *Ingeborg Holm*, of 1913'. And now we're in 1968. That's about fifty years ago, rather more than fifty years ago, and for twenty-five of these years I've been making films myself. That's to say, I've been at it during half the entire epoch in which films have even existed as an art-form. And that feels strange.

J S : Where do I come in?

I B : At the time you wrote something a trifle ironical about 'magisterial utterances'—or something of that sort. It feels strange sometimes, really it does, that the cinema should be such a young art. The moving picture was only invented in 1895. And Chaplin is still alive!

It's extraordinary: 1895—the life-span of one man! Seventy years, during which the film has existed as a medium. Strange, isn't it?

T M : Jazz is younger still, but already it's finding existence problematic.

I B : It has fallen into a decline, they say; but the film has gone on developing all the time and is flourishing—things are always happening in the cinema.

T M : And this brings us to *Music in Darkness*.

J S : Dagmar Edqvist wrote the script. Did you have a hand in it?

I B : Yes, I did.

J S : And Mai Zetterling was the star?

I B : Yes.

J S : And Bengt Eklund plays a left-wing socialist.

31

IB: I had nothing to do with that.

TM: I remember that scene where Birger Malmsten gets shot . . .

IB: But Lorens cut almost the whole of it. Originally there was twice as much. It was a long nightmarish story. I'd made it up.

TM: I find the film a trifle dull.

IB: Don't let's talk about it. It was a silly little film, but it was my first popular success. It went rather well. Very well, even. And it was then, I remember, that Svensk Filmindustri came forward. What's the name of that fellow with the perennials?

TM: Olle Länsberg.

IB: Yes, he'd sent in a manuscript an inch thick, called *The Gold and the Walls*, and they asked me if I'd make a film of it.

JS: So it was this scenario which became *Port of Call*?

IB: Yes, and it was fun going about Gothenburg with Länsberg and looking at the place from the inside. It was true I'd been living there for years, but I detested the place.

SB: Obviously you were still going to the cinema a lot. It was made in 1948; and 1947, one could say, was the year the neo-realists made their breakthrough.

IB: Exactly.

JS: Which undoubtedly influenced the film.

IB: Influenced it—it's in the spirit of Rossellini throughout.

TM: It came so close on his heels, yet you had already snapped up the new style?

IB: I still had nothing of my own to offer.

TM: But to achieve that style so quickly, and be so receptive to it!

IB: Well, I hadn't any of my own. Each time I went to the cinema I thought 'this is what I must do, this is how it's got to be'. I felt every camera angle was a reproach to my own. I was staggering about, quite lost, and clutching at anything I could. It wasn't my fault. Things had just turned out that way, without me knowing how or why, and I couldn't do a thing about it. I had no independence at all. I was helpless. A technical half-wit.

SB: As can be seen in the first four of your films I've seen . . . I haven't seen *Crisis*. The style varies enormously. It changes all the time.

IB: Yes, I even changed style within one and the same film. The same thing can be seen in the young directors of today. They're staggering about, can't find themselves.

Port of Call: Nine-Christine Jönsson

TM: Perhaps they're trying out different methods?

IB: In my case I wasn't even trying them out. It was sheer necessity. I just grabbed helplessly at any form that might save me; because I hadn't any of my own.

SB: And you felt the semi-documentary style would suit *Port of Call*?

IB: Yes, it felt good. And at that time I felt it was tremendously relevant. Rossellini's films were a revelation—all that extreme simplicity and poverty, that greyness. At the same time my studio work at SF stuck to *Port of Call*, so it was a queer sort of hybrid.

SB: But one thing which really is characteristic of *Port of Call* compared with your other early films is that the people in it are less romantically conceived. *Port of Call*'s chief characters have much more inner maturity and awareness. They don't act so intuitively as the people in your earlier films did. There's a sort of consciousness behind their decisions.

IB: I've Länsberg to thank for that. The only bit of *Port of Call* which I wrote—and which is bad anyway and clashes with the rest of the film—is the hero's experiences when he gets drunk with a whore. It's really a miserable piece of work, thoroughly stylized and semi-literary, utterly out of tune with the rest of the film.

A Sven Nykvist composition in *Persona*

At that time I was producing a lot of plays, and I was already a good theatrical producer. I knew my instrument, knew how to get on with the actors at rehearsals, and had acquired some sort of artistic morality. I'd also begun to apply a certain intellectual awareness in relation to authors and their works. Here the years had had a decisive effect—those years when I'd been sowing my wild oats at Hälsingborg and then come under Torsten Hammarén's strict discipline and his ensemble of very, very strong personalities. They insisted on me giving an account of myself: Why do this? Why do you want it that way? Why do you see it like that? My collaboration with Anders Ek had taught me a lot, too. He was a tough and critical colleague; at once gentle and ruthless.

JS: And when you were filming you lacked that sort of guidance?

IB: Yes, completely—except for Lorens Marmstedt.

JS: Was it the technical aspect which was so troublesome?

IB: Yes, everything! I had such a passionate longing to make films. And at times, for brief moments, I even fancied I was having some success. But the moment I entered the studio I felt weighed down, obsessively weighed down by the clumsiness of the apparatus. I got cramp, began compromising. I compromised so that the fellows should have lunch on time, I compromised

34

to try and get the day's work done on time, I compromised to prevent the mike casting a shadow—everything and anything became more important than realizing my own conceptions. I was wholly in thrall to the machinery—while in the theatre I felt free and uninhibited.

TM: I thought maybe we could talk a bit about your cameramen. I suppose you must have your own attitude towards film photography and cameramen, and of course your own photographic vision. Could we hear a little about it? How much do you work together with your cameramen? Do you do all the visualizing of the various scenes—do you do everything yourself?

IB: This is a chapter on its own, and a difficult one. It's also a sensitive one.

For me, two things about a cameraman are fundamental. The first is that he shall be technically absolutely perfect, and at the same time first-class on lighting. The second, that he must be first-class at operating his own camera. I don't want any camera operators on my films. The cameraman and I come to an agreement about what is to be included in the image. We also go through everything to do with lighting and atmosphere in advance. And then the cameraman does everything in the way we've agreed on.

For me a film's suggestiveness lies in a combination of rhythm and faces, tensions and relaxations of tension. For me, the lighting of the image decides everything. Little by little Gunnar Fischer's ideas and mine parted company; and this meant that the solidarity, the feeling of personal contact and interplay between us, which was so necessary to me, became slack—largely, perhaps, because I became more and more domineering, more and more tyrannical, and more and more aware that I was humiliating him. Sven Nykvist is a much tougher personality. I've never had any reason to be nasty to him.

But the light in the images is something I hardly think can ever be attributed to just one of us. Perhaps I can put it like this: the impulse comes from me, and the enormously careful, subtle, and technically clever execution is all Sven Nykvist's work.

TM: So the simple fact of the matter was, you couldn't agree with Gunnar Fischer's vision? Yet he's widely famed for his style.

IB: He's an extraordinarily fine artist; a soft, silent, and introverted musician-type, always discussing, always diffident; while I become more and more domineering and overbearing, and less and less pleasant to have to do with. He, more and more withdrawn: I, more and more aggressive. In *The Devil's Eye* this almost led to a total breakdown. If anything worked at all, it was because he's an artist, because I could appeal to him all the time. But in my collaboration with him I was always unsure of myself, which I never am when working with Sven Nykvist.

JS: Let's talk about *Eva*, 1948. It has a certain proximity to the war. There's a soldier who drifts ashore, exactly as in Alf Sjöberg's *The Island*, whatever that may be due to.

A Gunnar Fischer composition in *Wild Strawberries*

Sven Nykvist with Bergman

IB : Well, it happens . . . a few soldiers are apt to come drifting ashore.

SB : Anyway it was your scenario?

IB : It's my script.

SB : It has a lot of Bergman touches in it.

IB : Yes, it has. There's a childhood fragment there which I think is quite fair. But otherwise the film is rubbish.

SB : The children on the railway engine?

IB : Exactly.

JS : But how can it have been a commissioned work, if you wrote the script? The idea was yours, wasn't it?

IB : The idea was to follow up the success of *Woman Without a Face*. Gustaf Molander and I were to have made another film together.

JS : This brings us to *The Devil's Wanton*, 1949.* And now, if you'll forgive

    * '*Fängelse*', 1949.

38

me for saying so, things begin to get more exciting. Is that a film with which your cinematographic relations are still cordial?

IB: Yes, I think I can say they are. It was the first time I was ever allowed to make my own script from an idea of my own. The whole thing was my own from beginning to end. And Lorens Marmstedt was as generous as could be.

JS: Was the script written about that time, or had it been lying in your drawer?

IB: I wrote *Port of Call* in the early summer. In the autumn I went up to Dalarna and wrote *The Devil's Wanton*. I think we must have shot it late that autumn. To get started on a film wasn't such an elaborate business in those days. We even walked on to each other's sets and shot scenes on them. I was thinking the film out during *Ship to India*, when we were working at Novilla, out in Djurgården.* Things weren't so genteel out there in those days as they are now. In fact it was an unusually scruffy sort of place. The high-tension cable taking electric current up to Skansen† ran underneath, and if someone carried a mike across it, it said *Brrr*; which meant that all the sets had to be built in such a way that the mike-lead didn't have to cross the main Skansen cable. All the sets for *Ship to India* had been built out at Novilla, so we had to shoot one set while standing inside another. It was all madly cramped. And then there was only one spot where one could even use the dolly at all—the floor went in waves; and all the time we were on location, the No. 7 tram kept jamming on its brakes outside. The moment after one had said 'Action!' one could hear the No. 7 coming along—*wowowowowowowo-brrrr!!* as it stopped right outside Novilla. There's a steep slope, too, and all lorries taking provisions up to the restaurants on Skansen went roaring up it flat out. The soundtrack of *Ship to India* contains a sort of chart of all these outside disturbances. Besides which the entire sound system had something wrong with it. The first-night audience couldn't hear a word anyone in the film was saying!

JS: But in *The Devil's Wanton* you shut out the outside world...

IB: Yes. By then I'd learned more about how to manage the technical aspects. By then I wasn't at the mercy of all the gremlins any longer.

TM: Which studio was that?

IB: We must have shot it up at the old studios in Lästmakargatan.

SB: The film is based on a short story called 'True Story'?

IB: That's right. But it was never intended for publication.

SB: The title of the short story is a good deal more ironical and detached than the film.

* Old film studio in the city park.
† Amusement park, outdoor museum, and zoo.

IB: In those days weekly magazines used to publish short stories called 'A True Life Story'. It was a sort of abbreviation of that.

SB: 'The True Story of my Life' so to speak?

IB: Exactly—sob stories.

TM: And here your belief in the Devil makes its first appearance?

IB: Now let's get this Devil business straight, once and for all. To begin at the beginning: the notion of God, one might say, has changed aspect over the years, until it has either become so vague that it has faded away altogether or else has turned into something entirely different. For me, hell has always been a most suggestive sort of place; but I've never regarded it as being located anywhere else than on earth. Hell is created by human beings—on earth!

What I believed in those days—and believed in for a long time—was the existence of a virulent evil, in no way dependent upon environmental or hereditary factors. Call it original sin or whatever you like—anyway an active evil, of which human beings, as opposed to animals, have a monopoly. Our very nature, qua human beings, is that inside us we always carry around destructive tendencies, conscious or unconscious, aimed both at ourselves and at the outside world.

As a materialization of this virulent, indestructible, and—to us—inexplicable and incomprehensible evil, I manufactured a personage possessing the diabolical traits of a mediaeval morality figure. In various contexts I'd made it into a sort of private game to have a diabolic figure hanging around. His evil was one of the springs in my watch-works. And that's all there is to the devil-figure in my early films.

JS: Is there one in *The Hour of the Wolf*, for example?

IB: No, there isn't. There's destructiveness, materialized destructiveness—the figure built up round Johan Berg. But no devil-figure.

TM: You regard witch-trials as part of this phenomenon?

IB: Three little children go out for a walk together—two little girls aged four, with a little boy of two. They take a skipping-rope with them. They put it round the neck of the two-year-old and tie the ends to a couple of trees—just high enough for the boy to have to stand on tip-toe. And walk away. And we don't know what it is that *causes these two to agree* to do such a thing.

SB: The moors murder in England...

IB: There's been a whole series of such events. Unmotivated cruelty is something which never ceases to fascinate me; and I'd very much like to know the reason for it. Its source is obscure and I'd very much like to get at it.

JS: In many ways *The Devil's Wanton* is a resumé of the Swedish literature of the forties. It's the quintessence of the fortyist film—nihilism, for instance.

IB: And romanticism. And coquetry.

JS: And then comes the 'catharsis of impotence', as Karl Vennberg* called it.

IB: Precisely!

JS: Did you find it liberating to make these two films, *The Devil's Wanton* and *Three Strange Loves*,† both so close to the literary mood of the forties? And then go on from them into the brighter fifties?

IB: With me it didn't work like that. I wrote my films without really understanding what I'd written. Then I shot them, and they meant certain things to me. But *what* they meant—that I didn't really understand until afterwards. Long afterwards. If my relationships to my own products are so odd, it's because often when I'm writing and shooting a film I'm inside some sort of protective shell. I hardly analyse what I'm doing or why I'm doing it. I rationalize afterwards. But what my motifs really were, that's something, maybe, I don't get until long afterwards. I'd be only too happy if I could say 'then I felt this', 'then I did that', 'then I drew up *this* line and carried it out *here*, and *there*, and *there*'; and 'I've followed this to the bitter end . . .' But for me it hasn't been like this. I've followed a winding path between all sorts of considerations, possibilities, and impossibilities, quite simply.

Suddenly a desire comes along and hits you—'I must do just this, *now*!' A film which was one of my shadiest, it seems to me just now, was *The Virgin Spring*. I admit it contains a couple of passages with immense acceleration and vitality, and it has some sort of cinematic appeal. The idea of making something out of the old folk-song 'Herr Töre of Venge's Daughters' was a sound one. But then the jiggery-pokery began—the spiritual jiggery-pokery.

I wanted to make a blackly brutal mediaeval ballad in the simple form of a folk-song. But while talking it all over with the authoress, Ulla Isaksson, I began psychologizing. That was the first mistake, the introduction of a therapeutic idea: that the building of their church would heal these people. Obviously it was therapeutic; but artistically it was utterly uninteresting. And then, the introduction of a totally unanalysed idea of God. The mixture of the real active depiction of violence, which has a certain artistic potency, with all this other shady stuff—today I find it all dreadfully *triste*.

But when I'd finished making *The Virgin Spring* I thought I'd made one of my best films. I was delighted, shaken. I enjoyed showing it to all sorts of people. Only one person was really critical, and that was Vilgot Sjöman, who expressed these views I'm expressing now, though very mildly. But I just said he was jealous and an idiot. A fine example of how one's motifs can get all tangled up, and how limitations and weaknesses one isn't clear about—intellectual shortcomings, inability to see through one's own motives—can transform a work as it develops.

* Karl Vennberg, Swedish poet, one of the outstanding figures of the *fyrtiotalist* school.
† Also known as *Törst* (*Thirst*), 1949.

JS: In *The Devil's Wanton* you collected together all your earlier expectations and ambitions. At times it's a film of almost adolescent revolt.

IB: I wrote the script—that's to say the scenario—in two or three days. To work out the actual script took me a bit longer and the film was shot in 16–17 days. There was no time to recast anything, to transform it artistically, palliate or disguise it, as I've done since I've come to know more and have more insight into my motifs. In *The Devil's Wanton* they just lie there, crude and bleeding, and at the same time perfumed with that coquetry which was so characteristic of the forties!

JS: That same year—1949—you made *Three Strange Loves*, which also contained 'fortyist' elements. But there you did not write the script. It was Herbert Grevenius and Birgit Tengroth, from her own collection of short stories.

IB: Oh, but I had some say in it, too.

JS: Suddenly it's all about grown-up, fairly mature people—and about marital problems.

IB: I felt a lot for that film, because my own marital complications were rather analogous.

TM: But before we go on to *Three Strange Loves* I'd like to ask you a question. What did Lorens Marmstedt think about *The Devil's Wanton*?

IB: He was extremely interested! I remember we shot that 'silent' farce one morning, sent it off to the labs and then, next morning, developed and copied it. The same afternoon Lennart Wallén and I edited it, up in Terrafilm's editing room. As soon as it was ready we called in Lorens and had a première. Lorens laughed till he fell on the floor.

JS: It still has tremendous charm, that little farce.

IB: Méliès is one of my household gods. Fancy making a film one morning and having its première next evening and going on like that until one has made fifty-two films in a year! As for *The Devil's Wanton*, the whole film was great fun, up to the first night. After that it was just misery.

JS: Eva Henning has the star rôle in *Three Strange Loves*. Wasn't she Hasse Ekman's ...

IB: ... headache.

JS: Why did you choose her for your film?

IB: Partly because I liked Eva very much, she was an extraordinarily fine actress; and then, Hasse Ekman had just launched her in *The Banquet*.

SB: We've mentioned the Swedish writers of the forties. But *The Devil's*

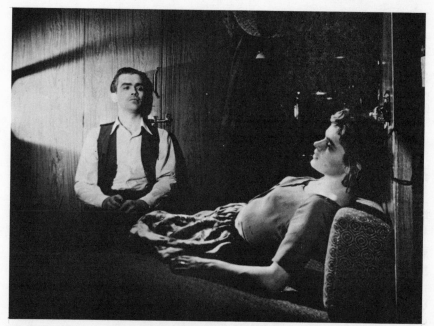

Three Strange Loves: Birger Malmsten and Eva Henning

Wanton also has links with Sartre and the existentialists—the spleen-filled intellectual, for instance——

JS: Not to mention the deterministic line . . .

SB: . . . you can see it, too, in the figure of Birgitta Carolina, the prostitute. I'm just pointing this out; but I suppose you chose her profession and social status consciously?

IB: The prostitute, the romantic whore, was dragged in everywhere in the forties. Birgitta Carolina is completely passive. She's just a catalyst, *i.e.*, the sacrificial lamb.

JS: That existential streak which Stig has just mentioned—were you deeply read in existential philosophy at that time?

IB: Very superficially, to tell the truth.

JS: Isn't there a paradox here? On the one hand the deterministic, fated life . . .

IB: I'd put it this way: I felt a strong affinity with Bernanos' and Bresson's *Mouchette*. It's a film I would have liked to have made myself, but which I didn't understand. In *Mouchette* the motif is expressed clearly and explicitly, free from all impurities. The girl in *Mouchette* and the girl in *The Devil's Wanton* are sisters, sisters in two similar worlds.

But while *The Devil's Wanton* is full of quirks and divagation and coquetry and jumps about all over the place, *Mouchette* is clear as daylight. It's a pure work of art. The religious motif only comes in for a moment, before the titles, as one sees the girl sitting there crying, and she says—'How will they manage without me?' How *are* you to manage without the saint, without the person who bears your sufferings? Just for a moment—and then all the rest of the film is completely undogmatic.

I'm also tremendously fond of *The Diary of a Country Priest*, one of the most remarkable works ever made. My *Winter Light* was very much influenced by it.

TM: By the film or by the book?

IB: By the book. I've seen the film seven or eight times, and it may well be that the film has influenced me too. But above all the book. I'm a mad fan of Bresson, yet at the same time find him insufferably dull.

SB: I would like to pause a moment on the dream in *The Devil's Wanton*. It's most unusual.

IB: No other art-medium—neither painting nor poetry—can communicate the specific quality of the dream as well as the film can. When the lights go down in the cinema and this white shining point opens up for us, our gaze stops flitting hither and thither, settles and becomes quite steady. We just sit there, letting the images flow out over us. Our will ceases to function. We lose our ability to sort things out and fix them in their proper places. We're drawn into a course of events—we're participants in a dream. And manufacturing dreams, that's a juicy business.

SB: The dreams in your films—are they your own or have you made them up?

IB: A bit of both. For instance in *Sawdust and Tinsel*,* in the episode with Frost and Alma on the beach, it's almost exactly something I'd dreamed, transferred to the screen.

TM: Do you still dream a lot?

IB: Yes, tremendously.

TM: And you remember your dreams?

IB: Sometimes . . .

TM: Do you write them down?

IB: Yes, now and again, when they may come in handy. Sometimes while I'm dreaming I think: 'I'll remember this, I'll make a film of it'—it's a sort of occupational disease.

* Also known as *The Naked Night*.

TM: The surrealists were also able to make concrete ...

IB: Yes, but they're doing something different.

TM: You're not influenced by surrealist art or interested in it?

IB: I think parts of Cocteau's *Blood of a Poet* are historic, remarkable depictions of dreams he made without any technical know-how, without technical brilliance, but perfectly astounding. Then I saw Conrad Rooks's *Chappaqua*. It's just a lot of crap from beginning to end. Very cleverly made, but crap. Laboratory work, a luscious bit of crumpet, the dark piece, who goes floating around in some sort of a nightie.

JS: *To Joy*. Seeing your first films in the light of film history, so to speak, this is a title which seems altogether admirable ... an opening into the future, toward your summer films: *Summer Interlude** and *Summer with Monika*.† And this tends to make one read too much into it. For the mid-fifties were a time of neo-romanticism and idylls. But *To Joy*, I suppose, is the invocation of these summer films?

IB: I was down on the Mediterranean coast, halfway between Cannes and Nice. In those days it was an even filthier place than it is today, a rather nasty slice of picturesque urbanization. And I was homesick. I'd decided to stay there for a couple of months and had really absolutely nothing to do and was feeling utterly miserable.

JS: What had you gone there for?

IB: Everyone else was abroad, so I thought I ought to go too. Birger Malmsten and I had decided to go abroad after we were finished with *Three Strange Loves*, so we went abroad. Birger found a bird who got her claws into him and chased him all over the place and gave him hell. But I was very much on my own. I had some flea or other, which was keeping me company. Couldn't get rid of it.

Then I met some friends down there—painters and so forth—they were hardly ever quite sober—so there I sat, and began to feel all romantic about my marriage—my then-marriage, that is to say the one I'd just taken extreme delight in ripping to pieces in *Three Strange Loves*. I got a bit sentimental and began thinking about my time in Hälsingborg, what fun it had all been, the symphony orchestra, and how I wasn't such a genius as I'd imagined. The first real setbacks, you see, had begun to put in an appearance.

But I thought to myself: 'even if one is only a mediocrity, still one must function'. So then I made up some sort of consolation for myself. That it's the infantry who are important in culture, not the more dashing cavalry. It all turned out into quite a harmonious film. The only trouble was, I couldn't find an end to it. So I made up that operatic ending with the kitchen stove blowing up.

---

* Also known as *Illicit Interlude*.   † Also known as *Monika*.

To Joy: Stig Olin and Maj-Britt Nilsson ...

TM: That was when Harry Schein was BLM's film critic. He pounced on you good and proper. He wrote a horrible review.

IB: Yes, '*To our joy*'—it was quite funny. But in principle he was right, though the film does have some nice bits in it. Something was beginning to stir inside my head. I was beginning to find my own solutions. Here and there, in *Three Strange Loves*, I had already begun to. I had begun to get a grasp of my medium. It was beginning to obey me, as it had in *The Devil's Wanton*. But more in *To Joy* than before.

JS: What line did Harry Schein take in his review?

IB: He thought the whole film suspect from beginning to end. Suspect and literary. And there I can agree with him. Beethoven shouldn't be mixed up with that sort of stuff. Harry was an artistic puritan.

JS: Victor Sjöström is in the film. But afterwards only in *Wild Strawberries*?

IB: Yes, only those two times.

SB: Your choice of him was some sort of homage?

IB: No, just appropriate.

JS: How did you two get on together?

46

... Victor Sjöström, Maj-Britt Nilsson and Stig Olin

IB : I don't remember anything about our collaboration. In *To Joy* Victor simply did whatever he liked. I remember when the film came out being deeply depressed. It didn't have much success and was badly mauled about by the critics.

SB : What qualities did you particularly appreciate in Maj-Britt Nilsson?

IB : Her way of letting everything be born on the spur of the moment. Her ability to express complexities. To look happy or sorry. To be appealing and at the same time split. She could do anything. She did it instantly, and delivered her lines with absolute naturalness. Not *there* or *there*—but precisely *there*! She played her rôle with force and self-confidence.

JS : In some interview or other you once said *This Can't Happen Here** is the only one of your films you wash your hands of altogether. That you'd like to forget about it, and have never seen it again. The last time I saw it was several years ago in a student film studio where it was being shown in a series called *Films Maudits*. As a matter of fact it's great fun—and I'm not being nasty. There's a lighthearted attitude to the material and to the secret agent story. Otherwise its theme was a pretty serious one, wouldn't you say?

* Also known as *High Tension*.

This Can't Happen Here: two scenes with Signe Hasso, Ulf Palme . . .

IB : I only had one enjoyable day in the whole shooting. Otherwise it was a nightmare! For one thing, I was dead tired. I had to go from *Summer Interlude* to *This Can't Happen Here* virtually from one day to the next; so I'd been preparing *This Can't Happen Here* while making *Summer Interlude*. The only bit of fun I had was the day I had forty cops under my command. They were to come rushing up in police cars, stop, dash out of their cars and up the gangway on to a boat. To see those fellows come driving like lunatics down to the quay at Stadsgården, jam on their brakes, rush out and dash up on to that boat, and then come up and ask—'puff—puff—was that OK?'— 'Well, a bit faster,' we said: and away they rushed and gave each other orders and got into their cars and started again—that was a delightful experience! I've always been a bit scared of cops.

When Signe Hasso came home from America—she'd been signed up without anyone having seen her and we were going to make the film in two versions, one Swedish and one English—it turned out that she'd just been down with thyroid poisoning. After a week I went in to the man who was production manager at that time—Helge Hagerman—and said: 'We can't go on like this. We'll just have to call the whole production off and pack the girl off home again.' He said: 'We can't do that!' So on we went. But something much nastier happened, too. I came into contact with some Baltic refugees. To them what we were just *playing* at was grim reality!

... and Alf Kjellin

J S : You mean, what happened to them when they came to Sweden?

I B : Yes. The Baltic refugees, and all the humiliations they were exposed to, both by us Swedes and by the Russians. That's something I'd really like to take up some day.

J S : In spite of Per Olov Enquist's documentary novel,* the episode is still politically inflamed——

I B : Bumping into the real thing like that, I suddenly felt I was making the wrong film. So I made it all into a lot of crap.

J S : Originally, then, it was supposed to have been a serious thriller?

I B : My light-heartedness, as you call it, put in an appearance just before we started filming—after I'd come into contact with those Balts.

J S : The film also has a farcical streak to it.

S B : What I remember best in *This Can't Happen Here* is one completely absurd scene, shot in the old Lion Cub Cinema in Stockholm. The cinema is showing Donald Duck and at the same time dramatic events are going on behind the screen.

* Per Olov Enquist: *Legionärerna*, 1968, deals with the post-war episode when a number of refugees from the Baltic countries were forcibly repatriated by the Swedish government at the demand of the Russians. Many Swedes have had a bad conscience about this ever since.

IB: I was dead tired and ill, and only made it for the money. Around Christmas time we knew the whole Swedish film industry was going to grind to a halt in protest against its economic conditions.

TM: Had the stoppage been planned?

IB: Yes, it was planned. In December 1951, all film production in Sweden came to an end until further notice. I had three families to support and six children and my finances were in a bad way and the child welfare authorities were breathing down my neck. Then came this offer of making a double version for which I'd get a little more money; so I felt I had to do it. But it was also an edifying experience, making a film to order, for money.

JS: Is there anything in the film you think is good?

IB: There's nothing in it I like at all. I think it's disgusting. I don't even recall the scene Stig mentioned ... I've quite simply repressed the whole film. But that, too, passed over, after a while. The film got a horrible bawling out.

SB: By the way, do you ever look at your old films again?

IB: Yes, now and then. I have reduction prints in my film library.

JS: Including *This Can't Happen Here*?

IB: No, not that one.

TM: But all the others?

IB: No, not at all. But quite a lot of them. I keep them out on Fårö,* and sometimes in the evenings when there's nothing on the telly and Liv† feels like looking at a film, we put on a little film show, either one of my own films or something else.

JS: How big is your film library?

IB: About 200 films. Certainly one of the largest private film collections in Sweden.

JS: *Divorced*: shall we touch on that?

IB: Märta Ekström was still alive in those days, and she was one of our greatest actresses of all time. She'd been seriously ill, and Herbert Grevenius was a close personal friend of hers. Herbert and I spoke of trying to get her back into films, to work of any sort.

So we had a word with Carl-Anders Dymling‡ and gave him the idea of this divorcée, and Carl-Anders agreed. But then Märta Ekström died—well, perhaps she didn't die just then. Maybe when it came to the push she backed

* Baltic island off Gotland, where IB now lives.
† Liv Ullmann.
‡ Managing director of Svensk Filmindustri AB from 1944.

out. But the film was already in production, and Inga Tidblad played the part instead. It was a commissioned job throughout.

JS: The original idea—was it yours?

IB: The fact is, I don't remember. But Herbert Grevenius wrote the script.

JS: So we've reached 'the Bergman summer'!

SB: But first we have the *Bris* films—the advertising shorts for soap you made during the film-strike: nine of them in 1951.

IB: Well, *Summer Interlude* comes before *This Can't Happen Here*. For me *Summer Interlude* is one of my most important films. Even though to an outsider it may seem terribly passé, for me it isn't. This was my first film in which I felt I was functioning independently, with a style of my own, making a film all my own, with a particular appearance of its own, which no one could ape. It was like no other film. It was all my own work. Suddenly I knew I was putting the camera on the right spot, getting the right results; that everything added up. For sentimental reasons, too, it was also fun making it. Far back in my past there had been a love story, a romantic experience.

JS: You wrote the scenario from a short story of your own. What was it called?

IB: 'Marie'—I'd written it at practically the same time as *Frenzy*.*

JS: You got some help from Herbert Grevenius?

IB: By that time the short story had gone through many different re-writings, but Herbert took the old version—the original version—and forced me to write a script straight off, on the original theme. He kept an eye on it while I was doing so, to make sure I didn't branch out or add any new ideas. Altogether, he has meant a tremendous lot to me. He was one of the best theatre critics Sweden ever had.

SB: Why did you choose the opera and ballet as its setting?

IB: Because I'd been assistant producer at the Opera for two years and was familiar with the milieu. But then a little problem arose—they wouldn't let us inside! At the last moment they refused, both the Ballet and the Opera. The story was regarded as degrading to the corps de ballet; young ladies in the corps de ballet simply don't have love stories. Nor do they ask to borrow half a litre of brandy!

SB: They'd read the script, anyway?

IB: They read the script and refused to let us in.

TM: Because of Annalisa Ericson's rôle?

IB: Precisely.

* Also known as *Torment*.

Summer Interlude: Annalisa Ericson and Maj-Britt Nilsson

TM: And she isn't even in the film!

IB: Unfortunately not—she was extremely gifted. But Maj-Britt Nilsson was wonderful. She really kept the two rôles, the older and the younger, quite distinct. Though we worked under primitive conditions, we made the film very quickly indeed. It was an unusually rainy summer, and every time the sun peeped out we dashed out to Smådalarö.*

JS: There's a diary motif in it, too?

IB: Yes, the girl finds her dead boy friend's diary.

JS: As I see it, the film's thematic idea is: to forget something that's happened, and be reconciled to it, one must first recall it.

IB: The original short story was written in diary-form and the part where the heroine is fully grown up is extremely sketchy. Obviously, it's influenced by Hjalmar Bergman—but I can't help feeling there's some sort of genuine core to it. Cinematically speaking, anyway.

JS: The flashback way of telling a story was very common at that time.

IB: It was very popular.

JS: *Woman Without a Face* is told in the same way.

IB: All films were being narrated in flashback in those days. Suddenly one sees an actor's face freeze, the camera zooms in, the actor becomes vague— and one understands: now we're going to see something which happened five years ago. It was the same thing in *Three Strange Loves*—it was packed with such gimmicks.

JS: The wonderful thing about *Summer Interlude* is that despite its superficial banality—for its framework is certainly banal—the girl in it is wonderfully sweet: the standard Swedish girl student in her summer paddock, student cap and all. Yet it feels so fresh, sets a string trembling deep down in one's teenage heart . . .

IB: Yes, it's close to the heart. Perhaps most of all because my instrument was working, because it obeyed me. But then, I'd had a lot of time to sit and think about it. The film stoppage had gone on for quite a long time.

TM: How did the public like it?

IB: A lot!

JS: Stig mentioned the *Bris* films . . .

IB: They yielded me the bare necessities of life. My income had dwindled to very little—I had many mouths to feed, and when Sunlight Soap asked me to make nine *Bris* films I was absurdly grateful. But the conditions were harsh— that little song about 'sweat doesn't smell, it's the bacteria, the skin bacteria,

---

* In the Stockholm Archipelago.

which do it, when they come into contact with your sweat' and '*Bris* kills bacteria! No bacteria, no smell!' had to be in every single film. And I had exactly 34 metres to work with—just over a minute—in which the whole sermon had to be squeezed in. To find nine different variations was quite a headache.

TM : They're all costume pieces, aren't they?

IB : No, only some. They're antiquated now. But in those days they were regarded as revolutionary.

JS : By the way, why did *Summer Interlude* have its première one year later than *This Can't Happen Here*, having been made before it?

IB : The company slept on the film. There was nothing I could do about it. The film stoppage was complete.

JS : But *Waiting Women** came out before *Summer With Monika*?

IB : *Waiting Women* came first. Immediately the film stoppage was over came *Waiting Women*, and then, almost immediately after *Waiting Women*, I started work on *Summer With Monika*. I finished *Waiting Women* in July 1952, and began on *Summer With Monika* in August.

JS : So you wrote the script of *Waiting Women* in a good mood after your success with . . .

IB : . . . the *Bris* films! It was written in a mood of bad temper, sheer terror, grim necessity. I felt I just had to have a viable script ready against the day when the film stoppage came to an end—to have something for us all to live on. It was no fun, I can tell you! It was some sort of gallows humour. Because it was my last chance. My finances were in shreds and my marriage badly frayed.

SB : Hadn't you a job in the theatre, too?

IB : I was being paid Sw.cr. 2,500 ($500, £200) for each play I put on. I had finished in Gothenburg and started in Stockholm at the Intiman Theatre as artistic director. After two programmes I got the sack. So I had virtually nothing.

TM : Sacked by Lorens Marmstedt?

IB : Yes. At that time everything was going to the devil. Only one thing mattered: to make something the public would like.

JS : But *Waiting Women* was a box-office success?

IB : It went like hot cakes. It was one of the happiest experiences of my life, to hang about in the foyer of the Röda Kvarn Cinema and suddenly hear people inside howling with laughter. It was the first time in my life people had ever laughed at something I'd made—laughed like that. One of my bitterest enemies at SF came out. Coming up to me, he threw his arms round me and said 'It's an indescribable pleasure to . . .'

* Also known as *Secrets of Women*.

Råsunda Studios, 28 June 1968

JONAS SIMA: Would you like to tell us a bit more about your collaboration with your actors? In his review of the book of the script of *Persona*, the critic Göran O. Eriksson writes: 'He is one of those directors—and it is his greatest weakness as a man of the cinema—who give the impression of being bigger than the sum total of all their actors.' What Eriksson seems to mean is that you reduce actors to mere instruments, and often not even to instruments who sound with their own voice or timbre.

INGMAR BERGMAN: In that case he knows nothing of the relationship which exists between myself and my actors. Just take a girl like Bibi Andersson. You can never get *her* to do anything she doesn't want to! If you try, all you get is an endless row. Her performance as Alma in *Persona*, alone, completely contradicts what he says. Bibi became something so infinitely better than her rôle. Gunnar Björnstrand, too, has a fine intellectual sharpness, an intense clear-eyed ability to see through things. Or take an intact *noli me tangere* fellow like Max von Sydow. Press him somewhere so that it hurts, or so that he feels he's in a straitjacket, and he rears like a stallion. Slowly, slowly, over the years, I've arrived at a technique for collaborating with my actors.

I sit quietly at home, make all my preparations in detail, plan the sets and draw them in detail, until I have it all in my head. But as soon as I get into the studio with the camera and the actors, it can happen in the course of the first run-through that a tone of voice, a gesture, or some independent expression on the part of one of the actors makes me change the whole thing. Even though nothing's been said explicitly between us, I feel it will be better that way. Such an awful lot of things go on between me and the actors, on a level which defies analysis.

Ingrid Thulin once said: 'When you begin talking to me, I don't understand a thing of what you mean. But when you don't talk to me, then I understand exactly what you're saying.'

That's how it often is between me and my actors. The fact is, I'm part of them, the complementary part.

Actors can be a great help, too. I remember—*A Lesson in Love* I think it was—coming to the studios one morning and saying to Eva Dahlbeck and Gunnar Björnstrand, 'this scene is so silly, let's cut it.' At which they both let out a howl and said—'Get out of the studio! Beat it! We'll rehearse it together. Afterwards you can come in and look!' So I went out and made four telephone calls and cashed some cheques. When I got back, they had rehearsed a wildly funny scene.

Take a thing like *Persona*. There were only the three of us—two actresses and myself. I was feeling poorly, anxious, unsure of myself. And you can see how, step by step, we got results. There it was a real case of give and take. First, we did a lot of work in the studio. But afterwards, when we were out on the island, we reshot almost three-quarters of the film.

STIG BJÖRKMAN: On the island, did you let outside circumstances influence the work? What changes did you make, compared with the scenes you had shot earlier in the studio?

IB: It's like this. As soon as you've done something, you've turned a blow-lamp on to the text, on to the actors, on to yourself. You get some material. You look at it. That time I saw the results afterwards, and since neither Bibi nor Liv wanted to see the takes, we talked the matter over. 'I wonder if we couldn't do this bit differently and better.' And they said: 'Yes, supposing we did it this way? Suppose we do it like this?'

JS: Isn't this the fact of the matter: as you've developed, you've arrived at a more open attitude than at the beginning of your career, you're more 'democratic' . . .?

IB: I see what you mean. But actually it has to do with something else altogether. Anyone who starts directing films—at least in the days when I began—is terribly scared. And if you're frightened and not sure of yourself, the last thing to do is to tell anyone you're frightened and unsure of yourself. Instead, you adopt the opposite attitude. Become dictatorial. Drive your actors hard. Get ruthless. It can also be a matter of circumstance. Right up to 1955 or 1956 I went on sawing away furiously at the very branch I was sitting on—never knowing for sure whether I'd be allowed to make another film or not. So my attitude to everyone became terribly hard, closed-up. I was on my guard all the time. Nowadays I'm as open as can be. The other way of going about things was such a strain, so dreadfully exhausting.

But you young people nowadays enjoy another climate, another starting point. Besides, we mustn't forget that fashions change. I was born and grew up under the shadow of the big guns. So, even if I was only a peashooter, it was only natural I wanted to become a big gun too and behave like a big gun. And in double-quick time I learned the trick of it.

JS: The little experience I've had of film work has made me frightfully unsure of myself in connection with all the technical aspects. One doesn't really understand, for instance, how the camera works. One clings to one's technicians. Gets a bit ingratiating—and so, maybe, a shade more 'democratically-minded' than one really is. But the whole time one is thinking to oneself: 'Just let me learn this job and then I'll . . .'

IB: In those days everyone tried to sit on you. Their attitude was: 'Who's this fellow coming along and trying to teach us our business? This is how we've always done it. It isn't for him to come along and think he knows better.' Everyone went on saying I was an idiot, until, ruthlessly, step by step, I had taught myself everything to do with my profession. No one can rap me over the knuckles in technical matters today.

And this means that nowadays I can behave much more like an orchestral conductor. Imagine a conductor who doesn't know how to play the various instruments, who can't show his musicians what they've got to do at various places, where the fellow who's playing the bassoon is to breathe, whether a note should be an up-stroke or a down-stroke, whether the tympanist is to use his arms or his wrists. A conductor who says to his musicians, 'Remember, this is a microcosm reflected in a macrocosm' or something of that sort, is finished. But if he says, 'Breathe here. Squeeze your lips together like this. Take an up-stroke here. Stress this bit of syncopation', then they know what it's all about. It's precisely the same with actors and technicians. In the first place always give them purely technical instructions.

TORSTEN MANNS: Learn their language?

IB: Exactly.

TM: Does it sometimes happen that you can provide alternative solutions when actually filming—shoot a sequence in two different ways and then decide which you prefer afterwards, in the editing room? Or have you always made up your mind in advance?

IB: It's a sport. If I re-shoot a scene, I never do it twice the same way; it would go dead on the actors. If a solution isn't to my liking, they must feel I'm tearing it up and doing it in some other way. Trying to figure out why it went dead. Often the things one does to it are quite simple and banal, but they help to change the whole climate and character of a sequence.

58

s B : Often there's a difference, I suppose, between your script and the final film? Does this vary very much from one film to another? Do you make cuts and changes while you're shooting? Or do you mostly wait until the final editing work?

I B : No, I never edit while shooting. I'd find it too depressing. Besides, editing, for me, is a sort of erotic pleasure. I like to save it up. But I often 'edit with the camera'. I imagine the scene-changes while I'm working on the scenarios and with the actors.

Once a script has been written I hardly even look at it until the evening before a scene is to be shot. *Then* I tackle it, get my sequence ready, scrub parts of the text and make alterations in dialogue. Sometimes when we assemble in the morning it can happen that I break up what the actors have already learned. They give me their opinions: 'Can't this be changed?' and 'these lines seem odd and hard to deliver . . .' Maybe I don't think it's odd at all and say: 'Supposing you make a pause there, just before you say it'; and 'that bit has to go very slowly'. Then suddenly they feel it's OK and can be done.

J S : You almost never use amateur actors, though it's all the rage with the new generation of film-makers.

I B : Well, not only with the new ones . . .

J S : But why do you use amateurs so little? 'Classical' directors like Bresson, Dreyer, and others often look for their instruments among amateurs.

I B : Well, if Dreyer does, it's very rarely indeed.

s B : But you've turned to professionals, virtuosi.

I B : As long as something unambiguous is required of someone in a film, an amateur will do. But the moment something complex has to be expressed, an amateur is no use. Actors are trained to express complexities.

J S : Are you saying, categorically, that an amateur is incapable of expressing anything complex?

I B : Yes, I am. You may be able to do it *with the help* of an amateur; but you can never get an amateur, on his own, to express something complex. This can be seen very clearly in the film I like more than any other, and which I suppose I must have seen a hundred times: De Sica's *Umberto D.* There he uses the old professor—who was an amateur—admittedly with a dubbed voice, the voice of a professional actor. One sees clearly how situations arose when De Sica wanted him to express certain things—and it's more than he can manage. That's why the film becomes flat and slack in a few places, particularly at the end.

I don't think one could find a single instance of someone having got an amateur to express something complex. It's simply beyond them.

Summer Interlude: Maj-Britt Nilsson with Birger Malmsten . . .

The moment I find I'm out of rapport with someone who's got to do something in front of the camera, I'm utterly lost. The whole situation becomes idiotic. If I get an actor—and it has happened—who becomes petrified in front of the camera, falls into a cramp, can't remember what he's got to do, or panics for some other reason, the whole thing becomes extraordinarily hard to clear up.

s b : Godard wrote a most appreciative article about *Summer Interlude* in *Les Cahiers du Cinéma*, called '*Bergmanorama*' (CC 85/1958). He attacks all patent techniques that regard the film as a craft, not as an art-form. He writes: 'The cinema is not a craft. It is an art. It does not mean team-work. One is always alone; on the set as before the blank page. And for Bergman, to be alone means to ask questions. And to make films means to answer them. Nothing could be more classically romantic.' Could we hear your comment on this? It's connected with what we were talking about just now, your working methods. But it also concerns the films themselves.

i b : I find Godard's way of putting things bewitching. It's precisely what he does himself, what he has fallen victim to! He's writing about himself.

60

... and with Stig Olin

You must never forget that my life has been lived in the theatre; and theatre—even if it's a protected world—is always a collective. Producing a play, one belongs in high degree to a group. In a theatre actors are never for a moment defenceless against a producer. They have all sorts of most effective ways of resisting him. In recent years we've seen several young producers torn to shreds by the opposition of their actors.

I have felt very much alone in other dimensions; but never in a professional context. I know one great conductor, whom I met, who talked about feeling all alone in front of the orchestra. That's something I've never experienced, either in the theatre or together with actors and technicians in a film studio. What I *am* deeply conscious of is the way in which, by using jargon, by routine, by strict observance of certain ritualistic rules, we are always trying to exorcise our aggressions. This is a fact, not just an idea we try to waft away.

The group feels a strong suppressed aggressiveness against the man in charge, and the man in charge can feel tremendously aggressive towards the group.

Walk on to a cramped set, where some twenty-five people are milling around you. You never see anyone trampling on anyone else's toes or bumping into anyone. Never a harsh word, never a sulky face, never a rude word, hardly a raised voice. If things are like this, it's because everyone knows he's dependent on all the others. Everyone knows they've got to pull together. So everyone knows they must be considerate and polite to each other, even if the temperature in the studio is in the hundred-and-twenties and everyone's dead tired.

No, I've never known that sort of loneliness. I've felt lonely in the outside world, and for that very reason I've taken refuge in a community of feeling, however illusory.

SB: Many of your films are expressive of loneliness and isolation, not least the artist's.

IB: It's a painful experience, which I think I share with most people. But I don't have to be film director or artist to feel isolated.

JS: The international press is always saying you're best in the world—world film champion, and so forth. Does it affect you in any way?

IB: Not much. Sometimes I read articles when they're sent me direct. But I never look for them. It's always as if they're about someone else. When one has had all the success, all the money, everything one has ever wanted, ever striven for—power—the lot—then one discovers (excuse the expression) its nothingness. The only things that matter are the human limitations one must try to overcome and one's relationships with other people; in the second place—also enormously important, of course—one's ethical attitude toward what one is doing, or not doing. What you say 'yes' to, and what you say 'no' to in your work; and to temptations outside your work. Nothing else matters. All the rest is completely uninteresting. Whenever I've attended film festivals, for instance, the effect on me has been catastrophic. I've wanted to stop making films altogether. It has taken me months to recover my health.

But then there's the play itself, and that can be fun. Now and again, one makes 'appearances'. People want you to play your rôle. And you do.

JS: Do you still enjoy playing yours? Or did you use to play it more?

IB: Let me tell you a story. It's rather long, but edifying. A Jewish story.

Once there was a Jew who came to his rabbi and said: 'I can't stand it any more, being so poor. I've no food, we don't know how we're going to manage, I've several children at home and my two old aunts and my father and my father-in-law.' The rabbi thought a long while, and said: 'I'll tell you what you must do. Take on two of your neighbour's children, and come back in a week.' And the Jew went off gloomily and took home two of his neighbour's children. And after a week he came back and said: 'I'm at my wits' end. Now I've got two of the neighbour's children, and all my relatives and my own children and my wife cries all day. What am I to do?' And the rabbi replied: 'You must take home your other neighbour's two old grannies.' And the Jew went away gloomily and took his neighbour's two old grannies into his house; and came back after a week, and said: 'Any day now I'm going to hang myself. I've my neighbour's two old grannies, and I've two of my other neighbour's children as well as all my own relations and my own children; and my wife does nothing but cry.' The rabbi thought a long while, and said: 'What you must do now is take your neighbour's four goats into your field.' The Jew went off in tears. After a week he came back with a rope in his hand, and said: 'Now I'm really going to hang myself. I've those four goats, and my other neighbour's two old grannies, and my first neighbour's two children and all my own relations, and my wife never does anything but cry.' Then the rabbi thought long and deeply. 'And now,' he said, 'you're to send those two children packing, and the four goats and your neighbour's two old grannies. Go home now, and come back in a week.' And the man came back in a week and said: 'Things are simply marvellous. We're well off! We manage wonderfully.'

That's how things are after one has been director of the Royal Dramatic Theatre for three years. After that, no really frightening problem exists. It was purgatory. Nothing worse can happen to me for the rest of my life. Now I've only myself to look after. And it all goes rather well. How are things with you?

JS: Some day I suppose I'll have to become head of the Royal Dramatic Theatre!

IB: It's a tough school.

TM: Or take a job at the Film Institute!

IB: Yes, that's another of the devil's playgrounds.

SB: Well, let's go back to *Summer Interlude*. Next to *The Devil's Wanton* it's among the most opulent of your films, both in motifs and formally. The film's structure is unusually rich in patterns. It's interesting, too, I think, because it's about this girl Marie who looks back on an episode from her own youth; and you were about the same age as Marie, telling a story you had written when you were about the same age as the Marie of the flashbacks. I feel the circumstances depicted in the film need placing in relation to yourself. Or did you dream it up?

IB: Superficially it was something I'd experienced—except for the boy breaking his neck. He didn't do that. But it was tragic, even so: the girl got polio. So I was writing about something which had hurt.

But there's an awful lot of myself in Marie, too. Marie, the ballet-master and the somewhat world-weary and scabby journalist—all three are projections of myself. The student boy, on the other hand, is just a coathanger. I hadn't much interest in him.

SB: Marie, I suppose one could say, has reached a point in her career where

Death in Bergman: Mimi Pollak in *Summer Interlude* . . .

she has gained more insight into the demands of her own profession? Just as you had in 1950?

IB: The compromise she'd made, even though she knew deep down inside herself it was wrong, had consisted in letting Uncle Erland look after himself while herself taking refuge in her profession and in the protection he offered her. And when the boy died, she'd died too.

At that time I was much preoccupied with the fear of death. Not of physical death—well, that too, we can come back to that in some other context—but this business of dying spiritually. That every action, every choice, either leads to an access of life or else to one dying a little.

SB: À propos films, you're often quoted as saying that you make every film as if it's to be your last. This remark, one feels, could well have its roots in this period. You let Marie suddenly be aware that her career will come to an end. She has seven or eight more years to dance. Then she'll be forced to retire. After this insight she goes on with her work.

IB: For a year and a half I'd been living without making any films, without knowing when they'd next let me start on one. It was utterly devastating. It was precisely during the film stoppage, I think, that this insight was born inside me: that this business of making films is frightfully transient and chancy. Also in connection with *This Can't Happen Here*. 'I'll never do that

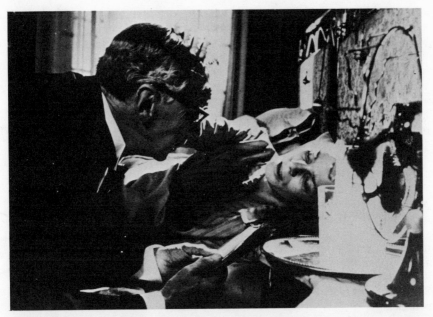

Håkan Jahnberg in *The Silence* ...

Bengt Ekerot in *The Seventh Seal*

again!' I said to myself. 'Never again will I make a film for money. No matter how insecure my material existence may become, never again will I let anyone buy me—no one—no matter for what money.' Making films is my justification for existing. If I start playing fast and loose with ethics, I'll lose my inherent value as a human being, everything that gives me the feeling I've a right to make films.

And this is why I must never forget that each film may be my last. Why I must have the courage to turn down the next one. To see I may be chucked out. If a project doesn't seem good enough, one must have the courage to scrub it.

It's a big wheel one sets turning; and all of a sudden one is spinning round on it oneself, and can't stop. One is helpless.

Starve—I've done that. When one is young it's not so bad. Usually one is pretty sure there's a loaf somewhere just round the corner. But not to be able to support the people you're responsible for, that's hell.

Personally I've almost no needs. Gradually one gets to be that way. I've my house on Fårö, it's true. It means a lot to me. I've my film library, which I love, my gramophone records, and my books. But I could leave the whole lot any day. Besides, the moment I've no other income, I've my State artist's grant: Sw.cr 25,000 ($5,000, £2,000) a year. I can never be penniless.

TM: In many of your films, minor figures, like Mimi Pollak in *Summer Interlude*, little old men and women, funny little trolls, seem to keep recurring. Are they always necessary? Or are they just for fun?

IB: That sort of thing just crops up as one goes along. Reserve exits ... The need to play ...

SB: In *Summer Interlude* Mimi Pollak stands for death—one of her scenes in the film, particularly, is very like a scene in *The Seventh Seal*, the one where she sits playing chess with the clergyman. The little old woman marked by death.

IB: Yes, she's Death. The moment the story darkens, she puts in an appearance. Up to the point where the chief characters have their first quarrel it's all very light and cheerful. And then Marie goes home to find Henrik; but meets that little old woman, Death, instead.

TM: You mean they're usually death-figures?

IB: No, just in this particular instance. The longer I go on, the less I figure out. Nowadays I let my characters look after themselves. In the old days I used to do a lot of building, planned my script, steered (as it were) people's fates, guided their footsteps. But now they have to look after themselves, and I let any characters come into the picture who want to and then float out again. I suppose I've a much freer relationship to what I'm doing. The climax of my 'constructions' is *Smiles of a Summer Night*, which is based on a play by

Marivaux, in the classical 18th-century manner. But when I'd done all that, it didn't amuse me any longer. It's the sort of thing one makes use of to train oneself; to try out one's capacities.

JS: All these motifs and themes in *Summer Interlude*, which recur in *Wild Strawberries* and in *The Seventh Seal*, for instance, have they any creative meaning for you today? Do you go back intuitively to your earlier works to find material?

IB: The longer I go on, the less my earlier work means to me. All the time I've a feeling of taking off in various directions, creating ever greater insecurity around the creative act.

JS: How did you work up that famous scene in the lift, the elevator in *Waiting Women*?

IB: Thanks to Hitchcock, particularly, I'd long been intrigued by shooting long sequences in difficult and cramped circumstances, weeding out everything irrelevant—quite simply, in making things hard for myself. (In *The Rite*, for instance, I've no décor, in the usual sense of the word: just blank walls, a curtain or so, and a few bits of furniture. It's a challenge, not having anything to play tricks with and get lost in.)

The episode in *Waiting Women* is based on a personal experience. I was to be reconciled to one of my wives in Copenhagen. We were staying in the home of some close friends, who'd gone away. They had given us their key, and when we got home in the evening, drunk and happy, with everything fully prepared, we put the key in the door—and it snapped off! No chance of finding a locksmith. So we spent the night on the stairs.

JS: Did the lift-scene involve any particularly difficult technical solutions?

IB: We shot it on slow film, which called for quite a lot of light. The elevator itself was a technical monstrosity. Several of us had sat down together and figured it out. But technical complications, no! And then Eva Dahlbeck and Gunnar Björnstrand were so sweet, and such fun to work with. It's mostly thanks to them the sequence turned out as it did.

Waiting Women wasn't really intended to be experimental in any way, it was meant to be a commercial success. But it contains another, more heavily disguised experiment. And that's the little bit with Maj-Britt Nilsson and Birger Malmsten. It has almost no dialogue, only some fifty lines. This really was an experiment, an attempt on my part to tell a story in pictures. An attempt I didn't repeat until *The Silence*, where there's very little dialogue. But it was a secret experiment, too—we didn't dare tell anyone we were experimenting.

JS: In *Journey Into Autumn*,* which is a technically brilliant film, there's a corridor sequence in which Susanne, played by Eva Dahlbeck, is going to see

* Also known as *Dreams*.

her ex-lover. I think the whole sequence is done with extraordinary brilliance, almost a textbook example of cinematographic art. Cinematic expressionism, without a doubt. Your experimental use of sound montage was remarkably independent.

IB : Sound has always been just as important as image.

JS : Only one word is said from beginning to end. She hears a voice inside her—her own or the man's perhaps—saying 'Susanne' . . .

IB : I don't remember that.

JS : Numerous close-ups of the door-handle of the railway carriage illustrate her suicidal thoughts.

IB : As in *Three Strange Loves*, where there are similar attempts. Trains have always had a most suggestive effect on me.

JS : How did you build up the corridor sequence in the script? Are the sound and camera montages included?

IB : No, I do all that afterwards. Whenever I have technical gimmicks of that sort, I just write down whatever occurs to me. I solve it technically, and then write an additional special script—a technical script . . . in which I go through everything that will have to be shot, letting a strip of film run through my head.

Waiting Women: three scenes with Eva Dahlbeck and Gunnar Björnstrand

Journey Into Autumn: Eva Dahlbeck in the train corridor sequence

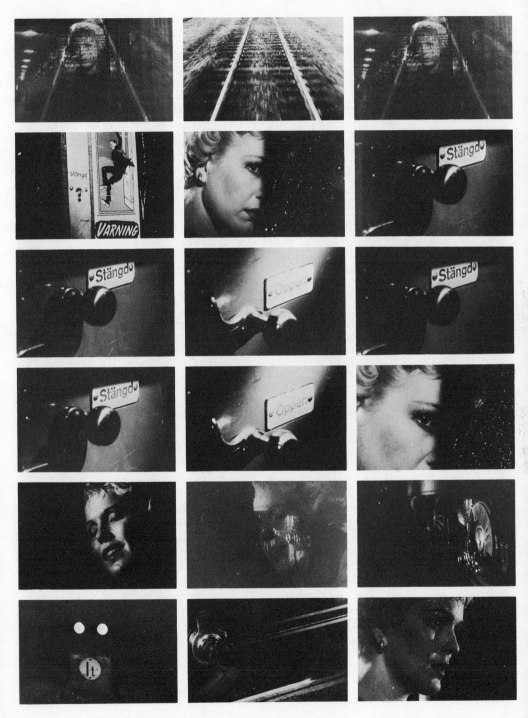

JS: Can you be sure of remembering the montage?

IB: Sometimes I write it down before I tackle it.

JS: Can you recall whether you put much work into the corridor sequence in *Journey Into Autumn*?

IB: All I remember is, we were in a hurry. In those days Sandrews used to put out twenty films a year, maybe twenty-five; and one had to nip in and out of the studio as if the devil was at one's heels. But if things are properly planned one can work fast. You just worked as long as they'd let you and then either got chucked out, or the film simply came to an end.

In the early years, both film negative and electricity were rationed. For *The Devil's Wanton* we were allocated 8,000 metres of negative, all in short lengths: Agfa and Kodak and Ferrania, anything that could possibly be got hold of. Each time Göran Strindberg switched on a photo-flood an old fellow specially employed for the purpose came up behind him and switched it off again. We were only allowed to do the last rehearsal in full lighting. If more than the calculated amount of current was consumed, it had to be paid for at a special rate.

SB: In *Waiting Women* you try to give each of the episodes a special character, reflecting the character of the three women who narrate them. All three are very different ways of telling a story.

IB: The first episode is very chaste; the second is highly mobile; and the one in the lift has a hot, slightly burlesque tone to it. It was just an idea I had.

JS: *Summer With Monika* is a film people are determined to regard as all your own work. How much of the script do you attribute to Per Anders Fogelström? Originally it was based, wasn't it, on a short story which, after the film was released, became a novel?

IB: Quite right—after the film it was turned into a novel. It all started one day when Per Anders Fogelström and I ran into each other on Kungsgatan.* I asked him what he was doing. He said: 'I've got a thing in my head, but how it's going to turn out I don't know.' 'Really?' 'Yes, it's about a girl and a fellow, just kids, who pack in their jobs and families—and beat it out into the archipelago. And then come back to town and try to set up in some sort of a bourgeois existence. But everything goes to hell for them.'

I remember jumping a yard high into the air and saying: 'We're going to make a film of this! Remember—we're going to make a film of this!' He thought so, too; but then other things came between. But each time we met, I asked him how things had turned out for that couple. And by and by, during the film stoppage I suppose it must have been, we got down to work on the script.

* Main shopping street in Stockholm.

Summer With Monika: Harriet Andersson as Monika

Bergman on location for *Summer With Monika*

I don't quite remember—he wrote so fast—whether the novel came out before the film stoppage was over, or not. Anyway I know the script was handed in to SF and Carl-Anders Dymling liked it. I told him that a few of us were going out into the archipelago, just a little gang, with a silent camera. It was to be very small and simple; the world's cheapest film. After the film stoppage things had begun to brighten up a bit, and SF wanted more films for its own cinemas.

At that time Carl-Anders Dymling's hands were strictly tied. He had a council, board-members, and others, who decided which films should be made. There was a hell of a hullaballoo over ours. But that time Carl-Anders Dymling won. Some members of his board, I seem to remember, even resigned. We shouldn't be allowed to make such filth!

I had just seen Harriet Andersson in *Defiance*, and no girl it seemed to me could be more 'Monika-ish'. Then one day Lars Ekborg and I met on the street, and I thought he'd do for the boy and put the proposition to him on the spot. Then quite a time passed before the project was approved and he was free, so we prepared the film while we were making *Waiting Women*. I was no little infatuated with Harriet—oh yes, we took our time when trying out costumes!

JS: How old was she then?

IB: Eighteen or nineteen at most, I guess. But she was devastating, and engaged to Per Oscarsson. And so off we went, exactly one week after finishing *Waiting Women*.

JS: Who had picked Harriet for *Defiance*?

IB: I think she'd been in *The Beef and the Banana* and *While the City Sleeps*, a whole lot of minor rôles, and all of us younger directors were very keen on her, for a number of reasons: Lars-Eric Kjellgren and Allan Ekelund—he wasn't a director, he was a production manager—we were all stuck on her. There's never been a girl in Swedish films who radiated more uninhibited erotic charm than Harriet.

So out we went in a boat and took lodgings in the parish clerk's house on Örnö Island. As I've said, we were costing the firm nothing. There were no sets. We had fun. And the script was as sketchy as could be. Altogether it was a romantic and somewhat exhausted little gang who assembled early each morning. That was a wonderful August.

Then, just as we were getting ready to come home, it happened. To save transport costs we'd let the rushes pile up over the three weeks. When it was developed we discovered that, on practically everything we'd shot, there had been a bad scratch on the negative. A message came out from Stockholm that we'd just have to re-shoot the whole thing from beginning to end—well, seventy-five percent of it. No film team ever shed bigger crocodile tears. We were only too happy to stay on!

Making *Summer With Monika* was a lot of fun. When it was over we came

Summer With Monika: Lars Ekborg and Harriet Andersson

Råsunda Studios, 28 June 1968

77

home and worked in the studio a bit. The whole film went like a song. And then—the censors cut it.

J S : What did they cut out?

I B : There's a sequence where Harry sits and gets drunk in the evening after the fight. The censor cut that, too: there are two fights between the boys, first the one where they tumble about all over the place, and then another bigger one. In this love-scene their passions reach a climax; they sit on the shore and get drunk and have a wildly orgiastic love-scene. The censor took it all out.

S B : Did anyone question the censor's decision?

I B : You're crazy!

S B : What, didn't either you or SF protest?

I B : Hell, no! How could we? There was no one to protest to. We just had to accept it.

S B : In connection with *Summer Interlude* and *Summer With Monika*, perhaps we ought to comment on the summer motif. It's quite natural that Swedish films should often be shot in the summertime. But in this case there seem to have been other reasons besides the purely practical ones. Sometimes I have a feeling there isn't all that much difference between the summer motif and, for example, the hour-of-the-wolf motif. There's something desperate about your way of experiencing summer, the clear, penetrating light.

I B : For me a Swedish summer is full of deep undertones of sensual pleasure, particularly June, the time around midsummer—May and June. But for me July and August, July especially, when the sun shines day after day, are a dreadful torment.

Sunlight gives me claustrophobia. My nightmares are always saturated in sunshine. I hate the south, where I'm exposed to incessant sunlight. It's like a threat, something nightmarish, terrifying.

J S : There's strong sunshine in your dream sequences, too.

I B : There's the same hard sunlight in *The Hour of the Wolf* and *Wild Strawberries*. When I see a cloudless sky I feel the world's coming to an end.

Throughout *The Silence*, for instance, it's blazing hot and the sun scorches down. Not until towards the end does the thunder come.

T M : In some way the sunlight goes right through your people and their actions.

I B : Yes, they're eaten out.

J S : Compared with the more adolescent revolt in your films of the forties, *Summer With Monika* suddenly seems much healthier. The revolt is no less violent, admittedly. But in some way healthier.

IB : And it was in the autumn after *Summer With Monika* that I started at the theatre in Malmö. After my time in Gothenburg I was tired of drifting hopelessly about in Stockholm.

JS : That was 1952?

IB : Yes, I think so; and then everything changed. And my spotty-faced period came to an end, at least to some extent.

Technically, what was interesting about *Summer With Monika*—besides being made by a little unit and a silent camera and dubbed—was that I'd lost my regular editor, Oscar Rosander, and was given another who was incompetent. Oscar Rosander had been magnificent. When you have a good editor you take it easy and let him help you. But now, suddenly, I was without one, and had to do my own editing. I was obliged to learn how to edit; why one made just this cut or that; changed shots at just this or that particular point. Instructive.

I don't suppose there's much more to say about *Summer With Monika*, except that it's close to my heart and one of my films I'm always happy to see again.

JS : Did *A Lesson in Love* grow out of the lift-sequence in *Waiting Women*?

IB : Yes, it did.

JS : At the same time the film seems to have acted as a sort of preliminary sketch for *Wild Strawberries*.

IB : It's possible. But *A Lesson in Love* grew out of my collaboration with Gunnar Björnstrand and Eva Dahlbeck, that's certain.

After making *Sawdust and Tinsel*, Harriet and I were down at Arild,* where we'd taken the outdoor sequences in *Sawdust and Tinsel*. Harriet was fond of lying on the beach and sun-bathing, and I wasn't. So she took up with Erik Strandmark and his wife and every day they toddled off down to the beach, while I rented a tower-room hanging out of an old villa, lay on my back and read amusing books and thought how agreeable life was.

Soon I began jotting down little scenes—marital scenes—which I found more and more amusing; and then I thought of Gunnar Björnstrand and Eva Dahlbeck, and they amused me even more. In a week the script was finished. I thought: I can always chuck this in to Sandrews and SF. So I sent it in first to Sandrews, and then, since there they were all away on holiday, to SF. Carl-Anders Dymling, who, for some reason or other wasn't away on holiday, read it in a flash, rang me up, and said I was to come up to Stockholm. A fortnight later the film was under way.

After ten days' preparation, I think it was, we got into production. The whole job was entirely frivolous. And that's just what's so good about the film, I suppose—its complete frivolity.

JS : I've seen *A Lesson in Love* several times, but in some way it soon fades from one's memory.

IB : It was only made for the passing moment.

* Small seaside resort on the Swedish west coast.

79

Råsunda, 3 July 1968

JONAS SIMA: In all your films about the artist's situation, the humiliation theme occupies a central place. I should like to pick up the thread of one of our earlier discussions: whether this view of the artist isn't really a romantic one? What I mean is: an artist enjoys a higher social status in our present-day society than he used to. Society supports him and he isn't too badly off—at least if he succeeds in gaining some recognition. Is this one of the reasons why you've often placed your 'artist films' in a historical setting? I'm thinking chiefly of *Sawdust and Tinsel* and *The Face*,* but also of *The Hour of the Wolf*, though admittedly the last isn't a costume film but is played out in a sort of fictitious environment.

INGMAR BERGMAN: You're always prodding me on this business of romanticising the artist; and it's quite possible my way of seeing the matter is out of date. I don't know. Obviously there's a more modern view of art and artists and of the terms on which the artist exists; but the humiliation motif is of the very essence. One of the strongest feelings I remember from my child-hood is, precisely, of being humiliated; of being knocked about by words, acts, or situations.

Isn't it a fact that children are always feeling deeply humiliated in their relations with grown-ups and each other? I have a feeling children spend a

* Also known as *The Magician*.

80

good deal of their time humiliating one another. Our whole education is just one long humiliation, and it was even more so when I was a child. One of the wounds I've found hardest to bear in my adult life has been the fear of humiliation, and the sense of being humiliated.

Every time I read a review, for instance—whether laudatory or not—this feeling awakes. A piece of criticism can be devilishly critical and yet not humiliate. I feel I'm learning something: 'Here's someone speaking direct to me.' But both positive and negative reviews can be humiliating.

My entire state of dependency on this company, to which I owed my existence up to 1955, I experienced as one long humiliation. Even when I was head of the Royal Dramatic Theatre, and was summoned to the Ministry to answer for something I'd done, or the auditors came along and wagged their fingers at me, I felt it was all ridiculous and humiliating, simply because I knew much better how things should be done than people who had nothing to do with the matter and didn't understand it, but still came along and interfered.

To humiliate and be humiliated, I think, is a crucial element in our whole social structure. It's not only the artist I'm sorry for. It's just that I know exactly where he feels most humiliated. Our bureaucracy, for instance. I regard it as in high degree built up on humiliation, one of the nastiest and most dangerous of all poisons. When someone has been humiliated he's sure to try and figure out how the devil he can get his own back, humiliate someone else in his turn, until, maybe the other feels so humiliated that he's broken, can't 'humiliate back' again, or doesn't even bother to figure out how he can do so.

JS: Well, the mechanisms behind humiliation and the aggression which creates a feeling for socialism, for social revolution and political awareness, are much the same. But in you, I should say, it has found other, more private expressions. And these are the ones I'd be inclined to call romantic!

IB: I stick to what I know. If I've objected strongly to Christianity, it has been because Christianity is deeply branded by a very virulent humiliation motif. One of its main tenets is 'I, a miserable sinner, born in sin, who have sinned all my days, etc.' Our way of living and behaving under this punishment is completely atavistic. I could go on talking about this humiliation business for ever. It's one of the big basic experiences. I react very strongly to every form of humiliation; and a person in my situation, in my position, has been exposed to whole series of real humiliations. Not to mention having humiliated others!

JS: We'll have reason to come back to this theme when we talk about your 'idea-films'.

IB: I imagine we shall, yes.

JS: The reviews of *Sawdust and Tinsel* must be one of the lowest low-water marks in the history of Swedish film criticism. 'Filmson' in *Aftonbladet*, for

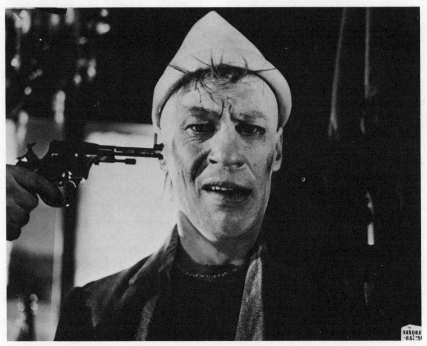

Sawdust and Tinsel: Anders Ek as the clown Frost ...

instance, wrote: 'I refuse to inspect the vomit Ingmar Bergman this time has
left behind him.' Besides which the film had no box-office success. How did
you try to protect yourself, on the personal plane, against such criticism and
setbacks?

IB: I thought I'd made a good, a vital film. I was perfectly well aware where
the film had its thematic and stylistic roots: in Dupont's old film *Variety* with
Emil Jannings, which I've treasured for many years in an old Pathé 9·5-mm
copy in four reduced reels. *Sawdust and Tinsel* was intended as a conscious
reply.

Naturally, I experienced both box-office fiasco and critical fiasco as catastrophes. Every time things went to hell I knew my chances of making any
more films had grown slimmer, that they became more and more uncertain
and risky every time it happened. My sector narrowed. And that was a most
unpleasant sensation.

TORSTEN MANNS: There's a definite hierarchy in the entertainment world,
isn't there? The circus, I suppose, is at the bottom. Then the film. And then
the stage, or vice versa?

IB: What was more to the point was that both sorts of entertainment artiste

.... and Albert (Åke Grönberg) contemplating suicide

were regarded as scum. Not quite so much during these last ten years, perhaps. But ten years ago an actor couldn't get a decent room at the town hotel in Jönköping. Perhaps you don't realize that? Anyway, that's how it was. And there are still large categories of people in this country who regard actors and entertainers of any sort as their lawful prey.

TM: There are suicides in quite a number of your films. Would you like to talk a little about that?

IB: Like all other children, it seems to me I remember deciding to go out into the forest and lie there and pretend to be dead until everyone was sorry. Everyone knows that all their lives artists—particularly if they're the sort that function as I do—retain a strongly infantile streak; or, to put it better, the creative streak is so deeply tied up with a sort of infantility, or a leftover of the child's attitude to the world about him, that the artist also retains a lot of marginal behaviour-traits.

STIG BJÖRKMAN: Your choice of artists as main figures in many of your films, and your way of making them concretely express the humiliation theme—is this due, then, to your regarding the artist as more exposed than other people? Professionally more exposed?

IB : Yes, exposed to humiliations.

SB : An artist is comparable to an engineer or an inventor. He works in a similar professional atmosphere. They, too, invent things; construct a new world. But they can always show results which, good or bad, can be objectively evaluated. . . .

IB : And are tangible, at least.

SB : The artist's work springs from more or less the same drives, but he is obliged to expose himself in quite another way—and in doing so experiences a whole complex of dependencies where he is in the position of a child. He is exposed to criticism, to humiliations, to curses or praise. An engineer or an inventor is not at all so insecure or alienated. They can say: It works, therefore it is good.

IB : And they've figured it out so that it will work in this way or that way. And there it stands, the finished job.

JS : You have razor-edged memories from your own childhood, haven't you?

IB : I'm deeply fixated on my childhood. Some impressions are extremely vivid, light, smell, and all. There are moments when I can wander through my childhood's landscape, through rooms long ago, remember how they were furnished, where the pictures hung on the walls, the way the light fell. It's like a film—little scraps of a film, which I set running and which I can reconstruct to the last detail—except their smell.

Many artists' faces are like the faces of grown-up, secretive children. Look at a face like Picasso's! It's a child's face. Or Churchill or The Swedberg*— another kid who's never grown up. Or Stravinsky, or Orson Welles, or Hindemith. One might even add a man like Mozart—but admittedly we don't know exactly what Mozart looked like—but from his pictures we can be sure it was so. Even Beethoven's face. One could call it the face of a wrathful infant.

When I come into the studios here with my camera and colleagues around me, we always seem to be starting a game. I remember exactly like when I was small, and took my toys out of the toy cupboard. It's exactly the same feeling. There's something analogous about it. The only difference is that nowadays, for some inscrutable reason, I'm paid for doing so, that some people treat me with respect and do what I tell them to, which now and then amazes me.

JS : A major motif in *Sawdust and Tinsel* is Albert's and Anne's longing, quite independently of one another, for a more tolerable, *i.e.*, a more bourgeois life. Each accuses the other of being frightened and longing to pack it all in. Have you ever longed to give up your own artistic career?

IB : No, never. I think I can say without boasting that, in relation to my

* Swedish chemist and Nobel Prize winner.

Sawdust and Tinsel: Agda (Annika Tretow)

profession, I've always been happily unneurotic. As far as the actual creative function goes, all this business of keeping going, of doing things, and then doing new things and getting rid of the old ones, and so on and so forth: in these matters—at least as far back as I can remember—I've always functioned normally; experienced it as my natural position in this world.

JS: If I understand you aright, you've a strict professional morality, which insists that 'the show must go on'?

IB: Professionally, morals aren't too much of a problem. Over the years one has learned certain things by experience. They mount up. And gradually they crystallize into a pattern of behaviour which afterwards—to use a superior expression—one calls one's professional ethics.

JS: I'd like to ask you a question in connection with what we've been saying about *Sawdust and Tinsel*. Albert's ex-wife, Agda, represents the bourgeois ideal. 'Everything stands still,' she says in one important scene. 'Everything is silence and maturity.' 'Emptiness,' Albert replies. Yet he has a longing for just that very emptiness . . .

IB: But having called it emptiness, he makes a desperate appeal to her to take him back. Yet all the time he knows it's meaningless. He has been so thoroughly poisoned by his own sort of life, where everything is in ceaseless motion. For him silence is emptiness. For him, everything must keep moving, always. Anne, on the other hand, has got it all wrong; she imagines actors are part of the 'establishment'. And then discovers it's all a lie. Both of them are under a delusion.

TM: Frost's dream goes back to a remote time?

IB: Yes.

SB: The action of *Sawdust and Tinsel* occurs within twenty-four hours, and the film's main figure is Albert. Almost the entire film is seen through his eyes. There are really only two episodes without him: the dream—the story about Frost and Alma—and the parallel action with Anne and Frans. In the immediately preceding sequence we gradually realize he has been eavesdropping the whole scene between Anne and Frans in the attic. Why did you choose this dream and the parallel action with Anne?

IB: I'm not at all dogmatic. Or at least I wasn't then, and still am not. But I went through an intensely dogmatic and formalistic period—a sort of attack of purism. It passed over afterwards. The dream was the starting point for the whole of *Sawdust and Tinsel*. It was the basis for the whole film. The dream is the theme. Then follows a series of variations. The business between Anne and the actor is one of them.

SB: In a parallel montage you tell us about Albert's visit to his wife and Anne's meeting with Frans. As you cut to and fro between those two scenes, you often juxtapose the two women. The image of the one conjures up an image of the other. When you bring the first part of the scene with his wife to an end, the camera moves up towards her face; and the sequence begins with a close-up of Anne. Afterwards, when you turn back to the wife, you again juxtapose the two women in close-up. Is this to underline Albert's dependence on them both?

IB: It's fascinating. A face, then suddenly another face forcing its way through and materializing. But one could also say it was for formal reasons; a gimmick, to tie the two actions together. But it is motivated by the same basic pleasure, which I exploited afterwards in *Persona*, in letting faces float in and out of one another.

JS: The famous flashback at the beginning of *Sawdust and Tinsel*, the story of Frost and Alma. Is it a dream?

IB: It's a story.

JS: Its montage seems to me to be influenced in various ways by Eisenstein—I'm thinking of the montage of the cannon firing, feet, and similar close-ups, just as in *The Battleship Potemkin*. Are you aware of this?

IB: At that time I was scornful of Eisenstein. I hadn't seen *Potemkin*. They didn't have it in the Danish film museum, the only place I could get films from.

SB: Your treatment of the soundtrack in that sequence is extremely interesting. The film opens entirely without dialogue. But there are sound effects. And music. But when the man has rushed up to the camp to fetch Frost, then the dialogue starts: Frost's Danish–Swedish mumblings, and then, for a while, you keep the speech going, chiefly at moments when Frost has a reason to say something.

IB: But when he stands shouting 'Alma!' down by the shore, you can't hear it.

TM: It's a monstrous effect. We certainly do hear him!

IB: Probably it's an echo of my original real dream. Haven't you ever dreamed you're trying to speak, but can't? That the words won't come? Or that you're speaking too softly? You must have dreamed that? Well, that's where I got it from. In the transitional period between the old silents and sound films, some sound films had only a certain number of spoken lines—otherwise only captions. There were also sound films that only used sound effects and music, but captions for the dialogue. I found the mixture quite fascinating. Frolicking about on the soundtrack is a sort of erotic pastime.

SB: How did you build up that montage for the Frost flashback story? You work with white over-exposures, the pictures seem to dissolve in blinding sunshine. Why did you choose that technique?

IB: I think I've already told you that for me bright sunshine is charged with anxiety. I wanted everything to be as white as possible; hard, dead, and white. Merciless in some way.

SB: Which cameraman shot that bit? Was it Hilding Bladh?

IB: Yes. Hilding Bladh was a magnificent cameraman. We mustn't forget that both Nykvist and Strindberg are Hilding Bladh's pupils. He trained them both.

SB: In *Sawdust and Tinsel*, which cameraman did what?

IB: I don't remember. I recall Sven Nykvist shooting everything inside the circus tent. But Hilding must have shot most of it.

SB: *Sawdust and Tinsel* contains a lot of very long and rather difficult shots. In the very first sequence, inside the caravan, when Albert wakes up and goes out; and then again, for example, in the scene in the attic between Anne and Frans.

IB: It was fun doing it that way. You'll find that out for yourself. At first, one wants to do everything; then gradually weeds out what one doesn't.

JS: What strikes me every time I see *Sawdust and Tinsel* is that the introduc-

Sawdust and Tinsel: 'the dream—the story about Frost and Alma'

Sawdust and Tinsel: the attic scene with Frans and Anne (Hasse Ekman and Harriet Andersson)

tory narrative is quite timeless. One has a feeling: 'this is the film that will never grow old.'

I B : You mean the bit with Frost and Alma?

J S : Yes. Here's a film-language with its roots deep down in the history of the cinema, yet which seems utterly modern.

I B : Yes, I have a great weakness for that little bit.

S B : At the end of the sequence there's what one would call some impudent editing. Right in the middle of the sequence where they've just come up with Alma and Frost to the circus tent, and the chap is coming last with Frost's costume, suddenly you cut.

I B : Yes, suddenly they're all gone.

S B : No doubt you cut in the middle because the procession was too long to be shown in its entirety?

I B : That sort of thing was completely forbidden. But I'm like Beethoven. I say: 'From now on it's permitted.'

92

JS: 'A film broadsheet,' it says in one of the sub-titles to *Sawdust and Tinsel*. Stylistically, it's a heterogeneous film. It contains baroque, naturalism, and expressionism.

IB: Listen to some piece of music by Stravinski—other comparisons aside—and you'll hear reminiscences from the whole history of music. Though he mixes up everything, he has an idea, a vision of his own. He has something to say. And he uses whatever he likes to say it.

SB: Stylistically, the film changes character all the time. In the sequence where Albert meets his wife, the film's style, too, takes on something of the character of a middle-class comedy. You use a narrative technique that was highly typical of the American films of the forties, particularly for comedies with a middle-class setting. The sequence begins with a close-up of some object typical of the milieu and the situation; then the camera pans away to include the room and the actors. In *Sawdust and Tinsel*, for example, you have the wife take out her sewing-box, you show the sewing-box in close-up, and then let the camera stray out into the room. But this narrative technique recurs nowhere else in the film.

IB: The simple fact is, one grabs at anything that suits for the moment.

JS: The scene where Albert shoots the circus bear, which Alma loves so, expresses a sort of vicarious death. But I feel the film is more mysterious than that. This sequence has always fascinated me; but I've never really come to any conclusion about it. What I can't make up my mind about is what you mean by the scene, what it symbolizes?

IB: For me it doesn't symbolize anything. Albert has got to hurt someone, and all the time Alma's talking about the bear being ill. He feels driven to commit some act of cruelty. And he wants to hurt Alma.

JS: But it's only once anything is said about the bear being sick.

IB: No, twice! Once, when they agree to hold a big parade. The second time, when they've erected the circus tent. 'What do you mean by this bloody bear?' I've been asked this question so often! People have a feeling I must *mean* something.

JS: An Andalusian bear!

IB: It was a Canadian grizzly bear. The only one of us who really made friends with it was Harriet. It was furious with all the rest of us, even with its keeper. But Harriet—she could hold a lump of sugar between her lips and hold it out, and the bear would take it elegantly, hardly even touching her . . .

TM: 'Andalusian bear' Jonas says. In *The Exterminating Angel* Buñuel has a black bear. It's the same bear.

JS: It's horrible! The first thing one hears is the bear howling, primitive heathen howls.

Sawdust and Tinsel: Anders Ek, Erik Strandmark and Harriet Andersson

IB: It's a remarkable film.

JS: And then one sees it's just an ordinary little bear!

SB: You mentioned *Variety*. It's pretty obvious that Åke Grönberg is a sort of Swedish Jannings figure. But why did you choose Grönberg? There were other actors just as big and fat.

IB: But not with his physical and histrionic capacity! The first thing anyone making a portrait of himself does is to choose a little chap who is fat and strong, manic-depressive and anti-intellectual. When I started writing the script I'd already made up my mind that Albert should be Åke Grönberg. That's how I saw him throughout—a big heavy bloke.

SB: That little knitted cap which Åke Grönberg wears—all through the film—is that a coincidence? Photos of you in the early fifties often show you wearing something similar.

IB: It was the first time Mago* and I had collaborated. Ever since then he has meant a good deal to me. He's a chap who finds it amusing to upset things and

* Bergman's costumier.

94

then put them to rights again, to invent people, fabricate costumes, pull things out of his cupboard—altogether a remarkable fellow.

TM: You have Erik Strandmark in the film, too. He was a very fine actor. In *Sawdust and Tinsel* and in *The Seventh Seal* he plays much the same figure. He's a sort of assistant—a clown figure. In *Sawdust and Tinsel* he's a clown and a coachman. In *The Seventh Seal* he's some sort of an acrobat who belongs to the troupe of players.

IB: Strandmark was an actor with a streak of real genius in him. In *The Seventh Seal* I remember how he grabbed that actor's rôle—really it's rather banal, a simple-minded, noisy, one-dimensional type—and turned him into a mediaeval jester, a ferocious, burlesque, bullying, dry, ill-tempered fellow, all quite different from anything I'd imagined. He did what he liked with it.

JS: Albert is a philanthropist ... He's the artist who points out what pitiful creatures human beings are, who have to live here on earth. And then adds: 'Everyone's so frightened. But I love people.' This is a travesty of Strindberg in his *Dream Play*, isn't it?

IB: Now and again Åke had difficulties in learning his part, particularly at points where he had to grimace, make gestures, and keep tabs on Anders Ek into the bargain, all at the same time. He had to try to keep them both in the camera's predetermined range of vision. That's why he sometimes only came out with certain words. But the noises he made sounded much better than my longer ravings, so I left it all as it was. On the other hand, when Anders comes in and babbles drunkenly, that's all exactly as I had written it. But Åke had made it all over anew, turned it into a series of four-letter words. He just enters in a rage and lets fly. I thought it sounded magnificent. So I let it stand.

JS: Yes, the monologue, or at that point dialogue, is fantastically tragi-comic. Though the situation is highly tragic and dramatic, the lines and the way they're presented produce quite a different effect. When Åke Grönberg, for example, shouts out: 'I love them!'

IB: That was something he suddenly thought of himself. Though it must have been in the script somewhere, I suppose.

Anders' circus-talk was never quite the same from one rehearsal to another; so they said things to each other more or less as it occurred to them. It was all one big 'happening'. So I shoved in a wide-angle lens and said 'move over here' and we shoved out a plank where they had to stop; and then Anders was to mimic the bear, as I seem to remember, and say: 'Everything can go to hell, you can go to hell, I don't give a damn for anything.' And then they were to come forward gradually and drive all that circus scum away.

JS: That the scene turned out so ambiguous must be because Åke Grönberg is an actor who functions, so to speak, on the surface?

IB: He'd got his teeth into the outburst of feeling in that scene. That was the main thing. What else might come out in the dialogue was of secondary importance.

J S : When they suddenly explode, the aggressions between Harriet Andersson and Åke Grönberg are delightful. Two temperamental people . . . By the way, where did you get hold of all those people for the film?

I B : We'd done a thorough job of chasing up every retired circus artiste in Sweden who was to be got hold of. Artistes on their beam-ends or out of work. At the turn of the century there used to be fifty-five circuses wandering about Sweden. When we made the film there were only three left. Immediately after the Second World War there'd been twenty at least. So there were circus folk all over the place. And then, I'd begun working with a man who is always my production manager nowadays: Lars-Owe Carlberg. He held the whole of this mob of chimpanzees, grizzly bears, parrots, circus artistes, and actors in a muscular grasp.

J S : So the film wasn't shot in an artificial circus milieu?

I B : No, certainly not. For four weeks we lived in a pension, down there at Arild, with the entire company. Afterwards we went up to Stockholm and shot the interiors. By then we knew each other like sardines in a tin. We'd eaten and quarrelled and got drunk and lived together and had a marvellous time; so the boundary lines between who were the circus artistes and who were the actors and who were film directors or monkeys were by no means clear.

S B : Are you personally fond of the circus?

I B : I prefer variety.

T M : In one of the two episodes in *Journey Into Autumn*—to go on to your next film—an entirely new motif appears: what might be called the wolf theme. In that episode Harriet Andersson acts as a stand-in daughter to Gunnar Björnstrand, who has a real daughter, who hates him. Kerstin Hedeby, who plays her, has a typical wolf-face, and there's a terrific confrontation between her and her father. Was that an old idea, or is it only typical of this film?

I B : That motif of the old man who overwhelms the young girl with jewellery just occurred to me. But altogether I don't remember much about *Journey Into Autumn*.

T M : I've heard it said there was originally another episode, with Naima Wifstrand, but it was taken out.

I B : I believe there was a third episode. I usually work with three . . .

T M : So it was to have been the three ages?

I B : Maybe, I don't remember too clearly.

Journey Into Autumn: Kerstin Hedeby, Gunnar Björnstrand and Harriet Andersson in the confrontation scene

SB: Anyway, nothing was shot with Naima Wifstrand?

IB: No.

SB: Kerstin Hedeby was an unusual choice. She's a painter and scene designer, not an actress.

IB: I'd known Kerstin for many years, ever since she was seventeen, I think. I thought she looked exciting. I'd often thought of putting her in some film. And here she suited perfectly. Here's a film where one really *could* use an amateur whose appearance and behaviour fitted perfectly into some particular context.

SB: *Journey Into Autumn* is obviously in large part an experiment. Not least its form, in relation to image-sound. We've already touched on the train scene with Eva Dahlbeck. There are also the completely silent introductory scenes, the section at the fashion photographer's. It is depicted in a model expressive montage. Not least one remembers Bengt-Åke Bengtsson as an enormously impressive fashion king.

IB: As I was telling you, in my childhood I used to draw films, and tried to narrate what happened without using dialogue. Otherwise, as far as I recall,

Journey Into Autumn: the fashion photographer's scene with Bengt-Åke Bengtsson, Eva Dahlbeck and Harriet Andersson

Journey Into Autumn is a dialogue film, so there wasn't much point in including silent sections to prevent the dialogue from seeming too compact. But it's a boring film. I must have been tired when I made it. That wasn't a good time. While we were filming there was an eclipse of the sun. On sub-standard film I have seven, eight, or nine minutes of the making of the film. And it's fun. I've 9·5-mm film from *Wild Strawberries* and *So Close to Life*, too.

JS: Which you shot yourself?

IB: Yes.

JS: Why just 9·5-mm?

IB: That was the size we used to have in those days. We can take a look at it some time, if you like. It's rather comical.

SB: Do you shoot a lot of film on the side?

IB: Yes, nowadays I always take along someone who wants to watch us, and he has a camera and instructions to use up as much film as he likes, for the archives.

98

J S : Why?

I B : It's like keeping an album. Not necessarily interesting to anyone but myself.

J S : Do you do it while preparing your films, too?

I B : No, only while we're shooting them.

S B : Do you make many films like this? We've seen the results of one: *Daniel*. Do you shoot a lot yourself?

I B : Yes, I do. But I've only a little 16-mm Bell and Howell, with cassette, foolproof loading, and one lens.

S B : Do you get ideas from the films you make like this?

I B : No. They're really only—to use a modern word—documentations. I do it for fun.

J S : So you don't go out and try out an idea and look for a technical solution with your own camera first?

I B : No, but I do think it's fun practising exposures, and seeing how colour changes in the course of the day. I have set up a stationary camera and gone out once an hour and pressed the button and noted down the lens aperture. But only out of technical interest.

J S : *Smiles of a Summer Night* has certain theatrical traits to it, so much must be admitted.

I B : The devil it has!

J S : Was the film influenced by any situations in your stage work at that time?

I B : Between my job at the theatre and my job in the film studio it has always been a very short step indeed. Sometimes it has paid off, and sometimes it has been a drawback. But it has always been a short step between. As for *Smiles of a Summer Night*, the situation was simply that I needed another success. *Journey Into Autumn* had gone to hell and I had to attach myself again to SF. It was one of the most difficult periods in my life. For a couple of years I'd been producer at Malmö City Theatre, the Harriet period was over, and I'd promised Carl-Anders Dymling that my next film wouldn't be a tragedy. He'd also intimated that if it was to be a serious piece, well then I hardly need bother my head about making a film that summer. I needed money, so I thought it wiser to make a comedy.

I felt it would be a technical challenge to make a comedy with a mathematical pattern—man–woman, man–woman. Four couples. And then muddle them all up, and sort out the equation.

So, after midsummer, we got started. The hottest summer in living memory. It was monstrously hot. Did I tell you about that street in *Crisis*?

Smiles of a Summer Night: the luncheon scene

They'd built up a store and a little studio behind it; and there's the theatre in *Smiles of a Summer Night*. We had gas lamps and it was so hot the gas went out—for lack of oxygen. When the actors were all ready I shouted 'action' and 'camera' and the sweat bubbled out on them. It was a great effort, and all the time I had something wrong with my stomach.

My assistant director was Lennart Olsson. Today he's a 'big director' down in Malmö, and he kept a pedantically detailed log book, in which he noted down everything about lighting and camera angles, sets, and everything that happened all round, just for his own pleasure. Today it's in the film history archives. We kept at it for fifty-five days until we were all on the verge of a nervous breakdown. The book's about as dull as Xenophon's *Anabasis*, but suddenly one reads such things as: 'Now we are all pretty tired, if anyone says "shut up" to Katinka Faragó [the script girl] she bursts into tears.' And then on it goes, just as drily as before. There's nothing in the film to show it was made during one of my blackest periods.

s b : You mentioned Katinka. Some colleagues of yours we haven't mentioned ... She's one of your gang, isn't she? Did she begin with you?

i b : She began with *Sawdust and Tinsel*. She was seventeen when she started. Now she's a production manager. We mustn't underrate Sandrews' activities in the late forties and early fifties. In those days Sandrews were spewing out twenty films a year, the studios were in use every day, and any poor blighter who could hold a camera or knew anything about anything was welcome to come and work there. This gave us a lot of capable people, who afterwards survived and were gradually promoted. Well, they thought *Smiles of a Summer Night* was costing a colossal amount of money, Sw.cr. 350,000 ($70,000, £30,000) or something of that sort; or maybe it was 400,000. Anyway, very expensive. A rumour had got around at head office that I didn't approve of the furnishings as they were, and wanted them all re-upholstered, because I'd got it into my head they had all to be very light—there was to be nothing black in the film at all, except this young clean-living man wandering through the picture like a public catastrophe. All the others should be light, everything had to be white, light, transparent. So I called up Carl-Anders Dymling and was bawled out. He asked me what the hell I meant by having all the furniture re-upholstered. There was a big row, and I had to promise I'd only change half of it. After which I took out the other half altogether. So it all looked very white in the end anyhow.

I remember how, afterwards, when they saw the film, head office told me it had all been a dreadful miscalculation. The film wasn't funny. It was stylized. It was too lame, and too long. They'd also tumbled to the fact that it was in period costume, and just then costume films weren't doing any box-office. Altogether, there was a bottomless pessimism. So when I came along with the script of *The Seventh Seal*, there wasn't the least question of my being allowed to make it. And then I had that bit of luck with the prize at Cannes.

SB: Swedish films weren't very much represented at festivals in those days, it seems to me?

IB: No, they were just excuses for managers to take trips abroad and air themselves. Usually they would take some film or other along with them and run it a bit shamefacedly; but no one saw it. As early as the spring of 1949, *Ship to India* had been sent to the Cannes Festival before it had its première.

JS: Had you had any other films at festivals in between?

IB: I suppose I must have, but I don't remember. What I do remember is that Lorens rang me up in Sweden and said 'it's gone all to hell, cut it by 400 metres': whereon, of course, I flew into a rage and said it was out of the question.

SB: That prize at Cannes . . .

IB: It was the jury prize. I was sitting in the shithouse reading the papers. And then I read: SWEDISH FILM GETS PRIZE AT CANNES, SWEDISH FILM CAUSES SENSATION, or something of that sort. What the devil film can that be, I wondered. When I saw it was *Smiles of a Summer Night* I couldn't believe my eyes.

So I took the script of *The Seventh Seal* and went along to see Carl-Anders Dymling—Sandrews had given me plainly to understand they were still counting their losses after *Journey Into Autumn* and *Sawdust and Tinsel* and weren't interested. I put it down on the table in front of him—Carl-Anders was sitting there selling *Smiles of a Summer Night* to every country you could think of and was in a state of euphoria, thinking how from now on he'd be able to sit on genuine Persian carpets and look at pictures by Picasso, and was as delighted as could be about everything. So I said: 'Now, Carl-Anders, it's now or never.' And plumped *The Seventh Seal* down in front of him, and said, 'Come on now, make up your mind!'

Råsunda, 16 August 1968

STIG BJÖRKMAN: Bibi Andersson plays her first rôle in any of your films in *Smiles of a Summer Night*, as one of the actresses in the little play.

INGMAR BERGMAN: Bibi has one or two lines to say in *Smiles of a Summer Night*, but she'd already been in one of my *Bris* films. Even at that time she'd been in a lot of films: *The Ghost at Glimmingehus* and *Dumbom*. Bibi had started when she was sixteen.

SB: In your next film she has one of the leads. How do you choose new actors for your films? Do you usually try them out in front of the camera? Or do you see them in other directors' films?

IB: It's all a matter of intuition. A trial film can turn out hellishly fine—but afterwards one finds one is dragging a cow through a whole production; or a trial film can be so miserable you couldn't stick it up in the shithouse, but afterwards can yield dividends in the long run. I've had experience of both.

One of my strongest cards—perhaps my strongest card of all—is that I never argue with my own intuition. I let it take the decisions. Sometimes I can say to myself: this is going to the devil, it's all completely up the spout. Yet I stick ruthlessly to my intuition. Over the years I've learned that so long as I'm not emotionally involved—which always clouds one's ability to decide matters intuitively—I can follow it with a fair degree of confidence.

But then, after one has decided something intuitively, it's necessary to

Smiles of a Summer Night: Bibi Andersson and Birgitta Valberg in the 'little play' scene

follow it up intellectually. Intuition reaches far out into the dark. Afterwards one must try to go on foot to the spot where intuition's javelin has landed, using one's common sense. In principle I can say that, in me, everything to do with actors takes place on the intuitive level. It's because I've never doubted my own intuition that my activities in the House of Bergman Ltd are so extensive and many-branched.

JONAS SIMA: But acting and directing actors is also a technical matter. You prefer to work with brilliant actors. But don't you also have to study their technical abilities and their way of working?

IB: I can't approach an actor with a lot of emotional guff, no. If I did, he'd spit me out on the spot. I must give him completely clear, distinct, technical instructions. By technical instructions I mean such things as the set and his relationship to the camera, both of which speak to him indirectly. Well, you've made films, so you know that. One sort of relationship to the camera can solve a whole sequence; another can lock the action and kill it. Actors feel this intuitively. Either an actor feels liberated or else he feels inhibited.

TORSTEN MANNS: Today, when one sees *Smiles of a Summer Night,* one is struck by how very funny and well-written it all is.

IB: It was an attempt to be witty. People were always bawling me out for being such a gloomy guy.

105

TM: There's nothing strained in it. At least not as far as I can see. It comes off; all its thematic material comes off, too, just as it does in *The Face*, which is also a light film, made with a certain radiance. But I've almost a feeling that when you make lighter films you're very much on guard against your own motifs.

IB: Of course.

JS: A propos the suicide scene, Jörn Donner writes in his Bergman book . . .*

IB: Yes, he writes off *Smiles of a Summer Night* as a dead loss.

JS: On the contrary. He writes: 'The incomplete suicide corresponds to his [IB's] doctrine of ceaseless humiliations.' It could be taken as meaning that failure gives new insight, that life can offer fresh starts and consequently possibilities for new attempts. As far as I can see it's an optimistic view of life. But there's another sequence in the film which I think paradoxically contradicts that attitude. I mean the key scene with Desirée's mother, when she's sitting up in bed—Naima Wifstrand, that is—and is visited by her daughter, the actress Eva Dahlbeck; and says that 'One can never protect anyone from the least little suffering, that's what makes one feel so infinitely tired.' No one can learn anything except from his own mistakes. And that's a pretty pessimistic view of life, isn't it?

IB: *Smiles of a Summer Night* is disillusioned. It's a series of bits of behaviour, which are followed up. The film isn't particularly psychological. It shows certain groupings.

JS: So the truths said in it are just make-believe truths?

IB: Yes, I think so. All that stuff with the suicide is nothing but a game. To make suicides in a film—a fictive suicide or some other horror—is just play, a game. One could talk for a long time about games.

What is so peculiarly stimulating about a game is that it must be taken seriously all the time, even though at the same time one is conscious that, even at those moments when one makes one's most searing announcements, it's all just a game. Everything happens by mere chance. That's how it is when one is writing a script. Maybe you're borne up on a wave. Then in comes someone and says the phone's ringing. When you come back, the wave has subsided, and something else has been born instead. It's all just chance. Or a game. I disagree deeply with commentators and critics—though I can only speak for myself, of course. They assume all sorts of conscious lines of thought, intellectual penetrations, carefully laid courses. But for me everything just happens unreflectively, formlessly.

Afterwards, in manufacturing the artistic product, one does one's utmost—often quite helplessly—to find out what it was one really meant. This purpose-

* Jörn Donner: *The Personal Vision of Ingmar Bergman*.

Smiles of a Summer Night: Naima Wifstrand

less game which is so serious, but which at the same time is so chancy and indifferent and pointless, is something one becomes more and more conscious of, I think, as the years go by. It would be crazy not to bear this constantly in mind, I think: that it's all just a game; that one is in the privileged position of being allowed to ritualize a lot of tensions and complications within and around oneself.

Perhaps I express myself clumsily—but you see what I mean? If you don't, please say so. I usually never talk about such matters.

TM: I don't quite agree with you.

IB: No, I'm only speaking for myself.

JS: I was just surprised, because it seems to me you've been answering quite a different question from the one I put to you.

SB: I'd like to pick up a thread here. I understand what you mean about it all being a game. But at the same time it becomes a sort of double-cross toward yourself, because the game is based on certain complications within yourself and at the same time gives rise to other complications, which are grasped by the public. If it was only the game they paid attention to, I fancy you'd be disappointed.

Smiles of a Summer Night: Harriet Andersson and Åke Fridell

IB: The melancholy fact about artistic creation is that there is so little of it that really gets under the public's skin. At most it can give people a momentary prod in one direction or another.

JS: But doesn't it also create a tendency for art to move more and more in the direction of entertainment, or what you call games? What penetrates beneath the skin, today, is the sort of reality we see on TV and in the mass media. As you've said at some time during these discussions of ours, one really ought to stop making feature films altogether and make something quite different instead!

IB: The drama has already taken shape. We see it being played out every day on television. Its ingredients are monstrous. And in this drama it's doubtful whether art has any rôle or occupies any real place in people's minds. The TV medium has turned all accepted concepts upside down.

JS: This fact, that while you talk about your intuition and your games, critics and viewers regard you as a tremendously conscious artist, contains, I think, a hidden paradox. One has a feeling that each little detail is where it is not by chance, but because you've decided that that's where it must be.

IB: What do you mean by that?

JS: What I mean is, you are not primarily an improviser, who creates a framework for a situation and then lets the situation itself work out its own content, adopts the content, and says 'Well, this has turned out fine!' That's the way many people in the newer films work. You're not exactly a happening-artist ...

IB: I said very clearly, didn't I, that in all circumstances the dream, the vision, the idea, the intuition comes first. Afterwards, as an artist, I've a need to give as conscious and powerful a form as possible to what has been born intuitively. This is a drive inside myself, and I can do nothing about it. But even this drive is part of the game.

SB: About *Smiles of a Summer Night*, I'd like to ask you a somewhat more technical question. In comedies, even in farces when they're good, the medium long shot is often a most effective way of describing a farcical or comic situation. It's one way of prolonging a situation, a painful situation perhaps, by which all the participants are obliged to remain inside the frame and sort things out for themselves. It's a method you use quite a lot in *Smiles of a Summer Night*. I find it most effective.

IB: The long shot is a remarkable instrument—Mizoguchi developed it to perfection. I suppose I must have hit on the idea long before I saw his films; but his technique struck me all of a heap. It was from him I pinched a long shot which I regard as among the most successful I've ever made; and that's in *Persona*, when Bibi lets the piece of broken glass lie where it is.
   But at the same time the long shot demands tremendous density and a high degree of awareness. It must never be used at random.

SB: In your earlier films you worked in long sequences, but generally using a very mobile camera and mobile sets. But in *Smiles of a Summer Night* you base everything on this farce-and-comedy principle. It comes off well. Afterwards it seems you realized just *how* well it works in dramatic sequences too, and how much elbow room it gives the actors.

IB: It was *The Seventh Seal*, I think, which first set me using it consciously. There's a scene where Bertil Anderberg has caught the plague and lies screaming in the forest behind a log. Originally I'd intended to shoot it in close-up. But then I realized its horror would be reinforced in a long shot.

JS: The long shot and mid-shot problem becomes extremely acute in TV. How should it be solved?

IB: Unfortunately TV doesn't work that way, I think. Viewing conditions are so utterly different. But on the cinema screen, where you sit staring at a point of light with nothing else to distract you, the medium long shot can be extremely suggestive.

SB: While we're on this technical question, I'd like to refer to a sequence in

109

Smiles of a Summer Night

Smiles of a Summer Night and ask you what your ideas are about camera set-ups. Obviously, the camera can be wherever one wants it to be, but every position it takes up adds different meanings to the sequence. In one scene in *Smiles of a Summer Night* you've a very high camera angle, the one where Björn Bjelvenstam, just before trying to commit suicide, sits playing the piano. Why did you choose that angle?

IB: We were in a hurry, and the sequence had been cut. Björn Bjelvenstam wasn't a success—today he earns his living in some other way. What I needed was a young Per Oscarsson, but I couldn't get hold of one. As it is, the rôle is mostly romantic. The sequence begins with him sitting there playing the piano; the candles are blown out and there's moonlight instead. Then he staggers up some stairs. As he comes towards the camera it pans up to a naked statuette. After absent-mindedly banging his forehead against it, he realizes he's resting his brow in the lap of a little 18th-century maiden with round breasts and thighs. In a state of some excitement he stands there poking at her with his forefinger: realizes what he's doing, rushes upstairs and tries to take his own life. But Björn didn't really understand what it was all about, so I had to cut the rest of the sequence.

SB: When I put that question I expected quite a different answer. Often, when one uses any other camera angle than a horizontal one, it's to define the situation more sharply in some way. A high-angle camera is often used to denigrate the actor slightly, make the audience feel sorry for him, or something of that sort.

IB: The longer one perseveres in this business, the more one realizes there aren't so very many places where you can put a camera.

If you don't mind, I'll make a little skip here. In *The Hour of the Wolf*, you may recall a sequence where Max von Sydow is sitting on the seashore trying to draw. Then Ingrid comes along. At first one only sees her feet; and she comes closer and closer. This is the only sequence in the entire film that was shot continuously. *I.e.*, there are two takes of the same shot and a dissolve in the middle, which one doesn't see, because the beginning of the second take was better than the beginning of the first, and the end of the first was better than the end of the second.

I'd envisaged that sequence clearly. But then the shore and the location looked different from what I'd imagined when I'd written it, so I began experimenting. For once I tried to improvise, and it didn't come off. That sequence was divided up into close-ups, fixed and moving camera movements. After pondering it for a couple of weeks, I came to the conclusion that the only way of doing the scene was to give it the whole feeling of meaninglessness, desolation, indifference and impotence which comes from seeing them at a distance. They are like black shadows over there against the wall. I think it works, and other people too have said so; some others say not.

JS: And this brings us to 1956, the year of *The Seventh Seal*.

The Seventh Seal: Max von Sydow with Maud Hansson in the execution scene

IB: I was teaching at the theatre school in Malmö. There were some young-sters there, eight or nine of them, and I was looking for a play to put on, for that's the best way of teaching. I couldn't find anything, so I took it into my head to write something myself. It was called *A Painting on Wood*.

It is a pure training play, and consists of a number of monologues. All except for one part. One pupil was being trained for the musical comedy section. He had a good singing voice and looked very handsome, but as soon as he opened his mouth it was a catastrophe. So I gave him a silent part. The Saracens had cut his tongue out. He was the Knight. I worked it up with my pupils and put it on.

Then, if I remember aright, it suddenly struck me one day I ought to make a film of the play; so I started on the script. The whole thing developed quite naturally. My stomach had been in bad shape and I sat writing the film in Karolinska Hospital in Stockholm while it was being put to rights. I handed in the script to SF, and SF said 'No, thank you.' But then came the success with *Smiles of a Summer Night* and I got permission to make it, providing I did it in thirty-five days. So I shot it in thirty-five days, and it was ever so cheap and ever so simple. Almost everything is shot on sets here in Råsunda, where they've built the new laboratory.

There was an old propman called Borax. Down there in the yard there were lots of original characters. He had a shed full of photographic back-drops. It was the apple of his eye. The old boy must have been over seventy.

113

The Seventh Seal: 'the dance along the horizon'

As you know, there's a stream in *The Seventh Seal*, at the point where they come tramping through the impenetrable forest with their cart and the Knight, before they meet the Witch on her way to execution. So we got hold of a fire hose and made a stream—just squirted masses of water until it began flowing like a stream—and it all looked highly effective. But if you take a close look at that mediaeval forest, behind a tree you'll see one of the tower blocks of flats out at Solna; or, to be more exact, a reflection from one of the windows. Suddenly we realized old Borax, a little white-haired fellow, was sitting there in the doorway of his shed with water flowing all round him. He looked like bloody old Noah himself! For years afterwards we kept the place for shooting exteriors, and the spot was known as Borax' Stream. It's in all the reports: Borax' Stream.

The place of execution was a little further down the yard; so we could only shoot from one side, the tower blocks being on the other. When the time came for me to inspect the heap of firewood, a crowd of little urchins were already there, clambering up on the fence and asking: 'When's the execution going to be, Mister?' So I said: 'We're starting at seven this evening.' And one little chap said: 'Then I'll go home and ask my mum if I can stay up a bit later!'

Things like that were all part of our way of shooting films in those days. It was as bohemian as that. Out at Solna we had the youngest fire-captain in Sweden, generally known as Squirt-Olle. He was given orders to prepare the

bonfire. Squirt-Olle turned out to be an inverted pyromaniac of the first order. For a week he put his whole heart and soul into preparing that bonfire. We'd arranged a fantastic camera-angle from above the bonfire and the girl hanging at the stake, and Gunnar Björnstrand and Max von Sydow and the cart with Åke Fridell, Bibi, Nils Poppe and Gunnel Lindblom in the background; plus the soldiers, of course, who had to light the bonfire. At exactly the right moment for exposure in the twilight I shouted 'action'. And out came Squirt-Olle and set fire to it and—puff!—not only we, but the whole of Solna, were swathed in a cloud of smoke stretching as far as Haga South. I was standing on a crane yelling 'Max, where are you?' And the stallion Fridell should have been riding, that was found right down by the pavilion, with Fridell hanging on behind. The trams all came to a stop, and for several weeks afterwards all the housewives of Solna were cleaning oil off their window-panes.

But the film got shot in thirty-five days. You know that scene where they dance along the horizon? We'd packed up for the evening and were just about to go off home. It was raining. Suddenly I saw a cloud: and Fischer swung his camera up. Several of the actors had already gone home, so at a moment's notice some of the grips had to stand in, get some costumes on and dance along up there. The whole take was improvised in about ten minutes flat.

JS: *The Seventh Seal* isn't only a legend, I feel, a fable about eschatological

115

questions—the film seems to me to contain more recent allusions. I'm thinking of Nils Poppe's clown. In one of his lines he says something of this sort: 'People aren't much interested in art in this part of the country.' He's the dreamer, the artist who dreams of the absolutely perfect trick of getting a ball to . . .

IB : . . . to stand still in the air, yes.

JS : This cheerful clown-like figure doesn't crop up anywhere else in your work?

IB : No, he doesn't.

JS : And clashes with your earlier pessimistic clown-figure—Jack?

IB : Altogether, this unneurotic, slightly barbarous, altogether square troupe of actors, with Jof and Mia, and Skat the black sheep, are a nice lot of people. Don't forget that at that time I was living in a happy symbiosis in the Malmö theatre—a form of theatre so robust and self-evident one can hardly even imagine such a thing today. In one huge theatre we were doing practically everything: operettas, operas, ballet, plays. As a theatrical existence it was completely unneurotic; the whole thing was a sheer joy, a sort of pure vitality. Even today those mediaeval actors still represent the sort of theatre I love most of all; robust, direct, concrete, substantial, sensual.

I don't know whether you've seen that statue of Thalia in the foyer of the Malmö City Theatre? She's wonderful—a huge, solid female of magnificent proportions, rushing toward you like a waterfall, with a gay, impudent face, a big mouth and a big nose, all the while holding both the tragic and the comic mask lightly in her hand. She's indomitable, free; her whole face is one tremendous laugh.

That's how I see theatre at its best, at its most genuine.

SB : The names of Jof and Mia aren't mere chance, are they?

IB : No, not at all. Naturally, they're Joseph and Maria, it's as simple as that. As a film it just happened. I can't remember any complications. The complications began when SF celebrated some sort of mysterious half-centenary by showing it. As a first night the atmosphere was less festive than murderous.

JS : It's the most rhetorical of all your films?

IB : Yes, I think so. It's based on a play, so that's natural enough.

SB : But essentially both the film, and the characters in it, are rather different from what they are in the play. The same rôles appear in both; but their relative proportions and their importance to the drama are different.

IB : Jof and Mia aren't in the play at all.

SB : And the relationship between the Witch and the Knight is considerably changed too?

IB: Yes, they're quite different. The play and the film have nothing to do with one another. Yet the film is obviously verbal, even so. They never stop formulating their ideas, they babble away like the very devil.

JS: In *The Seventh Seal* Jöns, the atheistic squire, says: 'We live in a ghost-world.' The Knight, Block, is seeking knowledge of a god who really exists. But the god remains silent. He exclaims: 'Why can't I kill the god within me?' But when he sees the happiness of the Jof family, he exclaims: 'Faith is great suffering.' In my view this is a rather unpleasant sort of faith, but in the film the Knight himself, on the contrary, is rather a decent fellow. We really feel he is a struggling soul. Chiefly I'm thinking of the execution scene, in which the Knight is more interested to know whether the Witch has really seen the devil, than he is in her physical sufferings. But Jöns, the atheist, gives her some water.

IB: It's two sides of the same thing. I couldn't agree with you more. To the fanatical believer physical and spiritual suffering is beside the point, compared with salvation. That is why, to him, everything happening around him is irrelevant, a mirror-image, a mere will-o'-the-wisp. But Jöns, he's a man of the here-and-now. He feels sympathy, hatred, and scorn; the other bloke is like the echo department of a large organ, placed somewhere up in the rafters.

JS: Which figure did you feel closest to at that time—1956?

IB: I can't say, really. I've always felt sympathy for the Jönses and the Jofs and the Skats and the Mias. But it's with something more like desperation I've experienced the Blocks inside myself. I can really never get shot of them, the fanatics. Whether they appear as religious fanatics or vegetarian fanatics makes no odds. They're catastrophic people. These types whose whole cast of mind as it were looks beyond mere human beings toward some unknown goal. The terrible thing is the great power they often wield over their fellow human beings. Apart from the fact that I believe they suffer like the very devil, I've no sympathy for them.

TM: Is *The Seventh Seal* a film which means a lot to you personally?

IB: It was a triumph to have carried through that large and complicated shooting schedule in such a short time, and so cheaply. It was fun reconstructing a whole epoch with such incredibly simple means.

TM: An epoch which really plays a functional rôle in the film.

IB: Yes, I still feel a sort of friendship for that film.

TM: The foreign press—not the ordinary press perhaps, but people who've written longer and more ambitious essays on it—say it's a film about the present, that it's apocalyptic, forebodes the nuclear catastrophe.

IB: That's why I made it. It's about the fear of death. It freed me from my own fear of death.

The Seventh Seal: Jof and Mia (Nils Poppe and Bibi Andersson)

s b : I'd like to touch on Max von Sydow's rôle, not only in *The Seventh Seal* but also in some of the films which followed it, like *The Face*, *Winter Light*, *Through a Glass Darkly*, *The Hour of the Wolf*, and *The Shame*—though not *The Virgin Spring* and *So Close to Life*. In all these films he gives the impression of being a very stable person both physically and mentally. But all the time these films reveal cracks in his stability. If one traces the development of his rôles, one sees these cracks have become bigger and more desperate. Have you put Max von Sydow into these rôles intentionally, because you personally feel yourself allied to them?

i b : The fact is, there's an enigmatic relationship between Max and myself. He has meant a tremendous amount to me.

Stravinski once said something good. I heard Blomdahl and him discussing Alban Berg's *Lulu*. They were discussing a singer. Stravinski said she was a bad Lulu, because she was so vulgar. But then Blomdahl, as I remember it, said: 'But Lulu's the vulgarest female alive.' And Stravinski said: 'Yes, and that's why she must be played by an actress who hasn't a trace of vulgarity in her—but can play it.'

I suppose that's exactly what I find in Max von Sydow. As an actor, Max is sound through and through. Robust. Technically durable. If I'd had a psychopath to present these deeply psychopathic rôles, it would have been unbearable.

It's a question of acting the part of a broken man, not of being him. The sort of exhibitionism in this respect which is all the rage just now will pass over, I think. By and by people will regain their feeling for the subtle detachment which often exists between Max and my madmen.

j s : I admire Max von Sydow a lot, but sometimes, when one sees the films at a certain distance, his statuesque rhetoric becomes a shade comic. I'm thinking chiefly of *The Virgin Spring*.

i b : Now I want to make it quite plain that *The Virgin Spring* must be regarded as an aberration. It's touristic, a lousy imitation of Kurosawa. At that time my admiration for the Japanese cinema was at its height. I was almost a samurai myself!

t m : In *Chaplin*, Victor Svanberg wrote that the film, far from being brutal, was sentimental.

i b : I think its motivations are all bogus.

j s : The film was made in 1959 and you got an Oscar for it. I was living in Paris that year and I recall that the reaction in Parisian cinéaste circles was the same as it was here in Sweden. Well, that's how it always is when an artist has had some extraordinary successes. People envy him. A sort of reaction sets in, his younger competitors must find someone to shoot at, and this film came just at the right moment—that was the year when an anti-Bergman wave was sweeping through the cinéaste world . . .

Max von Sydow: Martin in *Through a Glass Darkly*...

... Vogler in *The Face*...

... Johan in *Hour of the Wolf*...

... Jan in *The Shame*

IB: ... and Bo Widerberg wrote that amusing article about me being Sweden's chief tourist souvenir. À propos *The Virgin Spring*.

JS: The remarkable thing is that only a year after the New Wave had discovered you and admired you they were ready to drop you.

IB: Yes, but it's all quite logical, I think. They took what I could give them in the way of influences. And what they needed chiefly was this business of making films single-handed. The idea that there's nothing very remarkable about making films anyway. And having taken it they threw me away.

JS: Yet it wasn't the end of the story, even so. Two years later they took you to their hearts again, with *Through a Glass Darkly*.

IB: Did they? I didn't know that.

JS: I think it all had a lot to do with just those two films you made in 1960: *The Virgin Spring* and *The Devil's Eye*. The *Cahiers* group felt they were ...

IB: ... dead! And so they were! Both *The Virgin Spring* and *The Devil's Eye* are dead films. For many reasons.

TM: What was Birgitta Pettersson's attitude to the rape scene?

IB: There's a funny still, taken during the shooting. Birgitta's lying in the bushes and we're moving the camera. Up by her head sits Axel Düberg and, on top of her, Tor Isedal. Her skirt's pulled up over her stomach. All three of them are quietly munching their sandwiches, and they've put a fur underneath her.

JS: In *The Virgin Spring*—if I remember aright—you make use of models. Had you worked with model sets before? The farmhouse in the film is a model.

IB: Quite right. That's something we do now and again. P. A. Lundgren, our art director, is a specialist and incredibly clever at it. Did you know it was originally a Swedish invention? Julius Jaenzon invented it in 1919. Afterwards it was forgotten, and the French took it over. Later, little by little, we re-invented it again. It's known as mirroring in.

TM: The folk-song the film was based on was called 'Töre of Vänge's daughters'?

IB: There are twenty-seven versions of it. But in the one I read originally there were seven daughters and seven shepherds.

TM: What influence did Ulla Isaksson have on you?

IB: I suppose we each influenced the other in the wrong way. Which was rather unfortunate.

TM: Do you think the film would have been different if you'd made it all by yourself?

IB: No. I'd never any intention of writing it myself, and I find it very hard indeed to guess what might have happened. All I know is that my collaboration with Ulla in *So Close to Life* had meant an enormous amount to me. That time she was really good to me. But in *Virgin Spring* it may be we 'seduced' each other a bit.

SB: Most of your films are made from your own scripts. Why have you collaborated with other authors in some of them?

IB: Often because I've been short of time. At first it was necessary, obligatory; one of the terms on which I was allowed to make films. But later on, when I was allowed to decide things myself, it has been due to lack of time. Often I've made two films a year and put on three or four plays, besides a lot of radio plays—and that didn't leave much time to sit down and write scripts, did it?

TM: *The Face* was a tremendously vital film, I think. It's marvellously well-written, dense, polished in some way. Distinguished.

IB: It caused a certain amount of confusion when it came out. It was regarded as odd, artificial, complicated, and theatrical.

JS: It really hasn't faded at all. But I'd almost forgotten how funny it is.

IB: Unfortunately it's not so funny as I intended it to be. The actor who was the big comic rôle was so drunk all the time he couldn't remember his lines or what he had to do. So about a third of his part had to be cut, which meant that the film lost its balance and became too serious.

JS: For instance that bit about the coachman. When they experiment on him and tie his hands, he goes out and hangs himself. Then the witch, Naima Wifstrand, comes along and finds him. But in the script it says she cuts him down and breathes life into him again. Why was that taken out?

IB: In the film she became a somewhat crueller figure than perhaps I'd intended. In every way the film became a little crueller, a little blacker, a little more brutal than I'd meant it to be.

I tried to sell the idea to Carl-Anders Dymling, but he was extremely dubious. So I said: 'You understand, this is an erotic play, the whole thing's one big erotic game. When the entertainers arrive at the country house everyone becomes confused and sensually excited and crazy, and the result is a wild erotic explosion.' That wasn't just a pack of lies of course, it was also a bit like what I'd imagined. But then during the filming I suppose I must have gone rancid.

I've mentioned that those were the days when I was at Malmö City Theatre, and it was important to keep the ensemble together, so I went about promising everyone parts in my next film, even though I hadn't the faintest idea what I was going to make, and in the end had tremendous problems how to put it all together! In the end it had to be a picture in the round with masses

The Face: Vergerus (Gunnar Björnstrand) examines Vogler (Max von Sydow); Vogler's wife (Ingrid Thulin) in the background

of people in it. I fancy my entire Malmö ensemble must have been in *The Face*.

JS: Whenever you want to depict intellectuals whose attitudes are critical or sceptical you make them terribly sharp and icy, and a shade comic into the bargain; rather stiff and almost inhuman. I'm thinking of Erland Josephson, 'Anders Ellius' in *So Close to Life*; and also, since we're talking about *The Face*, the medical officer Vergérus, played by Gunnar Björnstrand. But there are other examples of the same thing.

IB: The fact is, I've every sympathy for the medical officer, precisely because he really has one great passion. In my films you'll find several of the Vergérus family, one of them comes into my next film, the one I've just written. He's an architect; but his hobby is photographing faces.

JS: Do you have some prototype in reality when you depict intellectuals in that way?

IB: Myself.

JS: It's been said that in *The Face* you were caricaturing Harry Schein.*

IB: I was just joking.

TM: It's said that Max von Sydow plays you, Björnstrand plays Harry Schein, and Ingrid Thulin plays Ingrid Thulin.

IB: I say like Flaubert: '*Madame Bovary, c'est moi!*'

SB: Ingrid Thulin hadn't had much success in Swedish films until she came to you.

IB: No, she was regarded as unstable and untalented, and it was rumoured she meant to give up the stage and films, anyway.

SB: How did you get hold of her?

IB: She went through the Royal Dramatic Theatre School, then she was at various theatres here and there, among them the Lilla Teatern, and generally flitted about. I got to know Harry Schein and Ingrid, and became friends with them. With Harry, to begin with, mostly because he was *Bonniers Literary Magazine*'s film critic and was always so critical of my films. I badly wanted to see what he looked like in reality.

TM: Sorry to interrupt you, but the same year she was in *Wild Strawberries*, she was also in *Never in Your Life*, a semi-pornographic film which the censor pounced on.

IB: Anyway, I lured her down to Malmö City Theatre and she 'recovered'. I'd always had a feeling that a person who looks like that must be extremely gifted. And I was right.

* Swedish film critic, later head of the Swedish Film Institute.

The Face: Ingrid Thulin as Aman with Toivo Pawlo

TM: I suppose it must have something to do with your way of confronting actors you believe in, your way of directing them. You must have rescued her out of some sort of despair?

IB: Out of something comes something; out of nothing, nothing; or, as my old teacher Torsten Hammarén, summing up his forty years of experience in the theatre, used to say: 'Some can come in, and others must get out.' He was speaking of actors. There was another good thing he used to say: 'The damnable thing about actors is that as soon as they've drunk enough to get a good face, they lose their memories.'

SB: *The Face* has both black traits and comic traits. But it also has one of the most overwhelming happy endings to be seen in any of your films.

IB: A bit like the end of *The Beggar's Opera*.

SB: 'Art wins out in the end.'

IB: That was mainly because I felt I was generally despised. Then all of a sudden I was given a grant out of the King's Fund, which put my shares up at home with mother and father, anyway. In *The Face* the actors are even invited to the Royal Palace on July 14th, my birthday. The command from the Palace is dated July 14th.

TM: I've the impression that Toivo Pawlo is a sort of Beethoven portrait ...

IB: No, not at all ... Incidentally, à propos this Biedermeier-milieu: every morning I used to take a morning walk from the Sofiahemmet Hospital out to Djurgården.* The street where the last sequence was shot is on Skansen.† Every morning I went inside that old Stockholm burgher house and walked about in its rooms, looking at things, sitting down, and listening to the clocks ticking there, looking at the old pictures and furniture and listening to the walls creaking. There was a very special atmosphere in there.

But *The Face*, when it came out, caused any amount of confusion, no doubt about that! And a certain amount of gloom and despondency, too. It seems to me it was in that connection the critics began really tearing my films to pieces and scaring the daylights out of the public.

JS: Perhaps it's a film that shouldn't be taken too seriously ...

IB: No, there's no reason to take it seriously.

SB: How much pleasure do you get out of summoning up a past epoch like that?

IB: An immense amount. But today it's forbidden. All that business of fabricating horrible things and yet not being particularly indignant about it all amuses me enormously. It comes natural.

SB: Would you like to do it again?

IB: Nowadays it costs such a tremendous lot of money, so it's out of the question. I couldn't imagine anything more enjoyable than presenting our Swedish 18th century. In fact this business of reconstructing past epochs is part of my professional equipment. I find it stimulating. But today no one can afford to invest in such stuff.

JS: Why do you keep turning back to a turn-of-the-century environment? Is it some sort of nostalgia?

IB: Mostly because it stimulates my imagination.

JS: You said earlier you grew up in a home where time had stood still for fifty years. Presumably this must mean you've some sort of personal experience of the turn-of-the-century atmosphere?

IB: Obviously. But in some way I feel at home in the Sweden of the Middle Ages too. I'm always poking my nose into our old churches on Gotland—there are ninety-four of them, none built later than 1395 or whatever year it was—and looking at mediaeval paintings and fonts and gravestones. All these are things people have lived with. The same applies to the 1850s, with their romanticism and ghosts, right on the brink of the industrial revolution.

* Park outside Stockholm.
† Stockholm's outdoor museum, where a number of historical houses are assembled.

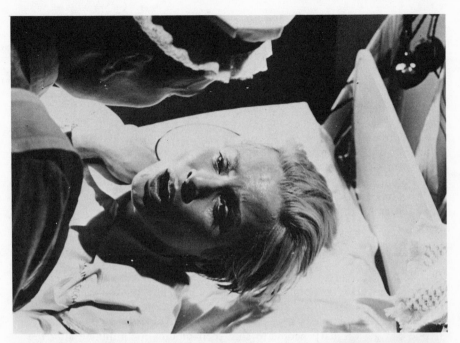

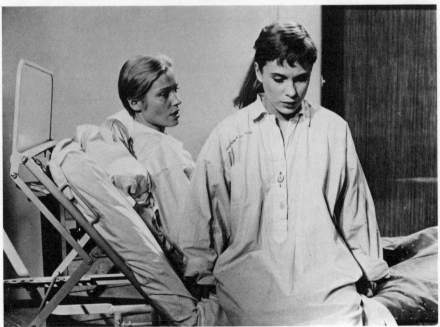

So Close to Life: two of the women: Ingrid Thulin and Bibi Andersson

JS: *So Close to Life* was shot in 1957. I saw it on TV recently. As a documentary it didn't feel at all so genuine or authentic any longer. It's theatrical in some way.

IB: I suppose I can say that compared with today's demands for authenticity it's extremely theatrical. No doubt about that.

JS: What moral attitude do you adopt toward the influence your films can have on other people—even though it may not have been your intention to influence them in that way? According to a psychiatrist I know, a young woman had a breakdown after seeing a scene in *Port of Call*, the one where the girl crawls under the bed when her parents are quarrelling. Or women who become scared of having a miscarriage after seeing *So Close to Life*. Stig Ahlgren has accused you, in *Through a Glass Darkly*, of bringing out latent schizophrenia in the viewer.

IB: Well, what of it?

JS: Haven't you ever felt any moral . . .

IB: . . . bellyache? No! If I weren't to be quite honest with you, I could say I've been in a state of moral conflict. But if I'm to be quite frank, no, I don't feel the least bit shaken by bringing out someone's latent schizophrenia just because someone in one of my films crawls under her bed—on the contrary. If one can get ordinary people to shut their mouths for a minute after the curtain has fallen, or get ordinary folk to make themselves a sandwich and sit together and have a chat in the kitchen for five minutes after seeing a film, or if someone is suddenly happy as he recalls certain scenes as he walks home afterwards, or someone suddenly cries, or feels shaken, or laughs, or feels better or worse—if people are influenced the least little bit, then the film has done its job.

JS: Even if, from the social point of view, its influence may be negative?

IB: I regard that objection as irrelevant. Inside the man who makes the product there's always a built-in censor.

JS: As an artist, have you ever been faced with a situation in which two solutions have occurred to you, so that you could have solved the problem in one particular way, but have chosen an aesthetically inferior solution for non-aesthetic reasons?

IB: No, that's something I've never done. I always choose the solution which will have the greatest impact. All that matters to me is to influence people, get into contact with them, drive a wedge into people's indifference or passivity.

Råsunda, 8 October 1968

JONAS SIMA: Today we thought we'd talk about *Wild Strawberries*. It's said that you had made quite a study of Victor Sjöström's life when you wrote the script for *Wild Strawberries*. Was the film intended as a monument to Victor Sjöström from the outset?—a demonstration of historical continuity within the Swedish cinema?

INGMAR BERGMAN: Not a scrap. *Wild Strawberries* had quite another starting point. You know that in my earlier years I used to be up in Dalarna a great deal. I'd grown up in a little village there with my grandmother, although in the wintertime she mostly lived in a big, old-fashioned flat in Uppsala.

Early one morning I had to drive up to Dalarna. So I took the car and drove out of Stockholm. I imagine it must have been between four and five in the morning—and got to Uppsala. You know Uppsala, two of you have been to university there. With its Carolina Rediviva Library, the cathedral, the castle, the Gustavianum building, the Gillet Restaurant, the river with rapids, and all those old cinemas—Fyrisbiografen, Eddabiografen (though that can't have been there in your day), Skandia, Röda Kvarn—the swans' pond, the Flustret Restaurant and the blue tram and the yellow tram and the green tram—it's a charming old town.

My grandmother lived at Nedre Slottsgatan 14, opposite Skrapan—you

131

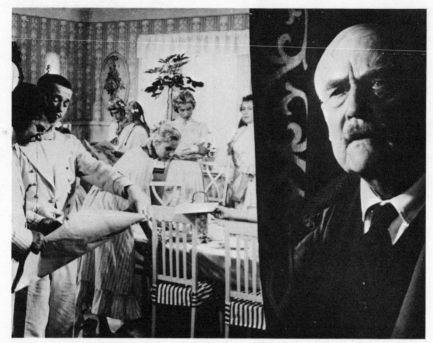

Wild Strawberries: Victor Sjöström as Isak Borg

know, the school. It was a very old house indeed, with an immense flat in it. In one of its long corridors there was a plush-upholstered toilet and lots of big rooms with ticking clocks, enormous carpets and massive furniture. It had all been standing there ever since she had moved in as a bride: the combined furniture of two upper middle class families, pictures from Italy, statues, palms.

That's where I lived as a little boy, and that sort of world had made a strong impression upon me.

That morning in the car I felt a sudden impulse to drive up to Slottsgatan 14. It was autumn, and a faint sun had begun to fall on the cathedral and the clock was just striking five. I went into the little cobblestone yard. Then I went up into the house and took hold of the door knob to the kitchen door, which still had its coloured glass pattern; and a feeling ran quickly through me: suppose I open it? Supposing old Lalla (our old cook, she was) is standing inside there, in her big apron, making porridge for breakfast, as she did so many times when I was little? Suppose I could suddenly walk into my childhood?

Nowadays I don't suffer much from nostalgia, but I used to. I think Maria Wine* has said somewhere that one sleeps in one's childhood's shoe. Well,

---

* Swedish poetess.

that's exactly how it was. Then it struck me: supposing I make a film of someone coming along, perfectly realistically, and suddenly opening a door and walking into his childhood? And then opening another door and walking out into reality again? And then walking round the corner of the street and coming into some other period of his life, and everything still alive and going on as before? That was the real starting point of *Wild Strawberries*.

JS: Which year was it you made that trip?

IB: It must have been the autumn of 1956. And afterwards, in the spring, as far as I remember, I began writing the script. I find dates difficult.

One of my best friends is a doctor, so I thought it might be a practical solution to make the main character a doctor.

Then I thought the old boy ought to be a tired old egocentric, who'd cut off everything around him—as I'd done.

JS: So, when you sat down to write the script, you didn't have Victor Sjöström in mind from the beginning?

IB: Well, I began to write, and then I thought: who the devil can do this? And then it struck me that Victor would be best. So Carl-Anders Dymling had a word with him and asked whether I could speak to him about it. Victor was feeling wretched and didn't want to.

JS: How old was he then?

IB: I can't say for certain, but I fancy he must have been seventy-eight. He was misanthropic and tired and felt old. So Carl-Anders had said to him: 'All you've got to do is lie down under a tree and munch strawberries and think of your own past, so it won't exactly be hard work.' Afterwards, when Victor had taken a look at the script, he wanted to back out. I had to use all my powers of persuasion to get him to play the part.

The first day we worked together Victor was in a vile temper. He said: 'I don't want to do this, I don't think you're right.' We fell out. I wanted him to do certain things he didn't want to do; or, to be more exact, I wanted him *not* to do certain things he wanted to.

JS: What, for instance?

IB: Oh, he was all tensed up and wanted to do a lot of things—I didn't want him to do anything at all. But after that he was wonderful to work with, ever so simple, sincere and fierce ...

I was a bit scared of those coffin scenes. For an old man to go and lie down in a coffin, that can feel tough. But he came to me and said: 'Shan't we do that bit with the coffin?'

He was delighted with Bibi Andersson, and Bibi was sweet to him. Bibi was no age at all at that time, only twenty-one. I've a bewitching scene which I shot myself on 16 mm: they're sitting waiting for a scene to be shot, with people walking about all round them, and there they sit flirting. He'd been a

Wild Strawberries: Bibi Andersson and Victor Sjöströ

great man for the ladies in his day, Victor had. There he sits making little approaches, and Bibi is delighted, taken with the old lion in the most womanly way.

As long as Victor got home at a quarter past five each day and had his whisky punctually, all went well.

The second time that things nearly went wrong was when we were to shoot a scene out here in the yard. In those days there used to be a little meadow there, and the light fell beautifully on that meadow just after five o'clock. It was the final scene, the one in which Victor looks so spiritual; but he was furious because he wouldn't get home to his whisky on time.

As soon as Victor had got a grasp on that old boy—and calmed down—he suddenly began to enjoy the filming. He'd been wandering about saying he felt rotten, and had gone to his doctor; and the doctor had said: 'But you're much better, Mr Sjöström.' Then he came up to me, ever so pleased and confused and said he felt better even though he felt worse. And that was the end of our difficulties.

I've always admired him so as a film artist. It was marvellous, having this inexhaustible wellspring near to hand every day. Unfortunately no one thought of sitting down beside him with a tape recorder, it wasn't usual in those days. I've often thought of writing about it, for he had so much to tell me about how he started and how his masterpieces came into being. Have you seen *Ingeborg Holm*? It's one of the most remarkable films ever made—1913!

TORSTEN MANNS: We find your meeting with him fascinating. Suddenly you're standing at the fountainhead.

IB: Yes, it's very strange, and I still feel it was one of the most important things that ever happened to me. Victor taught me a lot.

TM: In what way?

IB: Through his films.

STIG BJÖRKMAN: What is it you appreciate most in them? And which do you feel has meant something special to you?

IB: Above all *Ingeborg Holm*, as I've said, and *The Phantom Carriage*, but also *The Executioner*. *The Outlaw and His Wife*, too, a marvellously well-narrated film.

SB: But what, exactly, is it in Sjöström's films that has influenced you?

IB: His incorruptible demand for truth, his incorruptible observation of reality. His way of never for a moment making things easy for himself, or simplifying or skipping things or cheating or succumbing to mere brilliance. In *Sons of Ingmar*, for instance, there are some incomparable sequences, as there are in *Karin Daughter of Ingmar*, too. Have you seen *The Wind* with Lillian Gish?

136

JS: Here we have the traditional perspective backwards in time. So you are conscious of linking up with a tradition in Swedish films?

IB: Yes.

JS: But more with Victor Sjöström than with Mauritz Stiller?

IB: Well, I think Stiller, with his *Erotikon* and *Herr Arne's Treasure*, is a lot of fun. And his *The Atonement of Gösta Berling*, too, is a fresh, powerful, vital film. But time has left Stiller's films behind much more than it has Victor's. *Ingeborg Holm* is still true and gripping; remarkably modern. If run at its proper speed, which is 16 frames a second, it is photographically and scenically quite perfect. Often he works on two planes—something's being played out in the foreground, but then, through a doorway for instance, one sees something quite different is going on in the background.

TM: What attitude did Victor Sjöström have to your films?

IB: We never talked about them.

SB: If you were to point out the historical influences you have been aware of in the art of cinema, where are we to find them? Have you been influenced by any particular directors, any special period? You have mentioned German expressionism. But have the Russian silents, for instance, or the early Americans, meant anything to you?

IB: Not until 1949, when I first went abroad. I was in Paris a couple of months and was always running to the Cinémathèque in the Avenue de Messine. That was when I seriously began to study cinema. I'd never seen any old films before, only our Swedish silents. I was working in Gothenburg and Hälsingborg, and it was hard to get hold of the classics there.

JS: But you've seen them since?

IB: In 1952 I went to Malmö. There was the film museum in Copenhagen, just across the water. Here in Sweden we only had the Historical Film Collections, but those were all stills.

SB: But they had screenings, hadn't they?

IB: I never got to any of them; and I didn't belong to the student film studio, either.

It was in 1948, I believe, that Selznick wanted me to write and Sjöberg to direct Ibsen's *Doll's House*. I wrote a script for which I got the fantastic sum of Sw.cr. 30,000 ($6,000, £2,000), an enormous fee in those days. With it I bought myself my first proper 9·5 mm projector. Have you ever seen that sort of film, with the perforations down the middle? Pathé's? Then I bought *Caligari* and *Variety* and *The Niebelungs* and a lot of Chaplin films.

JS: Have you still got them?

IB: Yes, I've still got them. And I've still got an old 9·5 mm projector I can use. Such projectors are utterly impossible to get hold of today.

SB: Looking at your films for influences from the past, one finds expressionist traits going back to the Germans.

IB: That may be. The influence I'm most conscious of, though, is from the French. But then the French, in their turn, had been greatly influenced by the Germans.
Then there's one film I still think is fine in parts. And that is Machaty's *Ecstasy*. It came to Sweden in 1935 or 1936, I think; and it made such a vivid impression on me that, though I've never seen it again, I can still remember parts of it, image by image. It narrated in pictures. And then of course there was that naked woman one saw suddenly, and that was beautiful and disturbing.

TM: Your feeling for images is stronger than—how shall I put it—your verbal memory?

IB: I've no verbal memory at all. I can only recall images. But that faculty is well developed.

JS: Supposing we talk a bit more about the influences perhaps to be discerned in *Wild Strawberries*? You have said you think it was fairly free from influences. But of course there are traces of Strindberg?

IB: Obviously.

JS: *The Dream Play* and *To Damascus*.

IB: Naturally. Not to forget Jonas Love Almqvist.*

JS: Let's talk a bit about the ideas to be found in *Wild Strawberries*. It's a psychoanalytic film, with both religious and psychotherapeutic implications.

IB: That wasn't how I experienced it when I was making it. I made it as a run-down of my earlier life, a searching, final test. As for the psychoanalytical aspect, I had no real grip on it. It's other people who've stuck that on afterwards. For me the film is tangible, concrete.

SB: Just how conscious or self-critical is one, I wonder, when working on the various stages of a film script, filming, editing? It is only afterwards that all the theories begin to sprout. We were talking about dreams, how important they are. Certain dreams one writes down, maybe one reflects on their meaning for oneself in one's current situation. While one is writing a film, maybe, it's easy to relate it to one's surroundings, expose it to outside pressure. In a film, perhaps, one expresses oneself in much the same way as one treats a dream one has been interested in? But does this coincide with the theories

* C. J. L. Almqvist (1793–1866), Swedish novelist, poet, and dramatist.

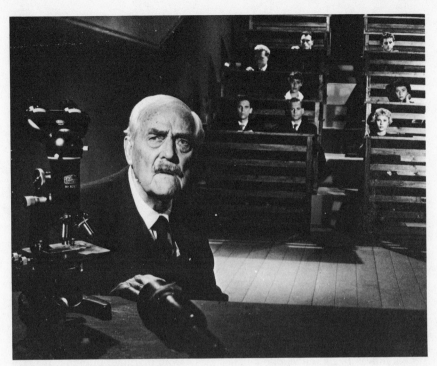

Wild Strawberries: Victor Sjöström

people make up around a film? How much theorizing does one really indulge in while working on it—if you see what I mean?

IB: I see perfectly.

SB: About a lot of it one can say afterwards 'That wasn't in my head at all— all that's been made up by critics and wiseacres.' But one must have had *something* in one's head while at work on it. How much connection do you think there is between the theories on which one bases one's work and the theories built up afterwards?

IB: I'll try to be as concrete as I can. While I'm writing, I'm immune to all marginal discussion. It hardly exists at all. If it did, I think I'd fall into such despondency, such a feeling of exposing myself and others, that I'd simply cancel the whole production out of sheer bashfulness. Actors get their teeth into it at quite another level. From their theatre work they're used to getting to grips with an author and a rôle and to asking themselves 'What's really behind this, why has he written this or that?' They come up and say things which can be painful, and often one shies away and says: 'That's not how it is at all, that's not right.' But secretly one often has to agree with them. All the

Wild Strawberries: the engineer Ahlman (Gunnar Sjöberg) with wife (Gunnel Broström)...

time a film is being made, one flinches away from marginal thinking. If I rely on my intuition I know it will lead me in the right direction. I don't need to argue with it. If I begin hesitating and discussing, I get so tangled up in personal complications and become so crudely aware of what it really is I'm depicting, I can't go on. Afterwards, I can often realize what I've really made, what I've depicted, or written. Obviously I was perfectly well aware from the outset, on the other hand, that Engineer Ahlman and his wife are a scurrilous portrait of Stig Ahlgren* and his wife. Stig Ahlgren had just beheaded me for some reason or other. And this was my revenge.

S B : Yes, and if one remembers that episode in *Wild Strawberries* very clearly, it's because it's like a short story going on on one side of the main action.

I B : Dead as a doornail.

J S : Well, it's highly dramatized—an ominously threatening scene, most unpleasant.

S B : For it you use two actors we haven't seen in your films before. You must have had some definite purpose in choosing them?

I B : Gunnar Sjöberg resembled Stig Ahlgren, and Gunnel Broström had the

* Columnist and critic, known for his scathing articles.

... and with Isak Borg (Victor Sjöström)

exact manner of speaking I needed. So it was a sensuously conscious act. Besides which I suppose I must have been splashing about in psychoanalytical ideas. I'd just begun to be discovered by the *Cahiers du Cinéma* gang, so I wasn't entirely immune to the critics, either.

The idea was that when Victor and Stig Ahlgren/Gunnar Sjöberg walked through the dream landscape to reach the boulder where Gertrud Fridh and Åke Fridell were copulating, one should discover snakes all over the place. So in the big studio we constructed a terrarium and managed to get all the snake-fanciers in Sweden to bring their protégés. I should think we must have had between two and three hundred adders. When the time came to let them out— phut!—and all the snakes had vanished! It turned out there was a hole in the terrarium. For weeks the snake-fanciers were out here at Råsunda collecting their little darlings.

That was one of the times I was given hell for playing up to the critics.

JS: You were on the way to doing the same thing in *The Hour of the Wolf*, weren't you? You'd scraped together a mass of birds that never appeared ...

IB: True. Another moment of aberration. But it passed over. Sin punishes itself.

JS: Otherwise the narrative in *Wild Strawberries* is psychologically constructed. The entire film is quite simply about this Professor Isak Borg and his relations to himself and those closest to him.

Wild Strawberries: the dream sequence

IB: After I'd been at it quite a while, writing the script, I discovered an innocent coincidence in one of the details: namely, that Isak Borg has the same initials as myself. I certainly hadn't intended it consciously. I chose the name Isak because he seemed icy.

JS: It was a matter of settling accounts with yourself in such a way as to gain insight that could bring peace to Isak Borg. That's why he travels through this childhood landscape.

IB: The film was based on my experiences during that trip to Uppsala. It was all as simple, concrete, and tangible as that. And I had no difficulty at all in carrying it through.

That dream about the coffin is one I've had myself, a compulsive dream of mine. Not that I was lying in the coffin myself. I made that up. But the bit where the hearse comes along and bumps into a lamp-post, and the coffin falls out and tips out the corpse. I had dreamed that many times.

JS: The psychology has almost catholic implications. How conscious were you of them?

IB: Not at all.

JS: The business about Isak Borg's guilt feelings being punished by emotional frigidity and fear of death, and the confession, which is what the journey really is ... He seems to want to justify himself before dying; to gather some spiritual capital by doing at least one good deed ...

IB: All that about his son owing him money and wanting to repay it, or Borg cancelling the debt—is that what you're thinking of?

JS: No, I was seeing it more in a theological light.

IB: I've never been much smitten by catholicism. I've never been committed to any religious dogma of any sort. The film has an underlying religiosity—a basic attitude—of course it has. But it doesn't clash with the general psychological approach.

SB: It's along these lines your catholic exegetes have interpreted the film ...

IB: For years the catholics had me on their blacklist. Then along comes some sharp-witted pater and says 'Let's take this lad into the business, instead.' And I've been plagued with catholic interpretations ever since.

JS: You've never felt any inclination to convert?

IB: No, I've never felt any attraction to catholicism. Catholicism, I think, does have its attractions. But protestantism is a wretched kettle of fish.

TM: To me the *Wild Strawberries* narrative seems entirely classical in structure—its purification process, its catharsis-scheme, are almost Aristotelian. Perhaps because you've had so much to do with the theatre?

I B : One finds a loose end, tugs at it; and it all comes out quite simply, hangs together from end to end. All one has to do is follow it carefully to the end.

S B : Its structure is very concrete, has an almost classical filmic simplicity— this journey which allows digressions in every direction. Films like Rossellini's *Voyage to Italy* and Godard's *Pierrot le Fou* have much the same. They are tremendously different, but both make extremely conscious use of their journeys.

I B : Many of my films are about journeys, about people going from one place to another. What is stone-dead in *Wild Strawberries*—as far as I now remember it—is the three youngsters. Not the one played by Bibi in the flashbacks: she's rather a sweet girl. But these three who are supposed to represent modern kids. Even at that time the image was utterly outdated.

T M : Many people see *Wild Strawberries* above all as a film in which you take stock, look back. And when one goes back to the sources one has been drawing inspiration from, or thinks one has, to one's childhood and its events—what happens? Well, one discovers a petrified world. Only bits of it are of any use. I experienced this in the summer of 1968 when visiting my father. All of a sudden something wasn't working. Now I ask you—can an artist, even so, make use of this, turn it into something vital? Well, *Wild Strawberries* answers my question. It's so enormously vital, so sensitive and deep.

I B : To me it seemed to be two quite different things. When I used to go home to my parents—my mother's dead now—and visit them in their flat in Storgatan in Stockholm, where I'd grown up, and found everything there just the same, everything standing in the same place; then, like you, I felt it was a petrified world, something I no longer had any contact with.

T M : It gave you no inspiration?

I B : There was just a sort of twilight, and something infinitely sad; but nothing stimulating or exciting. A world which has already sunk and only exists in memory, on the other hand, that's always alive. Admittedly, it's a closed, secretive, averted world. But its implications are stimulating.

T M : Though you re-evaluate it?

I B : Of course. I take up the images from my childhood, put them into the 'projector', run them into myself, and have an entirely new way of evaluating them.

S B : And having them at a distance, you can also control them . . . it doesn't hurt in the same way?

I B : Not in the same way. But it hurts.

TM: What I'm thinking of particularly are Borg's two disappointments: his wife's infidelity—that comes in the second place—first comes the story with Sara. These are the two excesses he has committed. And he's always regretting them.

IB: Certain painful experiences are so blocked they're immobile, impossible to handle.

JS: The son Evald, played by Gunnar Björnstrand ... it's obvious that his emotional frigidity, his inability to create a genuine emotional climate in his own marriage, have their roots in the old home. On both sides there's a sort of attempt to find love-compensation—on the father's, who has never been able to show love or create an emotional situation in his home, toward the son and his emotional inhibitions?

IB: Exactly.

JS: In many ways I see this as a criticism of the traditional structure of the family, centred on a patriarchal father-figure.

IB: Obviously. But all this business about Evald and his father is so tremendously personal, I can't sort it out. Nor can I sort out the relationship between Isak Borg and his old mother.

TM: Isn't it so that the sort of frigid interpersonal relations we see in this film get passed on down the generations, almost serially? It infects the relationship between Evald and Marianne. If it looks the same, it's because he carries within himself the chill from the father, as the father in his turn does from his mother.

IB: Marianne is different. That's why it changes; and the vicious circle is broken. A study has been made of the effect of beating children—those who've been beaten become the beaters. It's horrible.

JS: Why do you let Isak Borg's mother be alive still—I don't remember whether the film says how old she is. She must be over ninety?

IB: Well, I suppose we imagined her somewhere between ninety and a hundred—almost mythical. She says: 'I feel so horribly cold, what can it be due to, particularly here in my stomach?' The notion occurred to me that some children are born from cold wombs. I think it's a horrible idea, little embryos lying there shivering with cold. It was out of that line in the dialogue that the mother came into being. She ought really to have died long ago.

Marianne sees her standing there among all the toys, and sees the connection: the icy chain of aggressions and boredom.

TM: Do you think Marianne can save Evald?

IB: I think it's possible.

TM: I don't ...

J S : There's something paradoxical here. Marianne stands for someone who is more positive to life; a warmer, more modern person. But for this rôle you chose an actress who in herself doesn't represent these qualities, and whom you afterwards used to express a certain chilly intellectuality . . .

I B : Ingrid Thulin is a magnificent instrument. What was crucial was that she should be a person of firm, strong character, and who knew how to express it—Ingrid emanates something substantial; and I suppose that was what I wanted. Not anyone would have done to play against so overwhelming a personality as Victor.

J S : Well, shall we take *The Devil's Eye*?

I B : With *The Devil's Eye* things were like this: When I went to Carl-Anders Dymling with *Herr Töres döttrar i Vänge*, first he said no. So I said: 'Well, supposing I make a comedy afterwards, can I make it then?' And he said yes.
   In SF's archive there was a wretched old play called, I think, *The Return of Don Juan* or something of that sort—by a Danish author. I thought it might be rather fun to make a comedy out of it. In the early spring or late winter I was up in Dalarna writing on *The Virgin Spring*. I've been in the theatre so long and at one time used to write plays. Sometimes I've a longing to write plays, real plays. By plays I mean, in this context, something projected through words; in which the word takes priority. Naturally, it's hard to say exactly where the boundary goes for a play—so of course I tumbled into that hole. I wrote a play to which I just about managed to give a cinematic form. Being really a stage-play and, I'm afraid, not a particularly good stage-play either, it has all sorts of shortcomings.
   First I wrote a script. Then Ulla Isaksson and I wrote *The Virgin Spring*. Then I tore up the first script and rewrote it with parts of the first one, so it became a patchwork, though I didn't notice it at the time. I thought it admirable.
   So everything was fine and Jarl Kulle was in it. Then, at a very early stage—almost before we'd begun shooting it—Jalle said: 'Look, I can't do this rôle. This isn't a young, vital Don Juan! It's an old burnt-up fellow, completely worn out, a tragic figure. He's not my type. I can't do him.' Jalle's comments were instinctively right, but I waved them aside. He was right and I was wrong!
   Then I made *The Virgin Spring*, in May and June I took a month or so off, and then got busy with *The Devil's Eye*. And that's not good either.
   After shooting a film, it takes time—quite a lot of time—before one has collected oneself. So the film was rather weary, flabby in form, I think. It's not that I'm ashamed of having made it; it's simply that it turned into a series of mistakes and misunderstandings. Otherwise, I think it does have a few good qualities. But it's certainly one of my films I haven't much feeling for.
   I remember I was excessively tired during the filming. After *The Face* my films had been 'discovered' in America. There were lots of Americans here,

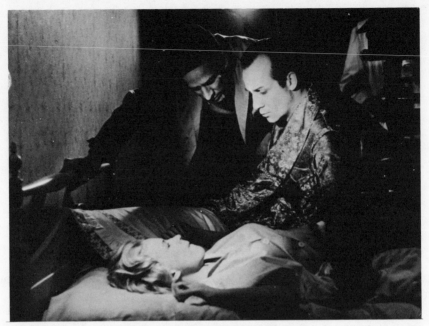

The Devil's Eye: Bergman directing Jarl Kulle and Bibi Andersson

and I had to have lunch with them. And *Life* was here and made a reportage. And *Newsweek* and *Time*. They simply wouldn't leave me in peace.

And then—I'd been uprooted. I'd just been engaged by the Royal Dramatic Theatre and had put on a dreadfully unsuccessful, tired and flabby production of Tchekov's *The Seagull*. I was unhappy at the theatre and thought everything was wrong.

TM: You must have been thoroughly rested, though, when you started on the trilogy: three fantastic films, all highly condensed, solid and fine.

IB: Suddenly one realizes something's happening that isn't right. I never planned those three films as a suite. They just followed one another. My down-period had begun with *The Virgin Spring*. At the time I'd thought it a good film, one hell of a fine film! I considered it one of my best films. I thought it was magnificent. Only much later did I discover it was all exterior scenery and no inner content. It was a washout.

TM: Unclear in a way.

IB: Yes. My mind must have been confused—largely because I'd left the Malmö City Theatre. I no longer had a secure anchorage. I was being moved about, had pulled up my roots, and had begun moving into the villa in

Djursholm* and was embarking on an entirely new way of life. I didn't really know whether I was fish or fowl, or where I belonged. And all this must have infected my work.

TM: Instead of just saying there's something wrong with *The Devil's Eye*, perhaps we should try to find out *what* is wrong with it. But you simply blame it on lack of inspiration?

IB: The worst of it is, one almost never knows—until afterwards—whether one has made something bad, or merely something one can't feel for. Only *once* has it happened that I've made something I've known from the beginning would be rubbish: and that was *This Can't Happen Here*. Otherwise I've always started out with the certainty that I'm about to make the best film in the world. And still do.

TM: Such a film gives the Bergman-hecklers grist to their mill. And of course they seize their opportunity!

IB: And don't mince their words, either!

TM: *The Devil's Eye* was the second film to be taken up by *Chaplin*. Victor Svanberg wrote about *Virgin Spring*, and *The Devil's Eye* figured in connection with the anti-Bergman number.

IB: Ernest Riffe—he's a Frenchman! The name dates from 1949. I was in France with a girl and she had a dreadful longing to go to a fashionable hairdresser called Ernest Riffe. She had very lovely hair, slightly reddish, long and thick. He must have been a pederast. He flung himself on this fantastic womanly head of hair—and cut it all off. I swore I'd be bloodily revenged; and christened my adversary Ernest Riffe.

JS: *The Pleasure Garden* and *Now About These Women* are written by the same author, Buntel Eriksson, who—we know now—is identical with yourself and Erland Josephson. Can you tell us something about the genesis of this man and how he came to write his two films?

IB: Erland often used to say he found it hard to think up stories but found writing dialogue fun; while I find it easy to think up stories, but a bore writing dialogue. So we started, mostly for fun.

When Carl-Anders Dymling fell seriously ill, SF didn't have a single script worth shooting. But they had Sickan Carlsson† and Gunnar Björnstrand on their payroll; so we had to make something. Since I'd been there for years and the organization was on the verge of falling to pieces altogether, we formed an interim government out of our business manager Birger Jukberg, Harald Molander, Allan Ekelund, and Hasse Ekman. Out at Råsunda everything was at a standstill—we had a hundred and thirty-five people on the payroll, all wandering about doing nothing. *The Pleasure Garden* was shot, as far as I recall, while I was making *Winter Light*.

---

* High-class Stockholm suburb.   † Swedish comedienne.

TM: Why did you choose a pseudonym instead of your own two names?

IB: Just for fun. We kidded ourselves into thinking we could keep it a secret. We had big plans for a lengthy collaboration covering the entire field of radio plays, films, ordinary plays, everything under the sun.

SB: Buntel Eriksson wrote two pastiches.

IB: Today I think *The Pleasure Garden* was unreasonably mauled about by the critics. It was a completely innocuous film, but got a dreadful bawling out. I think it's a bit boring, but quite sweet. Sickan is unusually good in it and Gunnar is quite funny and Bibi is charming. It was our first colour film—we'd just started our colour film school, too.

SB: *The Pleasure Garden* became a weapon in Bo Widerberg's hands when he wrote his book *Visionen i Svensk film*, about the situation in the Swedish cinema at that time.

IB: To Sickan Carlsson and Gunnar, who really was good in it, it was a nasty blow under the belt. So to hell—that's what I say!

TM: And she's not made any more films?

IB: No.

SB: What sort of an image did Sickan have for you and Erland? Of all Swedish actresses she is the one who has really gone through all these comedies with a special image—who has set her stamp on a special type of comedy.

IB: Sickan emanates something robust, self-evident, not at all deep, but good. I think she had a fine erotic charm and there was every reason to exploit it.

SB: She was the eternal teenager—she went on playing schoolgirls for I don't know how long.

IB: But here we made her a grown-up female, with a daughter of twenty, even.
We really went to a lot of trouble to make a fine colour film: repainted houses, took endless tests, and God knows what else. The film was shown to the critics out at Filmteknik, the only place where there was a decent colour film projector. It was a horrible, cloudy, cold evening, just before Christmas. I saw the gathering as they arrived, and afterwards as they were standing out there on the slope after the show was over, waiting for taxis. Well, that's a sight I'll never forget! A gathering of black, frozen crows, standing there glowering.

SB: You were acting as producer at that time?

IB: There was no one else. There was nothing for it, I had to stand in.

SB: Alf Kjellin was working here, and Hans Abramson was making his first film, and so were Vilgot Sjöman and Gunnar Hellström. How far did you follow what they were doing, as production supervisor? I don't know whether you directly collaborated in certain scripts; but anyway you contributed to them. You were responsible for *The Mistress*, surely?

I B : Certainly, I insisted on *The Mistress* being made. No one knew what Vilgot was worth. He'd never made a foot of film before. But he'd written to me and said: 'If you don't do this, I'll make it myself.' So I thought SF really ought to make the film, and pushed it through. I promised to take over as director myself, if it turned out Vilgot couldn't manage it.

Vilgot took his job tremendously seriously, and made, I think, a wonderful film. I was acting as producer, and was responsible for it; so there was a hell of a row when the State Railways refused to lend us a sleeping car.

S B : But did you act as producer for *The Pleasure Garden* and other films, too?

I B : One might say so, yes. In the last resort it was I who was responsible for the productions which started with *The Brig 'Three Lilies'*.

S B : And were also responsible for the engagement of certain directors?

I B : Yes.

S B : Shall we take *Now About These Women*?

I B : Well, you're specialists on it!

T M : Yes, we find it very funny.

S B : It's like one of Stroheim's films. But softer in some way.

I B : It's quite putrid. It seems to me we've talked about that film already.

S B : We've talked about it, and you said there wasn't much to say; so we said we'd come back to it. Now I'd like to ask you what you think of farce artistes?

I B : When farce is good there's nothing better. But it's practically the hardest thing of all. It's a strategic gift, an intellectual strategic gift, to get things to begin in one corner and explode in another, often syncopatedly: to make the audience think something's going to go bang, and it doesn't: and then does.

J S : *A Lesson in Love* is rather burlesque?

I B : It is.

S B : Well, we've all grown up on the silent comedies, and Tati and Jerry Lewis are working in that tradition, too. *Now About These Women* also reaches back to the 'sources'. It's more of a pure farce than any of your earlier comedies.

I B : Yes, you can say that. The ones we've mentioned so far were something between comedies and farces. To me a farce can be defined as a comical-

Now About These Women: Jarl Kulle, Barbro Hiort af Ornäs and Allan Edwa

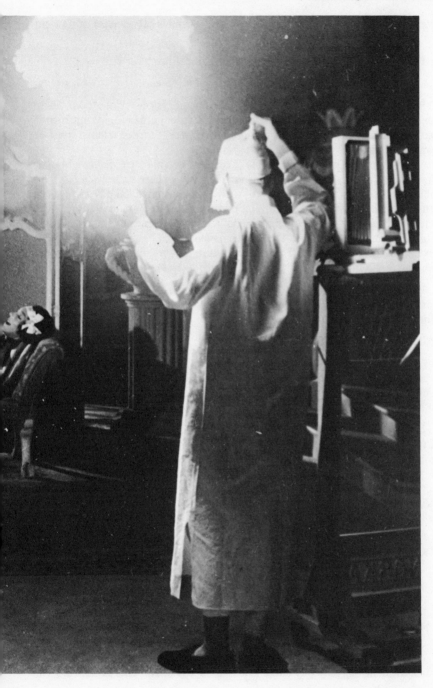

realistic situation carried to absurdity, where it comes off because of its rigid logic.

s b : I think *Now About These Women* is a logical film, too.

i b : Yes, it's completely consistent from beginning to end.

s b : But it seems to me a great many people misunderstood *Now About These Women*. It contains many elements of classical farce, it has logic: but then it ceases to make sense along the usual lines. The farce is turned against itself. It doesn't turn out as funny as one had expected.

In my view there are two very fine farce scenes which are on the verge of being funny, though they were never intended to be. There's always a *but*. The public is cheated of the effect it is waiting for. For instance, take Kulle's entry when he *doesn't* go into the swimming pool, and then his manipulation of the statue which *doesn't* fall to the floor. You keep these scenes in static pictures, teasing the viewer's patience. The viewer is cheated. His perfectly legitimate expectations find no outlet. Things never turn out as one expects them to, either for Jarl Kulle or for us. And so we turn against the film, instead.

i b : Besides which there is no one to identify with. The whole group is observed from without, completely objectively. We stuck to this completely mathematical formula throughout.

s b : It's frightfully chilly—though I don't mean anything negative by that.

i b : Very few people could swallow that film. And then of course its problems were altogether too exclusive. The whole of this question of the artist and his critics is totally uninteresting. To the great public the artist's concern for his own immortality is simply neither here nor there.

t m : You speak of identification in farces of this sort, and immediately I think of Chaplin. For a situation to be amusing, do you think we must be able to identify with it? In Chaplin's *The Immigrant*, he's leaning over the ship's rail and one thinks he's being sick; whereas actually he's just fishing. A different effect intervenes. And one can't help laughing. In *The Gold Rush*, when he's walking about on that precipice and a bear comes after him, one thinks the bear's going to attack him; but the bear wanders off somewhere else, and he just walks on. Do people really experience Chaplin as a human being? I don't.

i b : No, but they identify with him. That's the great mystery. They identify with Laurel and Hardy, and they identify with Harold Lloyd, and they identify to some extent with Buster Keaton.

s b : Not very much.

i b : Not very much, and yet Buster Keaton is the purer farce artiste.

s b : And a film director of genius.

i b : Just think how artistically choosy he is about his sets and his camera angles.

Now About These Women: Jarl Kulle

s b : I think Keaton is a cleverer film artist than Chaplin. Chaplin is warmer and perhaps more accessible to the big public. But he also has a heavy ballast of sentimentality.

i b : Yes, Chaplin is the genius—Keaton has a narrower sector and a more demonic sort of comedy, with something horrible about it. *The Navigator* is one of my favourite films.

s b : Or *Sherlock Junior*—have you seen it—where he walks into the film screen . . .?

i b : Then there's *The General*, with the train!

s b : *Now About These Women* is closer to a Keaton farce than any of your comedies.

i b : People made up their minds to loathe the film, and deliberately did so. Yet it was funny. I had two fiascos in one week!

s b : What was the other one?

i b : Harry Martinson's play *Three Knives from Wei*, which had its first night at the Dramaten and which I'd been working on all winter. Then, three days later, came *Now About These Women*! No one had the least intimation it would turn out an all-time fiasco.

Råsunda, 3 February 1969

JONAS SIMA: I'd like to discuss the problem of technique and method—or morals, if you prefer—taking as our starting point the slogans currently being spread in *cinegiornali liberi*, cinetracts, etc. Their attack on the commercial film includes the notion that they are being prevented from realizing their intentions, even on the technical level, by economic obstacles. Those of us who have done a certain amount of work in films and take this critical line feel that, if we could only afford it and had the chance to use a better camera, other lighting, and quite different technical facilities, we could produce more elegant—perhaps even more efficient—results. And this is what people find annoying. One must try to find a value in what is said in any film, however rough and ready. The rough and readiness may be due less to shortcomings in an artist's ability to express himself, than to purely technical defects—which can be explained economically.

INGMAR BERGMAN: Yes, but one must see it the other way round, too. If one *knows* one's material and *knows* the various elements involved in producing a film, it can be made with very, very simple means. I would even go so far as to say this. More often than not it's the people who know nothing or very little who use the most elaborate apparatus. It's their ignorance that complicates the whole procedure.

Take a cameraman like Sven Nykvist, a technically clever cameraman, one of the cleverest in the world. All he needs to work is three lamps and a little greaseproof paper. One part of knowing what to do is simply the ability to eliminate a mass of irrelevant technical complications, to be able to peel away a mass of superficial apparatus.

J S : It is true that someone who has a real grasp of technique can use grease-proof paper to make his effects. But if, for example, you want good sound, but can't afford a Nagra recorder and have to use a two-channel Tandberg, well, your sound simply won't be so good.

I B : That depends entirely on whether I've learned where to put the micro-phone.

J S : I don't think it's as simple as all that.

I B : Yes, it's as simple as all that. I think, though, that because of circum-stances and an inadequate nomenclature we are using the wrong expressions for matters which are really two entirely different questions. We agree, don't we, that anyone who makes films must have a goal before his eyes: namely, to try to get as close to the viewer as possible, to affect him as deeply as possible. We agree on that, don't we? What I call technique is knowing exactly *how* to affect the viewer. And that's why it's a wrong use of words to say that Arne Mattsson and Torbjörn Axelman are clever technicians. They are not clever at all—because they don't affect anybody.

J S : On that point I agree with you. Yet you're indulging in semantic sleight-of-mind here. In film technique you're including a feeling for suggestion-aesthetics and psychological mechanisms.

I B : And that's the crux of the matter. The rest is secondary. The one is something you can learn. The other is a matter of talent. All this technical business has become infested with gremlins. We must strip these words of their aura of anxiety.

J S : Now you've turned the problem upside down. Filmcentrum and all that radical lot are very strongly opposed to the sort of film fabricated by Mattsson and these so-called professionals. Obviously, you are much closer to the Filmcentrum position than you are to Mattsson's. So really the concept of technique is only a matter of interpretation.

I B : What I include in the concept of technique is also—can't we agree about this—what you called the aesthetics of suggestion.

STIG BJÖRKMAN : Professionalism isn't some sort of a miracle-working, a magical veil that can be drawn over any subject or film story you care to think of, to gild it. It's not a self-contained addition of technical virtuosity, the same for all films. One starts with what one has to say, and then uses whatever technical apparatus best suits the subject to say it. But first and foremost one must have something to say.

Through a Glass Darkly: Gunnar Björnstrand and Max von Sydow in the 'boat' scene and . . .

IB: It took me a hell of a lot of films before I succeeded in conquering and subduing the technical apparatus. As I've told you, it's been hard. And this is no pose on my part.

SB: In the introduction to *Through a Glass Darkly*, you present the four chief characters, the brother and sister and the father and husband. At the beginning the dialogue is highly condensed. The characters' relationships, their professions, everything is made plain in the first ten minutes. Got shot of, as one might say. Thereafter the individuals can function freely, each on his own account.

You also use different pictorial methods to tell us who they are. You place Max von Sydow and Gunnar Björnstrand in a boat and show, first, a mid-shot of the boat. Then you cut to and fro between very light pictures—you use a low camera angle up toward their faces and the sky. After that, in a very long panning shot, you show Harriet Andersson and Lars Passgård going off to fetch the milk, and the atmosphere and mood in that image are completely different from the other. Karin and her brother are integrated in the landscape in a completely different way to the father and the husband. In a highly conscious way you separate the characters out from each other and show their oneness, or lack of oneness, with the environment.

IB: That's correct. But I don't do it consciously.

... Harriet Andersson and Lars Passgård in the 'milk' scene

s B : But you don't do such a thing by trial and error, do you? Is it in the script? Take the scene in the boat, for instance—its form is closed, beginning and ending with the same mid-shot and with these cut-ins of Max von Sydow and Gunnar Björnstrand between.

I B : The fact is, I don't remember very much about *Through a Glass Darkly*. I'm a bit shy of it. But in the boat scene surely the crux of the matter is that important information is given about their relationships? We're told about Karin's illness and the father's flight, and that her husband really loves her. What is shown in the second scene is merely the contact between brother and sister.

s B : In the boat scene the characters are isolated from one another.

I B : Exactly. And in the second the characters are brought together. But one does that sort of thing almost instinctively.

s B : But when you shot the boat scene, did you take the whole scene from alternative camera angles, so that afterwards, in the editing room, you could be free to choose between different solutions? Or had you decided, even while shooting it, on the form to be taken by the boat scene, and reduced the number of camera angles accordingly?

IB : No, I've always made a sport of cutting with the camera. There's a special sensuous delight in scrubbing as few feet of film as possible, in knowing exactly where a scene is to change. In this way a film acquires its rhythm, even while it's being shot. Your actors get the feel of the rhythms you intend, and work with ever greater insight as the film proceeds.

In *The Rite* I've taken this to extremes. We only had nine days to shoot a full-length film, and I'd set the footage to a maximum of 15,000 metres. We used up 13,500 or something of that order, so I had to know exactly what we were going to include.

Obviously, one can't do this in a film like *The Shame*. So many irrational factors are involved. Things are quite different shooting outdoors. Usually one has to consume a lot of negative.

JS : The original title of *Through a Glass Darkly* is said to have been *The Wallpaper*, in which case it must have had its roots as far back as *The Devil's Wanton*?

IB : Quite right.

JS : Can you tell us something about how the film came into being, and the idea behind it?

IB : In *The Devil's Wanton* there was originally a sequence with a crazy painter. Birgitta Carolina has her night with the poet and wakes up in the morning. He's still asleep, so she thinks she'll slip out: it's just dawn, a spring morning. As she comes out into the hallway she's grabbed by the painter, played by Ulf Palme. He says to her: 'Come in here and I'll show you something.' Now it's just before sunrise. They stand there waiting, and the sun rises.

At that moment Birgitta Carolina hears voices beginning to whisper all round her. There are strange patterns on the wallpaper. Suddenly she sees how the patterns are transformed into a mass of faces, moving, strange, excited, raging, laughing faces, but diffuse and amorphous—movement only. Then, suddenly, the sunbeam vanishes, and it all becomes quiet.

That was the episode we made in *The Devil's Wanton*. But though we worked like hell on it, we couldn't bring it off technically. We simply didn't know how to. But we went on trying out possible solutions, until finally Lorens said firmly we must stop this nonsense, it was becoming too expensive—so the whole episode was cut.

But the things one has felt deep down are suggestive, they live on. By and by I thought I'd make a film about someone who floated quite naturally in and out of some wallpaper, and I must have seen Harriet Andersson before me as just that person. I saw a little door in the wall. Through this door she entered another world and then came out again. She lived quite happily in both worlds, but gradually the real world, the world of chairs and tables, became more and more unreal to her and the other world progressively took over. That was my starting point. My idea must have been that she would

Through a Glass Darkly: Harriet Andersson cowering into the papered wall

suddenly be transformed into the faces in the wallpaper and disappear into its pattern.

But while I was preparing the film I became interested in the human drama surrounding another human being who really was in process of slipping away—that is, in the whole syndrome of her sickness and the human groupings around such a syndrome. I felt I had to drop all artistic tricks and simply concentrate on the human drama. And that was how this play came into being—for a play it is. It's a surreptitious stage-play, you can't get away from that, with orderly scenes, set side by side. The cinematic aspects of *Through a Glass Darkly* are rather secondary.

Because I've always worked in the theatre and always had a longing to write stage plays, some of my films have obviously been surreptitious plays.

SB: *Through a Glass Darkly* could certainly be re-made as a play. But that it would be unfilmic I don't agree.

IB: *Through a Glass Darkly* I feel has a serious element of escapism and gross unveracity about it. A sort of desperate desire for security. An attempt to present a solution. A sort of weariness at always arriving at the question and never getting an answer. Like a circus performer who makes all his preparations for a somersault—and then, instead of making his death-leap, simply, with an ironical bow, climbs down.

The Germans have a good word for art which isn't pure but is infested with a controlling element. They say it's 'gewollt'. I think that's a fine expression. Naturally there's always a formal demand, an ordering factor: but this wilful imposition of ideas is something else. It's sterilizing, it's anti-artistic.

TORSTEN MANNS: The word '*gewollt*' appears in Heine's *Der Atlas*.

IB: You say so?

TM: I've a reflection I'd like to make, and a question to put. Some while back you were talking about the form of *Through a Glass Darkly*, how it contains various rhythms. That made me think of sonata form—is that what you're trying to achieve? You mention the Waldstein Sonata.

IB: You see there's a dedication on the film—it's dedicated to my then wife.* Just at that time I was beginning to penetrate music as a professional does; and obviously *Through a Glass Darkly* was affected by my almost daily association with music. It was also influenced, I think, by my production of *The Seagull* at the Royal Dramatic Theatre.

TM: As I see it, this film poses two central questions. Suddenly something appears that I haven't seen in your films before—a doubt whether the artist has the right to pry into people, as David certainly does. You reveal new forms of doubt about the artist's function. And this brings us to *The Hour of the Wolf*. The other central theme, as I see it, is a new sort of concept of God. Until then, God had been a tremendous authoritarian figure, with specified ethical principles. But here he suddenly turns into something ice-cold; a monster, an anonymous being, a spider-god. In Harriet's line: 'A rapist God.' Can you explain this change in your idea of God?

IB: As far as I recall, it's a question of the total dissolution of all notions of an other-worldly salvation. During those years this was going on in me all the time and being replaced by a sense of the holiness—to put it clumsily—to be found in man himself. The only holiness which really exists. A holiness wholly of this world. And I suppose that's what the final sequence tries to express. The notion of love as the only thinkable form of holiness.

At the same time another line of development in my idea of God begins here, one that has perhaps grown stronger over the years. The idea of the Christian God as something destructive and fantastically dangerous, something filled with risk for the human being and bringing out in him dark destructive forces instead of the opposite. Unquestionably this is one of the main motifs in *A Passion*.† Doesn't the parish clerk in *Winter Light* parody the confession in *Through a Glass Darkly*?

JS: In the diary Vilgot Sjöman kept while you were making *Winter Light*, he writes that while you were making *Through a Glass Darkly* you found great

* The Swedish–Esthonian pianist Käbi Laretei.

† Also known as *Passion of Anna*.

Through a Glass Darkly: Karin (Harriet Andersson) with her father (Gunnar Björnstrand)

Through a Glass Darkly: Karin (Harriet Andersson) with diary

security in this idea of God, the idea of God as love. But that as the filming proceeded you began to doubt it. And this, I think, leads to at least two questions. Is it still your principle never to change anything in the script while shooting? Do you still stick to the script as strictly as you used to?

IB: Nowadays I don't write that sort of script. Nowadays I don't write dialogue at all, only a suggestion of what it could be. The script is nothing but a collection of motifs which I work over with my actors as the filming proceeds. The final decisions I make in the cutting room, where I cut away all obtrusive elements.

What I write nowadays looks much more chaotic than the scripts I used to write. In the old days I stuck to a hard-and-fast line, and when it went badly the results were what they are in *Through a Glass Darkly*: it becomes '*gewollt*'. But *Winter Light* is not '*gewollt*'. Everything grows of its own accord. The drama has built itself. And there lies the big difference.

JS: The second part of my question is more theoretical. Why was it just while you were shooting *Through a Glass Darkly* you came to abandon the idea of a security-God?

IB: It must have been an insight, which gradually took form. It had a great deal to do with my private life. Previously I'd been living in Malmö. Virtually my whole life had been lived in the theatre. Then, suddenly, I veer off at a right angle, get myself a villa in Djursholm, set up house, and lead a bourgeois life which is the spit image of my notion of a secure existence—all this just as enthusiastically as I'd earlier lived quite another sort of life. I try to carry through my new rôle. Perhaps it can give me more security? I collect a lot of material things around me and around them I build up an ideology. Afterwards I discover that it's all utterly crazy, simply doesn't fit together. That it only corresponds to a narrow segment of myself—a sort of groping backwards into the bourgeois world I'd grown up in, and which I'd been trying to recreate. But then I see it doesn't fit, won't work at all. The result is a deep disappointment, and the entire ideology collapses. And there I stand suddenly, with a huge superstructure and no ideology to bear it up. The result, obviously, is anxiety.

There, I think, you have the exact reason why the intellectual content of *Through a Glass Darkly* collapsed. And why I carried the film through with such sullen obstinacy—a fierce effort of will, which is noticeable in the film.

T M : Yes, that's what happens with our desire for security——

I B : Well, we're grasping for two things at once. Partly for communion with others—that's the deepest instinct in us. And partly, we're seeking security. By constant communion with others we hope we shall be able to accept the horrible fact of our total solitude. We're always reaching out for new projects, new structures, new systems in order to abolish—partly or wholly—our insight into our own loneliness. If it weren't so, religious systems would never arise.

S B : The film certainly abolishes many rather weak and exposed sorts of security; but for many people it seems an important development.

I B : One could say so, yes.

S B : Right up to the final confrontation with the problem, the characters bear within them a sort of dishonest security.

I B : Exactly. But it was only when I began working on it that I realized just how dishonest the whole film was. That was why I couldn't give profile to my insight and rescued myself by regressing in the final sequence.

J S : You used the word *'gewollt'*—the effect of forced control. In his book *The Personal Vision of Ingmar Bergman*, Jörn Donner says how much he appreciates *Through a Glass Darkly*. Strictly speaking, he only has one objection to it; and that is Minus' final line in the film, when he says: 'Daddy spoke to me.' Donner regards it as a dramaturgical error. He thinks it lacks all basis in the preceding narrative. What would you say to that comment today?

I B : He's right. But wrong too. What makes him feel its inadequacy is that the film, as such, could never have been naturally one with its final sequence. They stand there side by side, quite dead. The simple reason is that there was

167

Through a Glass Darkly: Minus (Lars Passgård) against the background of the wreck and ...

no natural emotional bridge in me between the somewhat hopeful message of the end and the pessimism of the rest of the film.

TM: It's a sort of Beethoven effect. He often ends like that—he tires.

IB: I didn't tire. On the contrary. I devoted immeasurable energy to convincing both myself and everyone else.

TM: A theme, I mean, that you simply aren't up to, can't get a grip on. Beethoven often does it.

IB: Yes, we both do!

JS: You have called the trilogy a 'chamber work'. What Strindberg calls a chamber play is 'the intimate course of events'. What does the term mean to you? You've described as chamber works two films as different in form as *Wild Strawberries* and *Through a Glass Darkly*.

IB: *Through a Glass Darkly* and *Winter Light* and *The Silence* and *Persona* I've called chamber works. They are chamber music—music in which, with an extremely limited number of voices and figures, one explores the essence of a number of motifs. The backgrounds are extrapolated, put into a sort of fog. The rest is a distillation.

SB: Time is concentrated too.

168

... inside the wreck with sister (Harriet Andersson)

IB: Afterwards I abandoned that, maybe. But it was stimulating, too, to let things happen within a certain short period of time. As far as I can see, all three films in the trilogy have that in common.

JS: In some context I don't recall too well, you tied this up with *A Passion*.

IB: Yes, à propos the destructive effect of religious ideas.

JS: In that case I'd like to quote from Vilgot Sjöman's diary of the filming of *Winter Light*. At the beginning you say that 'this religious business comes in waves, like an ebb and flood tide'. After your trilogy and your new films, do you think you could succumb again to a religious 'flood-tide' in your film-making?

IB: No one is safe from religious ideas and confessional phenomena. Neither you nor I. We can fall victim to them when we least expect it. It's like Mao 'flu, or being struck by lightning. You're utterly helpless. Exposed.

As I see it today, any relapse is utterly out of the question. But I can't say it's out of the question tomorrow.

SB: I'd like to put a concrete question. It's about the way in which you give form to the mental syndrome exhibited by Karin in *Through a Glass Darkly*. How did you go to work—did you aim at clinical veracity, or did you dream it all up?

Scene within scene: Lars Passgard, Harriet Andersson and Max von Sydow enact Minus' play . . .

... in *Through a Glass Darkly*

IB: It's pure imagination. Naturally I knew a little about schizophrenia. But the medical basis is thin.

JS: À propos the big scene in the boat in *Through a Glass Darkly*, where David (Gunnar Björnstrand) and Martin (Max von Sydow) settle accounts, I've a feeling Martin's basic criticism of David is taken from various critical attacks on yourself, not least in the anti-Bergman number of *Chaplin*, which appeared in 1960. There the most personal criticism was made by the Frenchman, Ernest Riffe—according to certain usually well-informed circles identical with Bergman himself, and never convincingly refuted!

Many people have regarded the article less as a stroke of wit than as some sort of a black personal confession—and that's my question!

IB: That's your question, yes!

JS: Martin's criticism of David is tremendously personal!

IB: All the time you're producing, you're continually criticizing what you're doing. Where I've been successful, maybe, is in never allowing this criticism to have a devastating effect on my productivity. They're like two wild beasts. I keep them away from each other.

I love $8\frac{1}{2}$. One of the figures in it is that thin half-wit who keeps popping up all the time. Wherever the wretched director, Mastroianni, appears, this figure appears too, talking, criticizing, following him about. And Mastroianni gets wearier and wearier.

JS: Yet this article by Ernest Riffe seems to have been written with a certain relish, even so?

IB: Yes. But at the same time Fellini makes this fellow into something amusing, doesn't he, though you can be sure the background is black as midnight. It's a reserve exit: one can almost always transpose negative, unpleasant, brutal experiences into something productive; sometimes even into something amusing.

It gave me a special feeling of liberation to gather up all my own inner self-criticism, often synchronous with the criticism I was being subjected to from outside, and perform the little trick of verbalizing it as a bad Swedish translation from the French, and then to open *Expressen** and read: 'Nothing better has been said about Ingmar Bergman in recent years!'

SB: When you had made *Through a Glass Darkly*, did you know instinctively you would carry on the film's line of reasoning? Was the trilogy already planned? Or did each film arise spontaneously? And at what point in time did you feel justified in placing the three films together as a trilogy?

IB: Not until all three were finished. But then I was a bit astonished myself to see how unified they were. It must have been Vilgot Sjöman who first pointed it out to me. But when I was actually making them I had no such intention, no.

* Stockholm evening paper.

IB: *Winter Light*—suppose we discuss that now?—was conceived the following Easter. What year was it?

TM: 1961.

IB: The film is closely connected with a particular piece of music: Stravinski's *A Psalm Symphony*. I heard it on the radio one morning during Easter, and it struck me I'd like to make a film about a solitary church on the plains of Uppland. Someone goes into the church, locks himself in, goes up to the altar, and says: 'God, I'm staying here until in one way or another You've proved to me You exist. This is going to be the end either of You or of me!' Originally, the film was to have been about the days and nights lived through by this solitary person in the locked church, getting hungrier and hungrier, thirstier and thirstier, more and more expectant, more and more filled with his own experiences, his visions, his dreams, mixing up dream and reality, while he's involved in this strange, shadowy wrestling match with God.

We were staying out on Törö, in the Stockholm archipelago. It was the first summer I'd had the sea all round me. I wandered about on the shore and went indoors and wrote, and went out again. The drama turned into something else; into something altogether tangible, something perfectly real, elementary and self-evident.

The film is based on something I'd actually experienced. Something a clergyman up in Dalarna had told me: the story of the suicide, the fisherman Persson. One day the clergyman had tried to talk to him; the next, Persson had hanged himself. For the clergyman it was a personal catastrophe.

JS: But you invented the fisherman's motives?

IB: Yes, all that about the Chinese and the atomic bomb. But that's nothing remarkable in itself. Quite a lot of people, I fancy, have fallen into a state of anxiety about the Chinese and the atomic bomb. Not only my fisherman, Jonas Persson.

So we drove about, looking at churches, my father and I. My father, as you probably know, was a clergyman—he knew all the Uppland churches like the back of his hand. We went to morning service in various places and were deeply impressed by the spiritual poverty of these churches, by the lack of any congregation and the miserable spiritual status of the clergy, the poverty of their sermons, and the nonchalance and indifference of the ritual.

In one church, I remember—and I think it has a great deal to do with the end of the film—Father and I were sitting together. My father had already been retired for many years, and was old and frail. No one was there but him and me, well I suppose the clergyman's wife was sitting there too—no, she wasn't, it was the churchwarden; and I suppose a few old women had turned up too. Just before the bell begins to toll, we hear a car outside, a shining Volvo: the clergyman climbs out hurriedly, and there is a faint buzz from the vestry, and then the clergyman appears before he ought to—when the bell stops, that is—and says he feels very poorly and that he's talked to the rector

Winter Light: the clergyman (Gunnar Björnstrand) and fisherman's wife (Gunnel Lindblom)...

and the rector has said he can use an abbreviated form of the service and drop the part at the altar. So there would just be one psalm and a sermon and another psalm. And goes out. Whereon my father, furious, began hammering on the pew, got to his feet and marched out into the vestry, where a long mumbled conversation ensued; after which the churchwarden also went in, then someone ran up to the organ gallery to fetch the organist, after which the churchwarden came out and announced that there would be a complete service after all. My father took the service at the altar, both at the beginning and the end.

In some way I feel the end of the play was influenced by my father's intervention—that at all costs one must do what it is one's duty to do, particularly in spiritual contexts. Even if it can seem meaningless.

P. A. Lundgren built the church in the big studio, and together Nykvist and I began working on a completely new lighting technique. We studied light and began to figure out methodically how light functions, how it actually behaves, and how we could technically mimic its behaviour. We did this as some sort of an aggression against modern photography, which has given us an artificial idea of what real light looks like. Photography using ultra-fast film makes the bright side seem much brighter and the dark side darker than in reality. All that's very interesting. When it comes to the appearance of light, we've got a new lie instead of the old one.

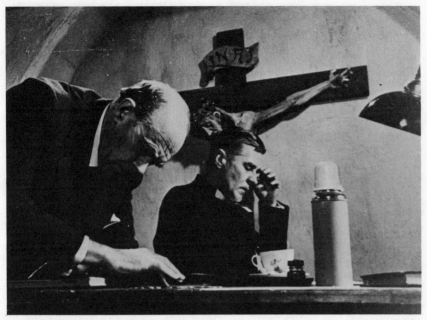

... Kolbjörn Knudsen and Gunnar Björnstrand

The shooting was extremely demanding, and dragged on for fifty-six days. It was one of the longest schedules I've had, and one of the shortest films I've ever made.

JS: What was so troublesome about it?

IB: For one thing, Gunnar Björnstrand was ill all the time. That autumn, or in the summer I think it was, he'd had severe heart trouble and was in personal difficulties. Besides which he detested the rôle.

JS: Why?

IB: The part really isn't a glamorous one, and he had a hell of a time; was forced to use other means of expression than he was used to. Throughout the filming Ingrid Thulin was a tower of strength.

JS: So she liked her rôle?

IB: The rôle appealed to her; but she was a moral support, too. So was Gunnar, with his professionalism—always ready, at every moment. But it was a heavy job.

I showed the film to my wife at that time, and she said: 'Yes, Ingmar, it's a masterpiece; but it's a dreary masterpiece.' There's some truth in that; but the importance of the dreary in art mustn't be underestimated. What amazed me

Winter Light: Märta (Ingrid Thulin) . . .

most—for I really thought I'd made rather a mature and lucid film—was the critics' reaction.

JS: Do you categorically deny the Christ symbolism in the figure of Märta?

IB: No, I don't deny it. But, it's a complete post facto rationalization. Märta is something of the stuff saints are made of, *i.e.*, hysterical, power-greedy, but also possessed of an inner vision. All that business about the eczema on her hands and forehead, for example, I'd pinched that straight from my second wife. She used to suffer from it and went about with big pieces of sticking plaster on her forehead and bandaged hands. She had an allergic eczema. But that it had anything whatever to do with stigmatization—that's utterly wrong. For me Märta is something furious, alive, intractable, pig-headed, troublesome. A great and—for a dying figure like the clergyman—overwhelming person. When she writes him a letter, it isn't three pages, but twenty-seven pages which flood his desk. At every moment her whole way of speaking to and being with him is overwhelming. When they sink down at the altar-rail she doesn't kiss him once. No, she kisses him seventy-nine times. Slops her kisses all over him. Not for a moment does she reflect that if there's one thing he really has no wish for at that moment, it's kisses. She won't give him up. At the same time I believe Märta constitutes the clergyman's only hope of any

176

... with the clergyman Thomas Ericsson (Gunnar Björnstrand)

sort of life. For me she's a monstrosity, a primitive natural force. But the poor clergyman's on the way out.

JS: Have you ever felt yourself to be some sort of religious preacher, a prophet?

IB: Certainly not! For me things have always been 'on the one hand, it's like this—but on the other, like that'.

JS: O'Neill is supposed to have said: 'Drama that doesn't deal with man's relation to God is worthless.'

IB: Yes, and I've often quoted him; and been thoroughly misunderstood. Today we say all art is political. But I'd say all art has to do with ethics. Which after all really comes to the same thing. It's a matter of attitudes. That's what O'Neill meant.

JS: Which—being interpreted—means today one could call you a political film-maker because you're preoccupied with the same sort of ethical problems as the young radicals are, though they've replaced the religious material with the political—something you've done, too, to some extent, in *The Shame*?

IB: All this talk about me standing aside, cutting myself off and so forth, has always amazed me.

JS: One has a feeling that all of a sudden, not least during all this lengthy interview, you are articulating these problems much more clearly, even to yourself. We've quoted other interviews in which you say: 'I'm not a political person, I don't bother about . . .'

IB: I've stated, firmly and clearly, that though as an artist I'm not politically involved, I obviously am an expression of the society I live in. Anything else would be grotesque. But I don't make propaganda for either one attitude or the other. No.

As I've told you, I vote for the Social Democrats. Their way of solving social problems comes closest to what I regard as decent. That I also find their actual solutions odd in many ways is another matter. Particularly during my time as head of the Royal Dramatic Theatre I really got to see something of the daily life of their political people and experienced their—I was going to say everyday moral validity.

JS: It can do no harm to point out now and again, I think, that ethical problems, moral problems—chiefly perhaps those of a religious nature in a certain social situation and a particular society—also admit of political solutions. Which is the same thing as saying one can't separate ethics from politics.

IB: I was going to say they're the same thing. It's a question of semantics. If we go on like this much longer I'll be getting socially conscious!

TM: In your view, though, there's no sense in you suddenly denying your bourgeois background? It is just simply there, and tremendously strong——

IB: Why should I deny a factor which has meant so much to me in every way?

TM: Some artists do, when they realize the wind's blowing in another direction.

IB: It's impossible to expatriate oneself, cut off one's roots; it'd be cutting oneself off from the creative elements in one's native soil. One must accept oneself as being like this or like that, and then try to keep a steady course in the unusually black and boisterous sea raging all around.

SB: We've talked about trilogies and trinities and your impulse to gather your film together thematically. Something crossed my mind which clearly doesn't seem to interest you at all, taking each work individually, and that is triangle situations. Your films always tend to be about either two or four people.

IB: They've just turned out that way. Marital relations, it strikes me, have been almost exclusively a subject for comedies. *Smiles of a Summer Night, A Lesson in Love* . . . It wasn't really until *A Passion* that I really got to grips with the man–woman relationship.

Råsunda, 10 February 1969

JONAS SIMA: What were you writing after *Winter Light*? What project did you have in mind? Not *The Silence*, was it?

INGMAR BERGMAN: Yes, as a matter of fact it was. It came very soon after. I began work on *The Silence*, I remember, at Christmas time after I'd just finished *Winter Light*.

After *The Silence* I received an anonymous letter, containing filthy toilet paper; so one could say the treatment accorded to this film, which by today's standards was pretty innocuous, was rather fierce. There were even people who rang up and threatened both my own life and the life of the wife I was married to at that time. Besides being subjected to a telephone-terror, I suppose I must have got about a hundred letters. So the sexual trauma in Sweden must have been acute. Things have changed radically these last years.

STIG BJÖRKMAN: It's said that both you and Kenne Fant regarded *The Silence* as a rather risky project financially.

IB: Catastrophic!

SB: Yet compared with your others it was a small film. How did you react, personally, to the way *The Silence* was received? And afterwards to this other sort of reaction?

The Silence: Gunnel Lindblom, Jörgen Lindström and Ingrid Thulin arrive at the strange city

IB: After Kenne and I had seen the film together for the first time, I said to him: 'Well, one thing you must realize. People are going to run their legs off to see this film.' And that was exactly what they did. You can see how one can misjudge situations!

SB: How did you experience people's reactions to it, personally?

IB: One is always glad when a film is a success. But then, when I discovered *why* it was a success, and how many of the people who were going to see it were saying furiously they'd never again go and see an Ingmar Bergman film, I was terrified.

JS: The serious discussion was mostly about the film censorship; less about the problems actually presented in the film.

IB: As usual, they were lost sight of.

JS: At least it had an important effect on the politics of film production—it torpedoed the censorship!

IB: Yes, I suppose it was the first definitive breach, through which a lot of other stuff then floated in. So it was some use anyway.

It's of no interest, perhaps, but yesterday evening I was reflecting on the origins of *The Silence*. I can no longer lay my hands on my work-books for it,

I don't know what I've done with them—but I remember that it was about Christmas time, and that *The Silence*, just like *Winter Light*, began with a piece of music: Bartók's Concerto for Orchestra.

My original idea was to make a film that should obey musical laws, instead of dramaturgical ones. A film acting by association—rhythmically, with themes and counter-themes. As I was putting it together, I thought much more in musical terms than I'd done before. All that's left of Bartók is the very beginning. It follows Bartók's music rather closely—the dull continuous note, then the sudden explosion.

Then I've always been fascinated by a strange city. As a boy I was often in Germany, Berlin exerted an almost demonic suggestiveness over me, due to an early collection of short stories about Berlin by Siegfried Siwertz. So Berlin wasn't the real Berlin at all, but a city of black destruction. Then there was Fallada's *Kleiner Mann was nun?* and *A Wolf among Wolves*, not to mention Brecht and Weill's *Dreigroschenoper*, which also isn't really about Berlin, as such, but London, and yet is entirely *berlinerisch*. My youth was spent to an accompaniment of Lotte Lenya and Lewis and that old Telefunken record of Ruth's Band.

As the train was approaching Berlin from Sassnitz, I remember standing looking out into the dawn over the huge grey suburbs as the houses grew taller and the train passed over viaducts until one felt the enormous dark suggestiveness of it all—you must have felt it too, I suppose? The sense of sinking into an enormous city, absorbing it, becoming anonymous within it.

A few years before, I'd written a film I never finished—the last third was lacking—about a pair of acrobats who had lost their third partner and were snowed up in some German city—Hanover or Dresden or suchlike, during the last stages of the war. As the end approaches, their relationship gradually falls to pieces. It was a bit of that idea I took up again.

Originally I'd imagined two men, one older and one younger, travelling together. One of them couldn't go on any longer, fell sick and ended up in a hospital; from then on it was to have been about the other man's experiences, how the city gradually draws him down into itself, and how their friendship goes to pieces as the older man gets sicker and sicker. But then, suddenly, I saw the contrast, the tension, the interesting aspect, the purely physical relationship; and had a strong sense of Ingrid Thulin and Gunnel Lindblom as two powerful poles and—primarily as a catalyst—the little boy. But I took many steps in various directions before I actually wrote the film.

At the film's bottommost layer lay the collapse of an ideology and a way of life. I remember writing down something I was tremendously pleased with, though of course it's nothing remarkable in itself: I wrote that *life only has as much meaning and importance as one attributes to it oneself.* There's nothing remarkable about that. But for me it was like a mining concession, full of potential wealth. But then everyone advised me against making the film. Both Käbi Laretei, whom I was married to at that time, and Kenne Fant, and

The Silence: the two powerful poles: Gunnel Lindblom and Ingrid Thulin

several of my friends. But I had a tremendous desire to make it. So I did anyway. And that's really all I have to tell you about *The Silence*.

TORSTEN MANNS: Doesn't it contain a fragment of the idea behind *The Shame*. Namely, the war motif? War is in the background in *The Silence*. One hears it gradually coming closer. Had you already thought of—or were you already thinking of—*The Shame*?

IB: Yes, of the war film I already wanted to make in connection with *The Silence*, and which I also wanted to make out of *The Shame*. And which I still haven't made. As a motif, war is something I'm approaching step by step— but perhaps I won't tell you about that. Doesn't Faulkner say 'stories you tell you never write'?

   I'm trying to find my way to a war film which would adequately cover the whole complex of experience which war brings to the surface. *The Shame*, after all, is more of a post-war film.

TM: There was a scene which was cut, wasn't there, at the end of *The Silence*, when tanks burst into the city?

IB: No, there wasn't.

TM: I'd heard so.

IB: But it's wrong. For me the important thing is that Ester sends a secret message to the boy. That's the important thing: the message he spells out to himself. To me Ester in all her misery represents a distillation of something indestructibly human, which the boy inherits from her.

TM: As far as I can see, quite a few things have become shitty—if I may use the expression—in *The Silence*. The spiritual has been replaced by the physical. One gets terribly close to these two women. The other thing is that language no longer functions.

IB: No, that's quite right, language has ceased to be a means of communication: they can't talk to one another. There aren't many lines of dialogue in *The Silence*. To some extent it was also a game.

JS: Has the language in *The Silence* any semantic authenticity?

IB: Timoka, the name of the city, I saw in a book belonging to my wife at that time. She's Esthonian. It was a book of poetry. The word 'timoka' stood there on a line by itself, and without knowing what it meant I baptized the city Timoka. Then I asked her what it meant, and she said—there are a lot of cases in Esthonian—it means 'appertaining to the executioner'.

Otherwise it was just a language I made up. You've seen that letter-game—I don't know what it's called? I jumbled up all the letters and laid them out in a long row and then divided them up as seemed neatest. And it became a language.

TM: Fellini has it in *8½*—'asa nisi masa'—it was written up on that black-board, and the telepathic character guesses what sort of a language it is.

IB: I used it earlier in *Wild Strawberries*, where Victor is taking his exam—he has to interpret something written up on a blackboard.

JS: The actors learnt it by heart from the script?

IB: Yes, except old Håkan Jahnberg, the waiter, who made up his own language because he couldn't learn mine.

JS: Is the language recorded on the soundtrack in the normal way?

IB: Yes.

SB: You never had any intention of placing the film in any particular foreign environment?

IB: No, never. About two years after the war I got stuck for a week in Grenoble. It was at the height of the summer. I was short of money and living in a nasty little hotel. I don't know whether you know Grenoble, but it's a hole. The only thing that reconciles you to it is that a 'Rapide' goes straight through the town. It's the only place the express stops at between the Côte d'Azur and Paris.

But then something very odd happened to me. The hotel room where they

183

had their amorous exercises—Birger Malmsten and Gunnel Lindblom—is copied from a hotel room in Paris where I once used to have a rendezvous with a woman. It was broad daylight, in fact blazing sunlight, a fresh autumn day; and we were billeted there, and I was ill. It was two floors up and the yard outside was the size of this room. At the bottom, overlooking the yard, were thick frosted glass windows, and looking straight down one saw people crawling around like worms in a corpse. It was the hotel kitchen and a heavy stench of food filled the room, which was narrow and coffin-shaped. When one turned round and looked out, one saw, high high up, a white autumn sky and, for a second, sunshine throwing reflections from a skylight.

TM: But the journey and this city in the film give the impression that the characters are travelling through an authoritarian country, a country to the east of the Iron Curtain, where armies are in motion, guns and tanks.

IB: It's a country preparing for war, where war can break out any day. Whether it's a civil war or what, I couldn't say; but all the time one feels it is something perverse and terrifying, these tanks in the streets. I happened to be in Hamburg just after the war, and one saw a lot of that sort of thing. The city had already been massacred; but at nights tanks drove about the streets, or simply stood silently sleeping at street corners.

SB: You spoke of trains. There's an important train sequence in *Winter Light* too. Märta and Thomas are halted in their car at a level crossing. A train with ore-wagons goes thudding by. They look like huge hearses, and you underline all this specially by showing them in an extra cutaway.

JS: Yes, you're really a technical virtuoso in railway matters! Somewhere there must be a stationmaster or an engine-driver lurking in the background of your life . . .

IB: There is. I grew up, as I've told you, at my grandmother's place in Dalarna, a little village called Duvnäs. Today it lies on the main tourist highway up to Leksand and Rättvik. But in those days it really was a little village, far from anywhere, with only two farms and a railway halt, because there was a small sawmill there too.

My maternal grandfather was a railway engineer. He built the Southern Dalarna Railway. Trains were something of a passion with him, so he built himself a house halfway along the line, and the trains went straight through his garden. There's a remarkable view out over the river, with heaths on the far side and the gravel ridges stretching for miles. The house had a veranda and there the old boy used to sit in the autumn of his days. I remember sitting on his knee. He had a big beard and a starched collar and was paralysed in both legs. He'd look at his watch, and four trains came puffing along in either direction, stopping at the little Duvnäs station to get their breath back.

My childhood has trains running all through it. Stationmaster Eriksson had been at Duvnäs for twenty years, but the peasants still regarded him as a newcomer, someone you couldn't talk to. The railway bridge over the river was so high it took your breath away, and far beneath the river swirled blackly. Those hot rails in summer and the wild strawberry patches down along the embankment . . .

TM: That calls to mind *Eva.*

IB: Right!

TM: Where the boy drives the engine . . .

IB: Now and again there would be a small shunting engine at Duvnäs station. Its name was Anna, a little engine which came puffing up with various loads—timber, I suppose, and such like—and then we were allowed to get on it and ride between Lännheden and Repbäcken and Duvnäs.

JS: So, when shooting *Winter Light,* you felt you needed to penetrate some aspect of your idea of God?

IB: It was more or less like this—as Torsten so rightly says—everything had gone to pieces. All this is so deep down in me, there was no question of 'penetrating' it. *The Silence* is simple. It tells its story by simple means, not with symbols and such antics.

JS: I'm inclined to see something positive in your capitulation—your insight into God's silence as expressive of some maturation process.

IB: Yes, in itself I believe so too, and I think it's to be seen already in *Winter Light.* Though it's very hard to say anything definite about this.

Out of all man's misery and conflicts and his insufferable condition is crystallized this little clear drop of something different—this sudden impulse to understand a few words in another language. It's remarkable, all that's left, the only positive thing. Just as the only positive thing in *Winter Light* is the clergyman standing up and holding his service—even though there's no one there to hear it.

SB: And this curiosity, one feels, is not merely momentary. It's something to build on.

IB: Quite. And for me it's the one essential positive thing in *The Silence.*

JS: On the abstract level, anyway, I see the trilogy as a sort of parabolic movement. Only as zero-point is reached does depression set in. We are back at square one. And so can look back, in a spirit of reconciliation, along the curve of conflict already travelled.

IB: If you see it that way, that's fine. But I didn't. Not when I made the film.

TM: Well now, this confrontation with the woman's world, which is so interesting in *The Silence* and which you've dealt with over and over again— *Waiting Women* and *So Close to Life* and all the rest—what chiefly interests

The Silence: the boy (Jörgen Lindström)—the catalyst . . .

me here is the women's relationship to each other. And, second, their position in the film; their position *vis-à-vis* yourself. I'm aware of a strong feeling of disgust, almost. Anna is incessantly preoccupied with her own body, washes herself and undresses and dresses again. Visually, too, there's all that business with the bolsters in the bed, a landscape of swelling femininity. Then again we have this tangible confrontation, this evil conflict between the sisters. The one sensual, rather sloppy, rather indolent. The other dry, intellectually tense. Do these represent for you two clashing ideals of womanhood?

IB: No, it's exactly the same as in *Persona*—they could equally well have been two men. The crux of the matter is that Ester—even though she's ill and inwardly decaying—is struggling against the decay within her. She feels a sort of disgust for Anna's corporeality. Tries to stave it off. She feels humiliated by her own attacks. And all the time she's trying to keep herself clean and nice. But Anna is uninhibitedly physical. She holds her little boy within the magic circle of her own animality, controls him. He's completely in thrall to it.

This physical disgust is Ester's disgust at her body having taken charge of her and exposing her to humiliating situations. But I don't feel put off by Anna—on the contrary. Possibly faintly sarcastic, the way she sits there after making love, reflecting on how clever she is to be able to drive a car, even though Ester thinks she's a nitwit.

... between the two women (Gunnel Lindblom and Ingrid Thulin)

TM: This is Gunnel Lindblom in a major rôle. Previously she'd only had small ones. It was during your Malmö period she came into the picture?

IB: Yes, she was with us during the whole Malmö period.

TM: And then she had some minor parts—well, quite a big one in *The Virgin Spring*.

IB: It's the second female lead.

TM: She's not quite in line with your major actresses. She's a bit bonier, and at the same time more rounded.

IB: Yes, she's a wonderful girl, austere and honest and magnificent.

SB: Nor does she exude a negative feeling in this film, either. As I see it, Johan is the chief figure. And it's through what she means to him that she too becomes a positive figure.

IB: Yes, because both women turn their best sides towards the kid.

SB: As I feel it, this curiosity is passed on to Johan, grafted on to a positive attitude to life.

IB: Yes, he escapes from the film almost unscathed. And all the time he feels a

187

certain curiosity. Starts seeing his mother a bit more objectively, but there's nothing inherently wrong in that. If he sees her clearly for the first time, it's because he sides with Ester.

JS: I'd like to follow up what Torsten had to say about the film's view of womanhood. When *The Silence* had just come out here in Sweden, I read an article on it by the sociologist Joachim Israel in *Stockholms Tidningen.** He saw *The Silence* as anti-sex. He wrote: 'By its negative attitude to sexuality *The Silence* becomes pornography.' He also said: 'The film is outspoken, but in a reactionary and anti-sexual way.' He thought it almost filthy. Do you regard yourself as morally hostile to sex, puritanical? Another article in the same newspaper, by the authoress Viveka Heyman, accused you in this film of taking a reactionary view of women——

IB: Some left-wing lasses went on the warpath after *Persona*, too; they said the women in *Persona* represented a reactionary view of woman. Kjell Grede, I think it was, put a stop to them by telling them the film wasn't particularly about women anyway.

JS: But are your morals puritan?

IB: Like hell they are! Wasn't I brought up in the twenties in a typical bourgeois environment? There were two things anyone who valued his own respectability never mentioned: sex and money. I could digress widely here, but I'm not sure anything is to be gained by doing so.

When I was fourteen I met a girl my own age, and to this day I bless her. During my four years at grammar school we came to some sort of a result— some sort of way of being together. From being comrades in contrition, sin, guilt and terror of sex, we arrived at an open, natural togetherness.

JS: Wherein you were certainly luckier than many of your schoolmates. Sexual experience in those days, it seems, came awfully late.

IB: She was big and fat and terribly kind and nice and not particularly beautiful. I even think I found her ugly. But if she hadn't existed I'd probably have gone out of my mind.

JS: It's odd, these frequent accusations of being hostile to sex. One reason, I suppose, must be the tremendous physical, at times even provocative, immediacy of your films. In showing how deeply it upsets them, your critics only reveal their own moral duplicity.

IB: Vilgot Sjöman's films really reveal and find cinematic expression for the nature of inhibition and hostility to sex. But it's you who're calling my films 'physical'—and that applies not only to sexual matters but all down the line.

My ceaseless fascination with the whole race of women is one of my mainsprings. Obviously, such an obsession implies ambivalence; it has something compulsive about it. But that I've any anti-sexual traits—that's a label I find it very hard to accept.

* Stockholm morning paper, now defunct.

The Silence: Birger Malmsten, Gunnel Lindblom and (on following page) Ingrid Thulin with Gunnel Lindblom and Birger Malmsten

JS: Deep down inside you, do you find it hard to accept the modern rôle which, according to current ideas, women should play in society?

IB: No, not at all.

SB: Yet the more self-aware and politically conscious sort of girl hasn't interested you in your films?

IB: No. Nor that sort of man, either. The people in my films are exactly like myself—creatures of instinct, of rather poor intellectual capacity, who at best only think while they're talking. Mostly they're body, with a little hollow for the soul. My films draw on my own experience; however inadequately based logically and intellectually.

JS: If one makes a 'close reading' of *The Silence*, with the sufferings of Christ as the answer to the question, one discovers some astonishing congruences.

IB: But I had no such intention.

JS: If one sees the trilogy as a Passion Story—Gethsemane, the sacrificial death and the grave—then *Persona* can be seen as the resurrection. The women stand for Christ—Karin in *Through a Glass Darkly*, Märta Lundberg in *Winter Light*, Ester in *The Silence*, and Elisabeth Vogel in *Persona*.

IB: No, not at all!

190

JS: Such an interpretation doesn't interest you a scrap?

IB: Not a scrap—it goes altogether too far.

JS: But your exegetes—educated ones—insist on it. They have demonstrated astonishing parallels.

IB: Maybe that's not so odd. I come from a world of conservative Christian thought. I've absorbed Christianity with my mother's milk. So it must be obvious that certain ... archetypes, aren't they called—stick in one's mind, and that certain lines, certain courses of events, certain ways of behaving, become adequate symbols for what goes on in the Christian system of ideas.

TM: The doctor in *Persona*, surely, is a projection of the God-figure. She intervenes so radically. It's really she who's in charge, isn't it?

IB: I say the same as I do in *The Rite*—I keep myself supplied with my own angels and demons.

TM: The boy in *The Silence* and *Persona* isn't merely played by the same actor; he has the same function. But then, one must bear in mind, there was to have been a film in between, which you didn't make: the one which afterwards became *The Hour of the Wolf*. When you made *The Silence* after *Persona* you must have taken him over from the one film to the next? He's not in the book version. In both films Jörgen Lindström reads the same book, acts as an identical catalyst. The only difference is that, in *Persona*, he's not there in person. He just evokes the course of events, conjures them up, sets them going; while in *The Silence* he's a link, definitely a very important person. Would you like to say something about his function in the two films?

IB: Yes; but that brings us directly to *Persona*. In *The Silence* he is what he is. He doesn't stand for anything. He's just a boy, at the point of intersection between the two women. He represents nothing beyond what is in the script.

JS: There's a connection here with the criticism levelled at the film: in his review of *The Silence* in *Dagens Nyheter*,* Mauritz Edström wrote something interesting. In his opinion you made a fundamental artistic mistake in depicting sick people and then pretending it was all a question of faith and doubt. He wrote: 'He lets schizophrenics struggle with the question of the existence of God, the sex-starved are put forward in the drama of faith and love, and over the solitudes of the death-doomed alcoholic the light falls at the last ashen grey, to the sound of the Last Trump.' What Edström means is that the clergyman and God's judgment seat are the wrong forum. These are human problems. As such, they should be treated by the doctor and the psychiatrist. How do you react to such a statement, to this type of criticism?

IB: Mauritz Edström comes from a nonconformist background. As far as I can see, he's suffering from a trauma on this point himself.

* The largest Stockholm daily.

The Silence: the boy (Jörgen Lindström) and dwarfs

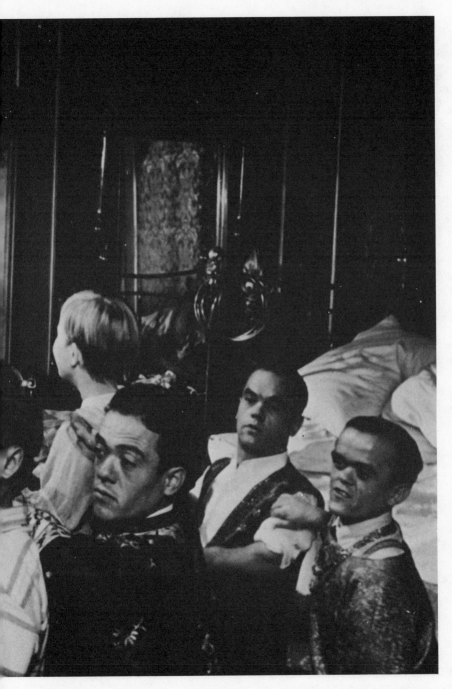

Bergman directing Jörgen Lindström in *The Silence*

J S : But Edström isn't the only writer to criticize you in this respect. Others too—not least abroad—have taken exception to your way of turning psychiatric into religious problems. Behind all this, of course, one perceives a sort of dogmatism.

I B : People think there's a solution. If everything is distributed in the proper quarters, put into the right pigeonholes, everything will be fine. But I'm not so sure.

J S : It's a common atheistic notion that religiosity is just a symptom of psychosis.

I B : Quite right! Precisely. And in religious circles, one might say, it's the other way round. I find this sort of criticism hard to understand. I don't even feel its relevance. I don't think it has anything to do with the motifs in themselves. To tell you the truth, I don't even understand what Edström's talking about. Do you?

J S : My interest is more in the problem of principle. May I ask, was it after *The Silence* you became an agnostic?

I B : What do you mean by an agnostic?

J S : Well, an agnostic, I suppose, is someone who, after struggling with a group of problems, just drops them. Since he has found no answer to them, he simply drops them.

I B : Or one might say the problem dissolves. Anyway the crux of the matter is—*the problem doesn't exist any more*. Nothing, absolutely nothing at all has emerged out of all these ideas of faith and scepticism, all these convulsions, these puffings and blowings. For many of my fellow human beings on the other hand, I'm aware that these problems still exist—and exist as a terrible reality. I hope this generation will be the last to live under the scourge of religious anxiety.

S B : Shall we push on to *Persona*?

I B : Supposing we begin with the film's actual genesis. The summer before *Persona* I didn't make a film at all. I only wrote a script, which I called *The Cannibals*. It was to have been a double film. My idea was to make a film lasting four hours. That was after my first year as head of the Royal Dramatic Theatre. It was planned that I should shoot the film the following summer.

Then, in January, I fell ill. Just an ordinary cold, but I went about with a fever. In early March I got very ill. I'd been going around with pneumonia for some while, it seemed. So I took sick leave, contracted penicillin poisoning, and a virus infection started up in my inner ear, bringing on attacks of giddiness. I was in a shocking state. All through March, April, and May I was in hospital at Sofiahemmet.* *The Cannibals* would have been a major project.

---

* Exclusive private hospital in Stockholm. IB's father was chaplain there in his childhood with a residence in the Sofiahemmet Park.

So in March, since no one could say when I'd be well again, we cancelled it. I administered the Royal Dramatic Theatre over the 'phone. For long periods at a time I couldn't read, couldn't look at TV. Just sat up in bed glowering at a black spot on the wall—as soon as I turned my head everything came tumbling down—I'd lost all sense of balance.

Bibi had been signed on for *The Cannibals*. I'd also met a group of Norwegian actors—I hope I'm not boring you by being so long-winded about all this? In the spring a group of Norwegian actors had been in Stockholm on a study visit, and I'd briefly met Liv Ullmann in company with Bibi. We bumped into each other at the corner of Almlövsgatan and Nybrogatan. Suddenly it struck me—'that girl Liv Ullmann—I ought to write a part for her'. So I asked her on the spot whether she'd like to be in my next film. And wrote a part for her, not a very big one, in *The Cannibals*. One evening I was at the home of my doctor, Sture Helander, one of my best friends, married to Gunnel Lindblom. He showed us some slides. Gunnel and he had been to see Bibi during the shooting of *Pan* or whatever the film was called . . . yes, up in Kärringöja the previous summer. Bibi and Liv had become fast friends; and Sture had taken a photo of them sitting sunning themselves against a wall. The moment I saw that picture I thought: They're devilishly alike! In a strange sort of way they resembled each other.

Afterwards I suppose I must have gone into hospital again and recovered from my giddiness. But then the resemblance began going round and round in my head. I thought it would be wonderful to write something about two people who lose their identities in each other; who are similar in some way.

Suddenly I got the idea of them sitting comparing hands. And that was the first image—of the two women sitting there comparing hands and wearing big hats.

I felt there was something in it, some sort of fertile material. I was so incredibly cheered by it I rang up Kenne Fant, and he came round to the hospital—it was April, with a touch of spring in the air—and Kenne and I drove out to Djurgården and into the Thielaska Gallery, and I said: 'Now listen, Kenne, do you think you could put some people aside for me until the end of July. And we could sign up Liv Ullmann and Bibi Andersson, and you could put up the money and maybe debit what it costs to my next film, if there is one?' Still being poorly, there wasn't all that much chance I'd be able to shoot it. Kenne was most sympathetic and asked: 'What's it about, then?' 'Well, it's about one person who talks and one who doesn't, and they compare hands and get all mingled up in one another.' 'Oh, really,' said Kenne. I said: 'It'll be a very small film, so it needn't cost much.' Kenne put up the money wholeheartedly. And that's something I'll never forget.

I began cautiously writing on it—I made a sort of therapeutic habit of forcing myself to go to the hospital writing desk and write for an hour a day. But I'd only seen Liv for ten minutes when she was with those actors, and had had ten minutes with Bibi; so I asked Liv to come over from Norway. We met

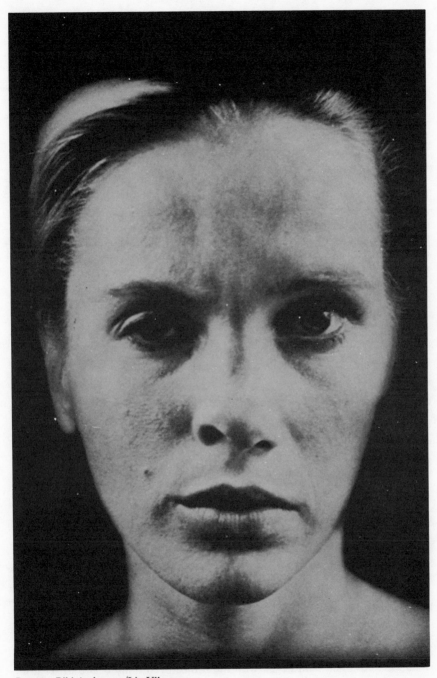

Persona: Bibi Andersson/Liv Ullmann

in my office at the theatre—they had let me out of hospital for a day. We met there and talked—well, I did the talking, and Liv sat there feeling embarrassed.

In May I was dreadfully bad again. All work was stopped, and Liv and Bibi came to the hospital to see me. I remember lying in bed, unable to turn my head, and how hellish difficult it was even to look at them while we were talking. But there was a little heap of manuscript pages, anyway, so I took it out and showed it to them—I didn't want them to get cold feet and think there wasn't going to be any film. Then they went off with their husbands to Czechoslovakia and Poland after Kenne had given them a guarantee they'd get paid, whether there was a film or not.

During the first days of June, I went out to Örnö, in the archipelago. The Royal Dramatic Theatre had closed for the summer. Though I still had attacks of giddiness, I began feeling a bit better. And suddenly the writing got going. I wrote the last half of *Persona* in a fortnight. After which it was high time to get started on it, because I had to begin rehearsals of *Hedda Gabler* at the Theatre in October, and Bibi had to play in *Duel at Diablo*, which she was to start in early September.

We began shooting on July 19, in a studio in Stockholm. The first days were nightmarish. All I felt was: 'I can't manage this!' And one day after another went by, and all the time we got only bad results, bloody awful results. And Bibi was angry, and Liv was nervous, and I was paralysed with fatigue.

JS: When you met Liv Ullmann on the street how could you be so sure she'd be up to such a major rôle?

IB: I wasn't. I just thought so.

SB: Isn't it rather rare for you to choose actors without having seen them in the theatre or in somebody else's film?

IB: I did see her, later. But not until after it had all been decided. Then I saw her in some films she'd made in Norway and in *Pan*.

JS: What was it about her sparked you off?

IB: You can see immediately whether an actor's any good or not. You've only to talk to them for five minutes, and you know. Not with pupils, not with beginners. But Liv was an experienced actress, and I knew her antecedents. She'd had a formidable success in Brecht's *The Caucasian Chalk Circle*. She'd just played Shaw's *Saint Joan*. She was the Nationalteatret's great young actress, opposite number to Bibi here. So it was no Pia Degermark I led out into the dance.

Shall we talk a moment about the boy in the film? Well, while I was working on *Persona*, I had it in my head to make a poem, not in words but in images, about the situation in which *Persona* had originated. I reflected on what was important, and began with the projector and my desire to set it in

Persona: Liv Ullmann

motion. But when the projector was running, nothing came out of it but old ideas, the spider, God's lamb, all that dull old stuff. My life just then consisted of dead people, brick walls, and a few dismal trees out in the park.

In hospital one has a strong sense of corpses floating up through the bedstead. Besides which I had a view of the morgue, people marching in and out with little coffins, in and out.

So I made believe I was a little boy who'd died, yet who wasn't allowed to be really dead, because he kept on being woken up by telephone calls from the Royal Dramatic Theatre. Finally he became so impatient he lay down and read a book. All that stuff about The Hero of our Time struck me as rather typical—the overstrained official lying on his sickbed. Well, all this is trivial. But that's how it works—and suddenly two faces are floating into one another. And that's where the film begins. As for the interpretation, you can interpret it any way you like. As with any poem. Images mean different things to different people.

s b : The film opens beautifully, I think.

i b : Yes, it's exciting.

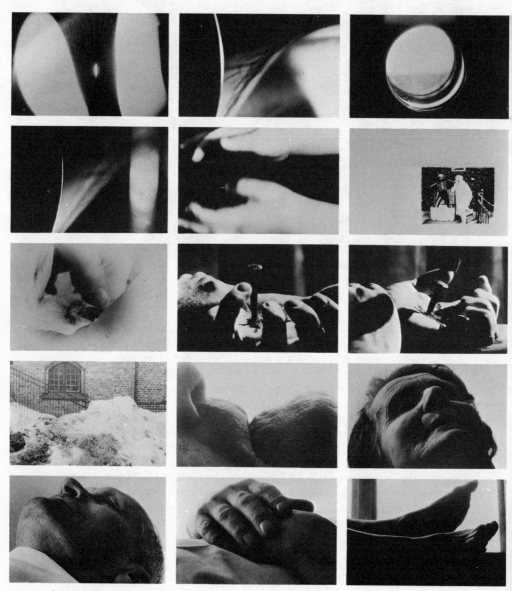

Persona: the opening sequence

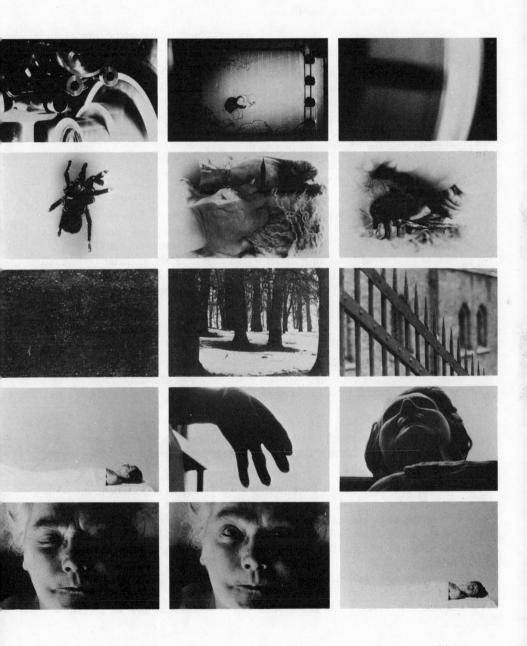

SB: The images have an extraordinary purity, emphasized by the way some of them fade into white.

IB: They even have a white border round them. They don't fill the whole screen. They're written into the whiteness.

SB: And the music is stripped of all inessentials. Just studio noises and music.

IB: Yes, the projector and the hand pierced by a nail. I wasn't used to writing that sort of poetry. No doubt I'll do it again when I feel it that way. It was stimulating to write a poem in images.

The same thing recurs when the film snaps and the projector comes to a stop. Inspiration had suddenly dried up on me. That was in May, when I got ill again, and the whole thing had come to a stop.

JS: Was it originally your idea to call the film *Kinematograph*?

IB: Yes, *Kinematography*. But Kenne had a fit.

TM: And that brings us to the title. Originally *Persona* means the mask used by actors in classical drama. It can also mean the various personages in a play. But Jung has a definition which I think suits your film admirably—I'd like to hear what you think about it. 'The consciously artificial or masked personality complex which is adopted by an individual in contrast to his inner character, with intent to serve as a protection, a defence, a deception or an attempt to adapt to the world around him.'

IB: It sounds good, and fits well in this case, too. There's something extremely fascinating to me about these people exchanging masks and suddenly sharing one between them.

TM: But they are also involved in a game—they're playing theatre *vis-à-vis* one another, and sometimes swap rôles.

IB: Exactly.

TM: Perhaps we should talk about the effect which occurs when Bibi Andersson's face suddenly flutters; and we see Liv Ullmann, and suddenly the image becomes static for a while.

IB: The girls didn't know I meant to do that. It was an idea came to me while we were shooting. We were out on Fårö and had sent that bit in—the bit where the dark side of one face is complemented by the light side of the other—to be printed. When the scene came back from the lab, we put it into the movieola and I asked the girls to come and see something amusing—a surprise.

We set the machine running, and Liv said: 'Oh look, what a horrible picture of Bibi!' And Bibi said: 'No, it's not me, it's you!' Then the picture stopped. Everyone's face has a better and a worse side, and the picture is a combination of Bibi's and Liv's less attractive sides. At first they were so scared they didn't even recognize their own faces. What they should have said was: 'What the hell have you done with my face?' But they didn't! They didn't recognize their own faces. I find that rather an odd reaction.

SB: So the scene is made in the lab?

IB: Yes, it was very easy to put the corresponding light sides together because one half of the scene is in virtual darkness.

TM: That's when Alma begins to become schizophrenic; her speech disintegrates. She notices that the other woman is projecting herself into her. With her.

IB: Yes, words cease to exist for her.

TM: But that's part of the schizophrenic syndrome.

IB: As I see it, Alma's aggressions in this dream situation take on such enormous proportions she finds she can no longer use words. She becomes violently disturbed; loses her ability to express herself. She's like a machine that has gone to pieces but just goes on turning madly, and her words, without any ordered context, just come tumbling out. Bibi found it frightfully hard to memorize those word-series. To learn a totally meaningless series of words by heart is said to be about the hardest thing you can do.

TM: It's to be found in Beckett's *Godot*.

IB: Yes, Lucky holds his long monologue—sentences all chopped up. He makes an endless speech made up of fragments of sentences. But in *Persona* there aren't even two words that fit together.

Well, the filming dragged on, and the results were miserable. But when we went out to Fårö things went fine. It was lovely weather, the filming began to flow, and we started re-taking everything we'd done in Stockholm. We were able to fix up the summerhouse more or less as it had been in Stockholm. The hospital set we arranged in the local museum, where we had our little studio. Afterwards, when we got back to Stockholm, we made haste to re-shoot even more of it. Half the film consists of re-takes.

JS: It cost more than you'd reckoned with?

IB: Yes, it was rather expensive.

SB: Those dreamlike night scenes, were they shot in the studio?

IB: Both on Fårö and in the studio.

SB: That scene, for example, where Liv floats through the rooms and one hears the foghorn in the distance?

IB: That's taken on Fårö. So is the whole crisis between Liv and Bibi. What we'd shot in Stockholm had been an utter failure.

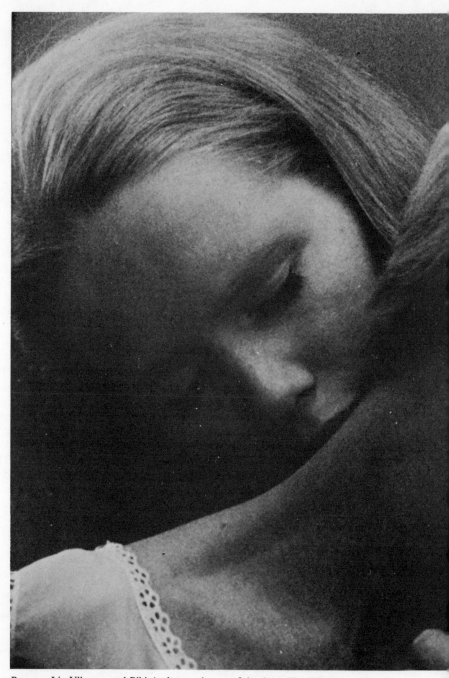

Persona: Liv Ullmann and Bibi Andersson in one of the dreamlike sequences

Persona: the oscillating relationship between Elisabeth (Liv Ullmann) . . .

S B : How far does Sven Nykvist inspire you—or do you inspire each other—in giving your films visual form?

I B : We've developed a private language, so to speak. We hardly need to say a word. Before the filming begins we go through the film very carefully, to see how we imagine the lighting, check the lighting conditions, and then solve all lighting problems together.

S B : *Persona* is almost entirely composed of close-ups and long shots, and its form is entirely congruent with its content. The relations between the women are shown in violent oscillations between close-up and distance, between intimacy and detachment. This way of telling a story, excluding the more 'normal' everyday mid-shot, was consciously intended, of course?

I B : Yes, long shot versus close-up arises out of an ambivalence in the director himself. You're a film director. You must have experienced the same thing. Suddenly one morning you can feel you're bursting with vitality. You're seized with a sudden need to get to grips with your devils, challenge them, force them up against the wall. In the best of humours you want to torment them till they yield their last possible ounce of expressiveness. To force them to burst their bounds. Sometimes in close-ups simply because the situation

206

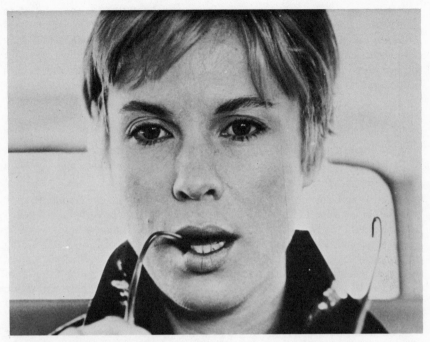

... and Alma (Bibi Andersson)

demands close-ups. Sometimes you feel a violent urge to burst all bounds, both your own and the actors'. If so, you know how immensely revealing, how dreadfully difficult the close-up is, not to mention the line of dialogue that belongs to it.

Some days you feel nothing but a huge revulsion and fatigue. Most of all you'd like to go home, or bawl everyone out, or just stand in a corner and whimper. Then suddenly you feel—'Ah, now I want to make long shots, now I want them at a distance, far far away!' And you ask yourself: 'But will it work? Yes, here it'll work, here it's even fine to have long shots.'

But what it really is that works—whether it's the built-in feeling for rhythm that's decisive, or whether you're being governed by personal, private impulses—that's something you have to make clear to yourself. You must use your ambivalence as something fruitful, something functional. A great deal of these swings to and fro, I think, are due to an interior rhythm. When you're in that rhythm—which you gradually get into, sometimes after three days, sometimes after a week, and in the case of *Persona* not until after we'd been shooting for about a month—you become dead sure of yourself. Then you can use either (*a*) your vitality, to jump in on them, or (*b*) your revulsion, to hold them at a distance. When shooting film you use everything you've got. Every cell in your body.

J S : When you've imagined a particular pictorial solution, or the solution to some scene, does it seem to you you're making a moral or psychological decision, so that you ask yourself: 'But is this solution motivated? Is it what I've got to have in this scene?' Do you think it out purely intellectually? Or do you rely on your sense of rhythm, your intuition? In my view there ought to be a moral and psychological congruence between form and content.

I B : I suppose it's largely built-in.

J S : It's Godard, isn't it, who has said this about form and ethic?

I B : I thought it was Antonioni—about it being an ethical decision. Hell, but Godard's morals must be low! But it's true. One discovers very quickly that a scene *can* only be shot in one way.

S B : I'd like to hear your comment on one particular scene in *Persona*: the one where Bibi is telling Liv what happened to her on the shore with the girl called Katarina, and the two fourteen-year-old boys. It seems almost studied, it's so precisely constructed. Then you move in to a mid-shot of Bibi, who's sitting in a chair talking. And out to a long shot of Liv and then to a medium shot of Bibi and a medium shot of Liv, and then a close-up of Bibi and a close-up of Liv. Then we see Bibi in mid-shot walking a bit dazedly about the room, smoking. Then comes a close-up of Liv, I fancy; and another shot of Bibi; and then they're lying in bed in close-up. And all the time she's telling her story.

You could have done this scene in a way similar to the scene in *Winter Light* where Ingrid Thulin reads out her letter. There you chose to exclude the listener; but in *Persona* you obviously regarded it as essential to show the listener too.

I B : If you look at Liv's face, you'll see that all the time it's swelling. It's fascinating—her lips get bigger, her eyes darker, the whole girl is transformed into a sort of greed. There's a profile shot of Liv, here, which is incomparable. One sees her face transformed into a sort of cold, voluptuous mask.

We called that scene the *fortellningen*.* The girls made a lot of jokes about it. When we were going to shoot it, I told Liv how she must gather all her feeling into her lips. She had to concentrate on placing her sensibility there—it's possible, you know, to place one's feelings in different parts of the body. Suddenly one can summon one's feeling into one's little finger, or one's big toe, or into one buttock, or your lips. And that was what I insisted she did—and what gives her her strange listening attitude. The important thing, after all, isn't Bibi's scared, faintly vulgar, and perfectly straightforward tone of voice or her amazement at what she has been through. Equally important, equally important erotically in that scene, is the woman who listens to her; the receiver, she is bombarded and stimulated.

S B : How did you go to work here, from the purely practical point of view? Did you shoot the whole scene in mid-shot, and then in close-up?

* Norwegian: 'the narration'.

IB: Oh, no, the sport is to go on up to a certain point, then break, and take the corresponding material from the other side. And so on throughout.

SB: The scene is constructed in a very architectural, or musical–architectural way. A construction you'd decided on in advance?

IB: The more excited, the more raw, horrible, brutal, or elaborate a scene is, the better it is to keep the camera an objective mediant. If the camera gets all excited and begins skipping about all over the bloody place, you lose a lot. It's you, the 'audience', who must feel it, whom it's got to strike. If the camera forces its way between and begins talking about its own emotions, usually it will just get in the way, and prevent you from experiencing anything. The story mustn't only have a suggestive effect on Elisabeth—it must have a suggestive effect on you, enable you to experience it all deep down inside you, in your own cinematograph—much more drastically, brutally, honestly, and voluptuously than I could ever show. Imagine a dissolve there, and the whole story told in pictures—what a horrible anti-climax! You'd have stepped straight into *The Naked Wind from the Sea*!

TM: You say some shots have arisen from your state of mind on one particular day. When you see the final material in the cutting room, how do you see it then? By then your attitude must have changed?

IB: By then they've been transmuted into something else. When I see the takes in the cutting room my attitude to the material is completely matter-of-fact. It's *before* it has taken shape, *before* the camera has absorbed it, that the great frenzy rages.

TM: With you, I never feel there are any alternatives. Everything has to be the way it is. In that long shot when Bibi comes out and knocks the glass over, you're busy with the camera down in the thicket. One wonders—what's the girl going to think up now? There she stands calmly waiting for the right moment. And it's not until the actual drama occurs, and Liv cuts herself on one of the pieces, that you come in with the camera.

IB: Right! Usually I'm only unsure of myself when I know a scene is bad in some way, or if I'm working with a poor actor, or have gone off the rails in some other way. Moments when I'm suddenly unsure of myself in some way ... you know, when everyone's cornered, and depressed and waiting for the director—that idiot—to hit on something at last, so we can all take a break for lunch.

TM: In a film industry like the American, which is so horribly commercialized and a film has to be shot at all costs and the dollars are pouring away—it's then, isn't it, they let the camera movements make good the shortcomings in the script and the vision?

IB: Take a look at any of Arne Mattsson's films, and you'll see how camera movement replaces almost everything.

JS: You said *Persona* was a poem in images. That's an observation I've really taken to heart, because *Persona*, while it's the film I intellectually least understand, is one of your films I most admire.

So I've some questions arising from this film. Elisabeth Vogler, the actress, has realized that her art is quite meaningless. Of her own free will she has chosen to become dumb. In the preface to the book we read, more or less: 'Religion and art are kept alive for sentimental reasons, as a conventional act of politeness toward the past, out of well-meant concern for the age of leisure's ever more nervous citizens.' In our conversations, too, you've said you doubt whether art is meaningful—at least we've discussed this point. Can this theme be discerned in many of your productions?

IB: At first I was quite simply entranced by the movement of the figures, and by being allowed to make films at all. Afterwards I've become more and more aware of the theatre's, film's, and TV's limited capacity for communicating fiction. Today, when I see how badly the novel has gone off the rails and how less and less able we are to experience and accept a fictitious course of events in an elemental way, the more reluctant I have become to tell stories with a beginning and an end—and the more dubious I've become.

JS: The Vietnamese monk who burns himself to death on the TV screen gives Elisabeth Vogler a nasty shock. The artist is struck down by reality. This confrontation in *Persona* is pregnant in a way we've hardly ever seen in your films before. So I think it's not altogether absurd—even if you think it is—to ask you what sort of reality it was, perhaps, that overwhelmed you when you were making *Persona*?

IB: It's not often I depict current events. Take, for instance, that poem which introduces *Persona* and depicts a situation at a particular moment. Art used to be able to be an act of political incitement, it could suggest political action. Today art, in this respect, has completely played itself out.

Political activity today is precipitated by the news, by television's immediate closeness to what is going on all over the world. In this respect art has missed the boat completely. Artists are hardly the social visionaries they used to be. And they mustn't imagine they are! Reality is running away from artists and their political visions.

TM: After Ruby's murder of Oswald, which we actually saw happen, that's absolutely true!

IB: Of course! And it's going on all the time.

JS: Anyway, you still think the artist has a function in society?

IB: Since society still thinks it needs artists, and even pays them for their services, and as long as people go to the cinema and see TV plays and fill the theatres and concert halls, the artist must be prepared to step forward, whether he's any use or not. And then, too, I think he must *reflect* a hell of a long time about *what way* he can be of use, and possibly *whether he can't be useful simply by taking a positive attitude to himself and just being an artist.*

JS : In *Persona* you have Alma say: 'I've a tremendous admiration for artists, and I think art has a tremendous value in life, particularly to people who are in difficulties.' The artist as therapist, quite simply. Are you just being scornful here? Or do you mean our view of art should really be as utilitarian as that?

IB : I'm joking. But that's just the sort of thing one hears. Where one feels most touched, and gets most furious, is when one hears people, decent people, who go toddling off to the theatre and fill the concert halls and go to evening classes, say: 'I've an enormous respect for artists and I love art and I think art is terribly important to people who're suffering.' There they sit patiently, patiently, waiting to be edified. But usually the artists, with their enormous vanity, are less interesting than the people who are sitting there waiting for them to edify them. I loathe the whole of this humble attitude toward artists, *who really ought to be given a kick in the arse.* Yes, one could say a lot about all this.

SB : And Bibi says it so naïvely.

IB : Yes, she's quite bewitching.

JS : But it's perfectly legitimate for the public, don't you think, to put art to therapeutic uses, if they want to?

IB : Legitimate, yes—if they can, it's marvellous. Then Elisabeth turns on a radio play—no, she's done that earlier. And Bibi makes a contribution there, the horrible inflexions of some star on the radio too; Bibi apes her tone of voice, then those horrible theatrical gestures and Elisabeth starts to laugh and gets all hysterical. It's exactly like when she plays *Phaedra*, when she suddenly hears herself—'What the devil do I sound like?' She sees her colleagues, their grease-painted faces—'What the devil are we really up to?' And then she thinks: 'There's no sense in saying anything. So I'll just keep my mouth shut.' Look at the first close-up, when she turns round. Suddenly she looks about her, and begins to smile.

SB : The doctor says the same thing too.

IB : And it's completely unneurotic, that's what's so important about Elisabeth. This silence she imposes on herself is unneurotic. It's a strong person's form of protest.

TM : In *Vertigo* Hitchcock has said this even more ironically about music, à propos James Stewart's catatonic depressions in the hospital. They've tried to lift these depressions by having him listen to music. But then the girl goes in to the doctor and says: 'Doctor, I don't think Mozart helps in the least.'

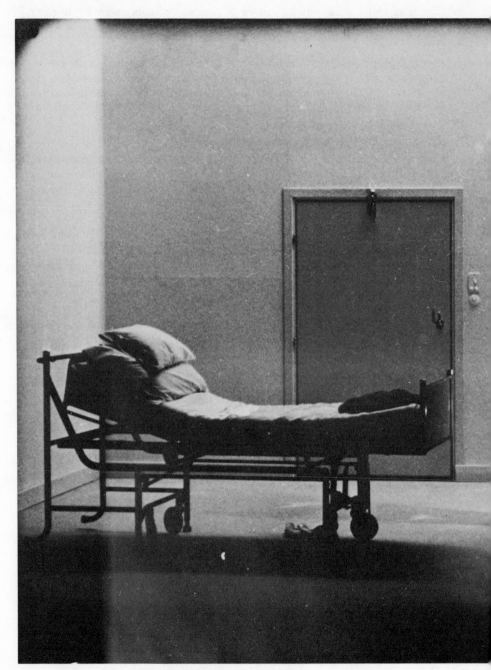

Persona: Elisabeth (Liv Ullmann) watching on TV the Vietnamese monk . . .

... and her reaction

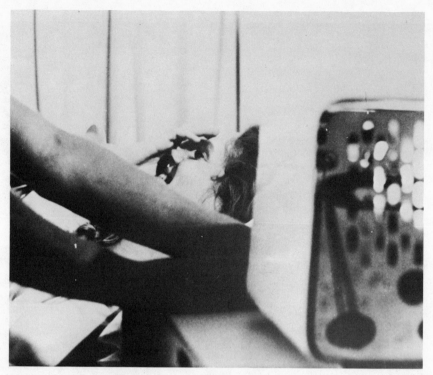

Persona: Elisabeth (Liv Ullmann) in the hysterical scene

IB : Mozart helps me tremendously!

JS : When you were preparing *Persona*, had you studied, as one doctor of theology maintains you had, Hjalmar Sundén's *Religionen och rollerna*, with its gestalt-psychological views?

IB : No, not at all. Not a word.

JS : But surely you've read that book? It's a standard work.

IB : No, I haven't. My literary baggage is rather light. People who studied the history of literature under Professor Lamm have only read *Harward the Harpist* and Ling's* dramas.

TM : What do you want with other people's baggage, when you've got your own?

IB : It enriches one's own, and becomes more important as the years go by. Little by little I'm discovering how legitimate it is to sit all day reading some book one likes. I used to get a bad conscience if I sat reading in the daytime.

* Ling (1776–1839) inventor of Swedish gymnastics, was also a dramatist of sorts.

First Meeting at Råsunda in January 1968

STIG BJÖRKMAN: The chief character in *The Hour of the Wolf*, the painter Johan Borg, is tormented by 'demons'. At two points in the film he calls them 'the cannibals'. You mentioned a project you had before you made *Persona*, called *The Cannibals*. Does the script for that film form the basis of *The Hour of the Wolf*, or have you taken motifs from *The Cannibals* both for *Persona* and *The Hour of the Wolf*?

INGMAR BERGMAN: This cannibal motif, the hour-of-the-wolf motif, goes back a long way. The same applies to the other motifs in *The Hour of the Wolf*: the redistribution of power, the identification problem, the silent as against the speaking rôle.

One can say that the script for *The Hour of the Wolf* is based on *The Cannibals*, which was never made. I wrote *The Cannibals* the year before I made *Persona*.

The Hour of the Wolf is extremely personal. So personal I even made a prelude and a postlude to it, playfully 'boxing it in'. Nothing is left of this but the dialogue which accompanies the titles. In this prologue and epilogue I was guilty of a self-deception. It was better not to play at any aesthetic games to hold this film at a distance. So I took these two bits away in two stages. The film was originally 2,850 metres long. I cut a hundred.

JONAS SIMA: What were these sections like?

215

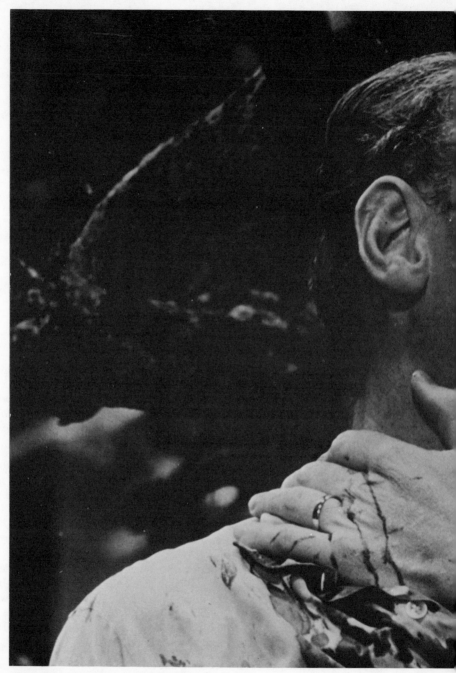

Hour of the Wolf: Max von Sydow attacked by birds

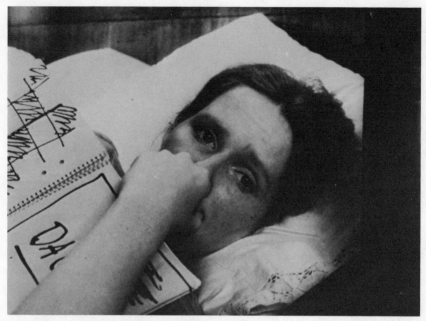

Hour of the Wolf: Liv Ullmann with the diary

IB: They were very simple. I sat in the studio, telling the actors how I'd hit on the idea for the film: about how a woman had handed me a diary—Johan Borg's diary—and how afterwards I'd got her to tell me, into a tape recorder, about their life together. All on the E. T. A. Hoffmann model.

TORSTEN MANNS: Hoffmann, Poe, Almqvist, where you feel at home?

IB: Of course! The allusion is quite conscious. The names of several characters in *The Hour of the Wolf* are taken from E. T. A. Hoffmann: Kreisler the 'kapellmeister', Heerbrand the curator, Lindhorst the archivist.

JS: During a sort of personal purgatory at the party in the castle, Johan Borg says that the artist, through no fault of his own, is a man apart.
He says: 'Nothing is self-evident in what I create—except the compulsion to create it.' Well, that's a romantic view of art, isn't it? Several of your earlier films reveal the same attitude.

IB: What do you mean by romantic?

JS: The idea of the artist as a man sent by God. Who suffers from a Platonic belief in inspiration.

IB: That's not how I mean it, even if in this case it may seem so.

218

JS: Otherwise your aesthetic position would be opposed to the one being adopted by so many artists today. By our young authors, Sven Delblanc, for instance, who calls authorship a profession, a job.

IB: As a craftsman, a film-maker, and a director, I share that view in high degree. What Johan Borg wanted to say was that he is faced with a 'must', an unending torment, toothache. He can't escape it. There's no question, that is, of a gift from on high. No other-worldly relationship. It's just there. A disease. A perversion. A five-legged calf. He takes a very brutal view of his situation.

I don't exactly recall what Johan Borg says in that scene. They're talking about the artist as one of the elect. I fancy he uses the expression in inverted commas. Anyway I know that when I wrote it I meant something tormenting. Something is going on that one can do nothing about. Afterwards one tries to give it professional form. And of course artistic activity is also a way of earning one's living.

My view of my work as an artist is that I make articles for consumption. If, in addition, a film turns into something more, that's nice. But I don't work 'sub specie aeternitatis'—with one eye on immortality.

JS: Hasn't your attitude to artistic creativity become somewhat less dramatic than it used to be?

IB: As the religious aspect of my existence was wiped out, life became much easier to live. Sartre has said how inhibited he used to be as an artist and author, how he suffered because what he was doing wasn't good enough. By a slow intellectual process he came to realize that his anxieties about not making anything of value were an atavistic relic from the religious notion that something exists which can be called the Supreme Good, or that anything is perfect. When he'd dug up this secret idea, this relic, had seen through it and amputated it, he lost his artistic inhibitions too.

I've been through something very similar. When my top-heavy religious superstructure collapsed, I also lost my inhibitions as a writer. Above all, my fear of not keeping up with the times. In *Winter Light* I swept my house clean. Since then things have been quiet on that front.

TM: You mention Sartre and the religious syndrome. I'd like to get on to the question of what view you take of the father, of authority, of the primitive father-image. In your first films, from your play *Jack and the Actors* to *The Hour of the Wolf*, you settle accounts several times with the father-image. There's that little creature in the wardrobe which Johan Borg speaks of in *The Hour of the Wolf*.

Many people have called you a Freudian; but they're wrong. You're really a Jungian. It's Jung who has these atavistic, primitive archetypes—which were originally individual and private, but have acquired a universal validity. This argument can be applied to the homosexual sex-murder which Johan

Hour of the Wolf: the 'boy demon' overcomes . . .

Borg commits on the little boy on the seashore. It's the father he murders—
the little chap in the cupboard who tries to bite his foot.

I B : I can't reply to that. For me that scene has changed meaning many times.
It is almost two years now since I wrote *The Hour of the Wolf*, and a year and
a half since I shot it. When I made that scene, it was a realistic expression of
Johan Borg's manic fear of being bitten. The boy was one of his demons.
Johan Borg couldn't make up his mind whether it was a dream or real,
whether he'd killed a boy who really existed or whether it had only happened
in his imagination. The boundary between dream and reality had been
blurred.

J S : The story of the beating in *The Hour of the Wolf*, the old man in the
wardrobe, is that taken from your own experience?

I B : I've experienced it myself. How I ever got out alive passes my understanding. In the original script I'd intended to show the whole episode taking place.
But I don't think I could have achieved the same result.

S B : Much of *The Hour of the Wolf* is built up like that: either you narrate in
images, in which case what happens is not commented on verbally; or else the
story is told in words, while the camera rests on a face. This gives it much
greater density and suggestiveness than if text and image had run side by side.

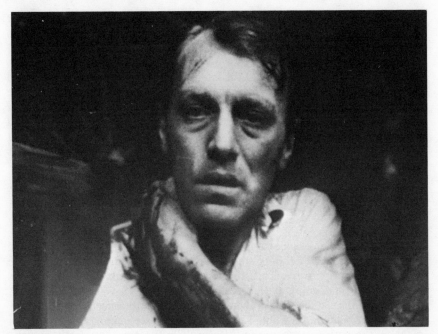

... Johan Borg (Max von Sydow)

By switching to and fro between things seen and things told, you set up a tension.

JS: In *Persona*, too, Bibi Andersson's erotic story is very much more exciting than any pornographic film could be.

IB: Which just goes to prove that in films one can do as one bloody well likes! Isn't that so?

TM: But think how few people exploit it!

IB: I was well aware how extraordinarily difficult it was going to be to make *The Hour of the Wolf*. But at the same time I felt it to be a challenge, both formal and practical; from the actors' point of view too. The whole time I was working on it I felt enormously stimulated.

SB: Yes, the film is a challenge—both for you and for the viewer.

IB: As it's intended to be.

TM: You have another play-within-the-play in *The Hour of the Wolf*. Are you a bit fixated on this sort of interlude?

IB: After one has been working awhile on a full-length film, it's a relief to interpolate something different. There sits your audience, looking in one direction. And suddenly you stick your head out and say—take a look over there for a while! And everyone turns his head. It gives them exercise. It's as simple as that.

There was a good deal of discussion about the bit in *Persona* where the film snaps. A lot of wiseacres thought the interruption silly. They said it distracted the audience from what was going on, etc. Personally I'm of exactly the opposite opinion. If you distract the audience temporarily from the course of events and then push them into it again, you don't reduce their sensibility and awareness, you heighten it. In *A Passion* I've four clean acts—the film is built up in four blocks, and each block is rounded off with an aria. The actors appear and comment on their rôles, place themselves slightly outside it.

s b : During the titles to *The Hour of the Wolf* we hear you talking to the technicians . . .

i b : . . . a few sound effects from the studio, yes.

s b : But before the titles come three blocks of text, in which you explain the film's background. Johan Borg's diary has come into your possession, you've heard Alma Borg's story. Then there's an exciting break. First you lure us into thinking we're going to see a realistic drama: 'this is what has happened'. Then come the 'studio noises' which immediately distance it aesthetically. What we are watching is a film. Then Liv Ullmann steps into the first shot and picks up the narrative where the titles broke off: a new, apparently realistic situation. It's as if you wanted to create a deliberate break between aesthetic detachment and emotional identification.

i b : It's good for people to be woken up a moment, then drawn back into the drama. I repeat the title, *The Hour of the Wolf*, in the middle of the film, for the same reason.

j s : You haven't consciously used this trick before?

i b : No, not before *Persona*.

j s : The French *nouvelle vague* experimented with these 'distancing' effects. Belmondo, in *À Bout de Souffle*, turns direct to the audience now and again and comments on what's going on. At the time this was regarded as something new and shocking.

i b : But it's as old as the hills, don't you realize that? In the theatre! The author turns directly to his audience. It's simple and delightful.

I used the method once, in *Summer With Monika*. Why, I didn't know; but I found it worked. In the scene where Monika has come back to town and is sitting in a café with a fellow she doesn't know. The chap sets the jukebox going. At that moment Harriet Andersson lights a cigarette, turns her face suddenly to the camera, and looks straight at us. In those days you just couldn't do that sort of thing. She looks at us in a long—in those days an indecently long—close-up.

Bergman and Sven Nykvist prepare Liv Ullmann for the monologue sequence in *Hour of the Wolf*

SB: Translating your development as a film-maker into the language of art, one could say you earlier worked as a sculptor. You gave form to space. You set up your tensions by the way you positioned your actors and their movements in space. You staged your drama. Today you also paint portraits.

IB: I concentrate on the face. The backgrounds are an accompaniment.

SB: The background is merely suggested, for instance in the first shot in *The Hour of the Wolf*. First we see the house with Liv Ullmann coming out of it, then she sits down at a table in the foreground and the camera settles on her face.

IB: If the background is in the picture at all, it's chiefly because of that strong wind which was blowing. It tore at the black bushes and gave an autumnal feeling.

SB: One must know one's actors well to work in this way. Know what one can get out of them. Know one can leave them alone with the camera for the long time needed. You write your rôles with an eye to certain actors; I know that. But can you tell us something about how you create these figures? Or we can turn the question upside down and ask can you envisage certain actors in certain films having been replaced by others; and what effect do you think that would have had on the films?

IB: It would have changed them radically. One gets A for a rôle, B for another, and C for a third. Then suddenly one sees how the magnetic field between A, B, and C changes, and switches from one to another of them. That's something one can do very little about. Consciously or unconsciously, one just has to go along with it.

JS: Whenever you've spoken of your actors it has always been with great respect and tenderness. Is this squeamishness, this loyal way of speaking about them, just part of the job?

IB: I realize how exposed actors are. They are the ones, always, who go on to the stage, or before the camera. Who have to strip themselves naked down to their very skeleton. *We're* protected. We can always make a grimace or resort to some verbal evasion. They can't. They can neither run away, nor explain things away. They just have to stand there, with their bodies and their faces. That's why the only respectable and decent thing to do seems to me always, unswervingly, unshakably, to stand up for my actors.

JS: Sometimes, in discussions about actors and with actors, I've felt irritated by their lack—not of intelligence—but of knowledge outside their profession and by their reluctance to broaden their knowledge. True, many actors today are taking an active part in the public debate, and not only when it concerns their own profession. But to many of them one feels like saying 'Read the newspapers!'

IB: The actors I have to do with aren't like that. But there *are* actors one

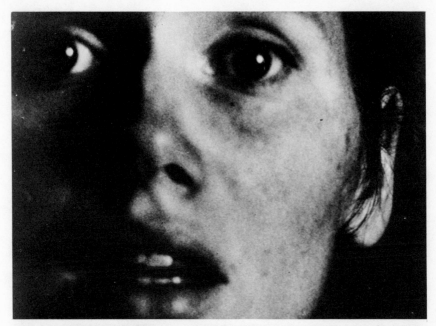

Hour of the Wolf: Liv Ullmann

shouldn't even try to discuss Vietnam with—there's no rôle for them in *that* drama!

J S : Are you sceptical of the intellectual type of actor?

I B : I'm sceptical of actors who replace intuition, sensuality, imagination with intellectual jargon, yes. Out of fear of shyness, or quite simply because they lack talent, they've hit on a manner of talking which helps them to survive. But sooner or later they all come to grief.

S B : Supposing we go back to our first question about actors: can you tell us something about how strongly actors influence their rôles when you're writing the script?

I B : Until I've decided which actor is to play which part I can't really even begin to write. But when I have, the rôle dresses itself up in his skin, his muscles, his special intonation; above all his rhythms, his way of being.

J S : In *The Shame* you are said to have improvised a good deal. Earlier you said 'Behind each improvisation there must be preparation.' About thirty technicians worked on *The Shame*. Isn't there something contradictory here? Mustn't such a big apparatus have an inhibiting effect on the improvisation, on the ability to listen, on the playful aspect? And aren't such improvisations something more in the nature of technical, tactical measures to create a better working atmosphere, rather than something aesthetic?

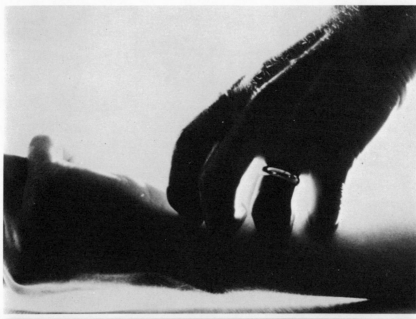

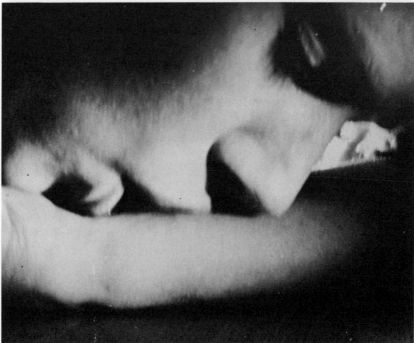

The element of violence ... in *Persona*: Elisabeth (Liv Ullmann) and Alma (Harriet Andersson)

IB: In *The Shame* we were all the time re-creating an illusion of reality. In such a film it's quite natural for actors to choose their own words. After all, each has his own way of hesitating before a word, his own characteristic intonation, his own speech-rhythm. Instead of containing a dialogue the actors had to follow, the script of *The Shame* tells them in indirect speech more or less what the conversation is to be about.

JS: Though fundamentally you did have a definite idea what the final result had to be?

IB: Yes. So must every improvisation—at least in this medium. We must be clearly aware of what it is we want to put over. After that it's another matter if we see sudden, amusing, characteristic, or exciting angles. But the goal must be fixed in advance.

SB: Do you feel stimulated by the new possibilities currently offered by the cinema? Things have developed rapidly these last few years. We've got faster film, more sensitive to light. Colour film has improved. Technical equipment has become lighter and easier to handle. There's greater variety in screen format. But so far—with the exception of *Now About These Women*—you've always stuck to black and white, and filmed for a standard screen.

IB: The other formats are beyond me. They seem artificial—and ugly, though I'd happily see the old silent screen format, which was a good deal taller, come back.

But I do intend to start with colour. There's a sensual erotic charm in colour, when properly used. But when there's nothing there except colour, then it's not amusing. For example, I think colour spoils a film like *Bonnie and Clyde*. That was a film, if any, which ought to have been shot in black-and-white, in coarse-grained black-and-white tones. But Arthur Penn is an extremely fine director.

SB: Penn's films and yours have certain traits in common. In Penn there are very strong elements of violence; not only outward violence, but also the inner unleashed sort, stored up in his characters. In both your latest films, too, one feels this very tangibly, not least in *Persona*, even though the violence finds no direct outlet. Are you strongly aware of the violence all round—and inside—us?

IB: Yes, I'm aggressive by nature. And I often find it hard to repress my aggressiveness.

The film as a medium is well-suited to destructive acts, acts of violence. It is one of the cinema's perfectly legitimate functions: to ritualize violence.

JS: Apart from your films, aggression in the Swedish cinema has been strongly inhibited.

IB: But the Swede's aggressions *are* inhibited. And so are our Swedish directors'.

Råsunda Studios, 24 February 1969

TORSTEN MANNS: What about the background to *The Shame*? We've asked you to tell us what triggered off each of your films. On several occasions you've said you had no intention of making it into a political film. So I see *The Shame* as a continuation of your earlier films—the depiction of two or more people's characters.

INGMAR BERGMAN: *The Shame* originates in a panicky question: How would I have behaved during the Nazi period if Sweden had been occupied and if I'd held some position of responsibility or been connected with some institution? Or had even found myself threatened as a private person? How much civic courage would I have been able to muster up under the threat of violence, physical or spiritual, or in the war of nerves in an occupied country? Every time I've thought about such matters, I've always come to the same conclusion: physically and psychically I'm a coward—except when I get angry. At moments I can get furiously angry. But I'm always a coward. I've a strong instinct for self-preservation; but, purely physically, my tendency to get angry can supply me with considerable quantities of courage. That's just physiological. But the long, cold, wearing threat—how would I survive that?

This is a question which has troubled me a long time, and I'm still not finished with it. The whole thing was precipitated by documentary film from Vietnam. It didn't show any war scenes. But it showed the third party to the

228

war. There was one horrible shot. An old woman and an old man, two South Vietnamese peasants, were standing holding a half-starved cow. Meanwhile an American military helicopter is starting up in the background. The cow passes water and tries to gallop away. The old woman, who's tough, clings to her cow, and disappears with it in a cloud of dust. The old man is left standing there, on the verge of tears, staring at this roaring helicopter and at his old woman disappearing with the cow.

JONAS SIMA: When did you write the script?

IB: I wrote it in the spring. The spring of 1967. But we mustn't forget one thing: at that time Czechoslovakia had still not been occupied. Nor had the Vietnam war begun to escalate. If those two things had already happened, the film would have worn a different aspect.

STIG BJÖRKMAN: In this film Max von Sydow plays a musician. Was that mere chance? Is its relation to the rest of the film fortuitous?—What I'm driving at is this. People have criticized you, in connection with *The Shame*, for once again taking artists as your main characters and depicting their problems within the context of the much greater problem of the threatening war situation.

IB: They could have been anybody. The main thing as I saw it was that an orchestra is an orderly, a disciplined world; a trifle authoritative, and with very strict working patterns. What I wanted to show most, I suppose, was that as long as Jan enjoyed such conditions, he hung together well. So does his wife, afterwards, too. The only connection with their personalities as artists is his fine 18th-century instrument, which has gone through the Napoleonic wars and survived all sorts of adventures, but which gets smashed to pieces. In some way the man is part and parcel of his instrument—the instant his instrument is smashed, his entire view of life crumbles too. He is transformed.

TM: You're building on what I should call a theory of catastrophe: 'these things happen to him, therefore culture is shattered'. But surely culture is only pushed aside for the time being? What we call the superstructure, after all— music and all the rest of it—that comes back. Surely you don't mean all culture could quite simply be wiped out by a war?

IB: And never revive?—No, I don't believe that for a moment.

TM: Take music, for instance. There are musicians who have the music by heart.

IB: As long as there are people, I believe there will always be reconstruction; culture will revive.

SB: The musicians Jan and Eva get into a short discussion or conversation with Jacobi, in which their artistic activities are put in question. Jacobi speaks of art's sacred flabbiness.

The Shame: Jan, Eva and Jacobi (Max von Sydow, Liv Ullmann and Gunnar Björnstrand) . . .

IB: Art's sacred freedom, art's sacred flabbiness, yes.

SB: This continues a familiar discussion of the artist's situation which we recognize from several of your earlier films. And it's this that makes us feel your choice of a profession for Jan and Eva *is* important; that it is precisely their status as artists which is crucial.

IB: For me it's a matter of no importance at all—well, perhaps not entirely. But it's secondary, or tertiary, or whatever you call it. What Jacobi means is simply that there's no freedom any more for the artist today. 'Don't come to me with all your grandiloquent talk about the freedom of the artist, it's sheer flabbiness. And please don't sentimentalize the situation either, just because you happen to be artists.' That's what he means, mostly.

JS: Of your films up to now *The Shame* must be the one which has been most criticized politically?

IB: Yes, it plumped down in the middle of *that* new wave.

TM: Of the various characters in your films, Jan (Max von Sydow) is a very interesting person, I think; and he recurs in a lot of them. In fact, one could say, you have him in most of your films. I see a certain resemblance to Caligula in *Frenzy*.

... Jan (Max von Sydow) confronted by the realities of war

IB: To me he seems a new creation. In point of fact, he came out of another film. Both he and Jacobi are taken from a film I'd begun writing when I was busy in Osló with a production of *Six Characters in Search of an Author*. It was about a scientist who makes psychic experiments. He shuts up two people in his laboratory, exposes them to various psychic pressures, and observes them. Well, I couldn't get a proper grip on that story. What I wanted was someone who had been put back to square one in some way. He returns in *A Passion*.

TM: But I didn't say he *was* Caligula—I never finished my question—what I said was he shared certain of his traits. People who are frightened and subjected to pressure, just like certain animals—black panthers for instance —only begin to defend themselves when they're attacked. Sadists function in the same way. Caligula is such a man. And so was Himmler. The evil in them only appears when they're attacked. When they've their backs to the wall.

Jan may be an amoeba, but he becomes either plus or minus—which is greatly preferable—when placed in a conflict situation. And still more so in a panic situation. This enormous pressure triggers him off, changes him in a very special way. And it's here his character shows small but none the less similar traits to such figures as Caligula.

231

For example, when he hides from his wife and sits there coddling himself, almost in tears. It's the same scene, isn't it, as the one in *Frenzy* when Jan-Erik comes home and finds Caligula sitting on the stairs: 'You must understand how things are with me, how bloody awful everything is for me, I'm maladjusted, I'm so unhappy and I'm so lonely.' It's an echo of this, I mean. But if these people get free hands and we lose control over them, then they turn into fascists, men of violence.

IB: Which is the whole point—how much of the fascist are you and I harbouring inside ourselves? What sort of a situation is needed to turn us from good social democrats into active Nazis? That's what I want to find out.

TM: A panic situation, one where we're suddenly torn right out of our own context and can no longer control ourselves.

IB: More and more I've a feeling that people, under the tremendous pressure they're being exposed to today, are acting in panic. Acting out of only one motive: self-interest. And that's what the film's about.

SB: The film describes a panic situation. In your view people in such a situation act one hundred percent selfishly. It's a very pessimistic view. And it's this attitude in *The Shame* that critics have attacked. Its chief characters lack any ideals or ideology. They are unable to choose. Unable to make up their minds which side they're on. In fact, the whole situation in the film is so involved they aren't even given a chance to take sides. But in such a situation I don't think people are only motivated by self-preservation. Naturally it's easier for us, standing outside the panic situation, to know which side we're on.

IB: I, too, think a faith, whether religious or political, is helpful in critical situations. It immunizes against psychoses.

JS: The film's pessimism offers no concrete alternative. When Eva and Jan put to sea and flee—what awaits them then?

IB: Nothing. We've disinherited ourselves. We're on the slippery slope. There's no stopping developments—things have gone too far already. The opposing forces are too few, too badly organized, too nonplussed, too helpless. What's going on in the West is all to hell. And we know it. And it's getting worse.

JS: I'd like to ask you rather a theoretical question . . .

IB: As long as it's not above my head.

JS: Well, let's see! This cleavage in your films between authentic reality and symbolic fiction was resolved in a very natural way, I think, in the chamber works, in the trilogy and *Persona*. Superficially, I think it's a question of greater precision in your means of expression; greater concretion, quite simply. That's why I personally react negatively to the final scene in *The*

The Shame: the final sequence

Shame. It's overburdened with symbolism. Suddenly the film goes all alle-gorical—and this is emphasized, not least, by the way in which your some-what lighter impressionistic dialogue is replaced by a heavier expressionistic way of speaking.

IB: Eva tells her dream. Nothing else is said. It's the only line of dialogue at the end.

JS: As the problems become more abstract, so does the film. A sort of conflict of illusions arises: the film passes from the authentic to the symbolic. Have you ever had any second thoughts about that coda?

IB: Not that bit, but at another point. Actually I got the final sequence from a photo series in *Life*. During the last war, or just after it, they'd photographed a torpedoed troop transport. They'd found masses of dead people floating about in the Atlantic. It all looks thoroughly stylized. Like those queues outside the crematoria in the concentration camps, or the pictures of those naked women standing with a grassy slope in front of them, half-turned toward the camera, with the gates of the crematorium to one side in the background. It's all so unreal it seems to have been staged.
  The shortcoming in *The Shame*, if I may say so, is a problem you've

The Shame: the execution scene with Jacobi (Gunnar Björnstrand) and military patrol leader (Sigge Fürst)

touched on and which I think you may have been more aware of on the instinctive level. And this is certain dramaturgic tricks, which annoy me today. They wouldn't have been there at all, if I'd taken half a year to make it in; or rather, if I'd made it six months later.

JS: Can you be more precise? You mentioned before that the occupations of Vietnam and Czechoslovakia still hadn't occurred, but if they had they would have influenced your whole formal conception of the film in a particular way. How?

IB: Well, I should have eliminated one of the basic elements which triggered off *The Shame*: the whole Jacobi episode. The film would have shown one day in the war. I'd have concentrated it on to the people, how they experienced war brushing them with its wing-tip. I'd have just told you about them, nothing else. As it was, I pushed the film in a particular direction, but that must have been because there were certain things I wanted to say. Certain matters I wanted to clear up. I shouldn't have bothered to do that today.

SB: Certain scenes in the film are tremendously expressionistic. They don't belong to the more documentary-like scenes with Jan and Eva. And they don't come off particularly well, either. The interrogation scenes, for example.

IB: No, they're no good.

JS: Suddenly you all seem so critical of the film—and of its director! I find that rather unjust.

IB: If one embarks on something so serious as the depiction of a war or a concentration camp, mental illness, cancer, or something of that sort, then the ethical demands become enormously stricter. Actually it's impossible to depict a war artistically, just as it's totally impossible to depict a concentration camp artistically, except possibly as a farce. If one starts describing a war, one just has to accept the fact that the moral laws which come into play are quite different from those governing one's other artistic activities. It was these laws I didn't pay sufficient attention to. I was aware of them, but I was scared of showing people dropping dead and all that sort of thing. There's only one real death in the film, and that's when Jacobi is shot. And that happens half a kilometre away, one catches just a glimpse of it behind a cart.

JS: It's a very effective scene.

IB: I think there are good things in *The Shame*. But it's not cauterized enough to have any broad validity.

SB: Would you like to tell us something about the film's dream aspects.

IB: One could say it was based on two dreams. It begins with the man's dream of his peaceful work in the orchestra. And ends with Eva's dream of lost love. Then, right in the middle of the film, she sits there saying 'Someone has dreamed this—oh, how ashamed he'll be when he wakes up!' And that, quite simply, is my aesthetic and ethical figleaf. I realized it was all an insuperable undertaking and that when I'd finished the film I should feel morally embarrassed—though—so much I can say—it all went better than I'd expected. And it won't be the last time I take up this theme, either. I have the necessary experience now.

SB: When you take the war motif up again, will it be in a similar context?

IB: Not similar, but in some way which enables me to formulate, even more clearly and concisely, my view of war and how it affects the human soul.

JS: To go back to the final scene again—Eva's dream. What are its ultimate implications?

IB: Eva says: 'I had a feeling there was something I ought to have remembered, which I've forgotten.' It's about the burning roses and the child she feels against her cheek. It's about everything that *is*—water, clear green running water, like a mirror. It's a dream I've had myself, a pure visual experience of something beautiful and delightful that has happened; something unattainable and which has been carelessly wasted. It must have something to do with love, I suppose.

JS: The resistance fighter, Sigge Fürst, jumps overboard voluntarily. Surely that's a desperate act, even if he has thought it over ...?

IB: Well, not desperate, but thought-out, yes! He's a fellow who has been on all thinkable sides and all the time managed to get away with it. As soon as everything gets tangled he takes the consequences, and clears out. He goes under.

JS: He doesn't swim ashore?

IB: No, he hasn't a chance. He's far out at sea. Jan just looks at him, doesn't lift a finger.

JS: Was the filming technically demanding?

IB: It's great fun, everything going bang and roaring and burning around you. It provides an outlet for a lot of infantile lusts.

TM: If this Jan fellow survives it all—will he become a leader?

IB: Never.

TM: You don't think so?

IB: No.

TM: That he'll grow ...

IB: No, never. He'll shrivel up again just as quickly.

TM: Under normal circumstances—but if this exceptional state of affairs goes on, then he won't ...?

IB: No.

TM: But you leave us with him—excuse me if my memory fails me on this point ...

IB: No, it's over. If you have a faith, if you've some deep conviction, whether you're a Nazi or a Communist or what the hell else you are—then you can sacrifice both yourself and others to your faith. But from the moment you've no faith—from that moment you live in a deep inner confusion—from then on you're exposed to what Strindberg calls 'the powers'.

JS: It wasn't your intention to stress the film's validity just for Swedish conditions? It wasn't the neutralist ideology you wanted to depict?

IB: Neutralist poison, you mean?

JS: By all means.

IB: Today it's extremely important that the social democracy shall really fix its ideals. In my opinion it's a shame it isn't doing so.

TM: The Swedish Social Democrats have no ideologist—well, Wigforss* perhaps.

* Ernest Wigforss, former Minister of Finance, veteran Social Democrat, now retired.

TM: *The Rite.* How did you come to make this TV film? When, where, and how did you get the idea for it?

IB: I'd written *The Shame* in the spring of 1967 and we were to begin shooting in mid-September. We were to take colour film along with us and experiment. On days when the weather was bad and we couldn't work, we were going to make a sketch together. We were going to take the interiors in a little film studio in the local museum on Fårö. I thought I'd write an episode about three variety artists who get mixed up in some fuss about public decency. So, in a rather vague sort of way, I began. And before I could say knife, there it was—a play! The direction script, it's true, reads like a film script. But there are no stage instructions. It's just dialogue, right through. Nine of them. It was a wonderful feeling, suddenly writing a play—to be able to forget all about cinematic considerations, and just write dialogue.

JS: Yes, when one sees the piece one has a feeling it could very well be staged.

IB: We discussed that, too. But I felt I wanted it in close-up.

JS: You wrote it while working on *The Shame*?

IB: I wrote it in July. We started on *The Shame* in September. And then, suddenly, I had a play, or a lot of dialogue. But we got so involved in *The Shame* we didn't even have time to look at it.

JS: When did you decide to shoot it as a film, and be your own producer?

IB: There's always such a lot of pretentiousness surrounding films. Such a lot of apparatus. Shooting takes forty-five days, fifty days, sixty-five days. For Fellini it takes twenty-eight weeks and there's a hell of a hullaballoo and costs God knows how much. So I thought: Hell, I'll gather four of my close friends and we'll rehearse for four weeks and then we'll shoot it. I figured out I'd be able to shoot it in nine days.

JS: And did you?

IB: Yes, out here at the Råsunda studios.

JS: On some occasion while you were working on this film you said it was a film without pretensions. But then you corrected yourself and said, 'Well, it's not quite as simple as all that!'

IB: When did I say that?

JS: One day.

IB: Godard speaks of those cinetracts of his. This is my way of making a cinetract, even though it isn't all that socially bloody conscious. Though of course it *is* about the artist and society.

TM: A handbook, if you'll pardon the expression—an anthology—in which all the time you're present in person. But what I've really worried about since

I saw the film is that these three artists are all definitely *functions* of yourself. All three of them. But I've wondered about Erik Hell, too, whether he too isn't a function in some way . . .

I B : Of course he is . . .

J S : If I wanted to stick a witty label on to this film, I'd call it a 'purgatory'.

I B : What comes out in it, I suppose, is what was pent up in me from my time at the Royal Dramatic Theatre. The ambivalence is in the judge. First we see him through the eyes of the artistes. Then we discover that both he and Björnstrand still have something human about them.

T M : The two others—Thea Winkelman and Sebastian Fisher—they're a couple of landmines. Tread on them and they blow up.

I B : They're artists on the way out. Between their profession and death they possess nothing.

J S : Have you assembled the evidence chronologically, so that one could say Anders Ek, as Fisher, corresponds to your Sturm-and-Drang period?

I B : No, what corresponds to what is very hard to say.

J S : But they're quite clearly distinguished in themselves. Anders Ek is the more romantic idea of an artist. Ingrid Thulin the neurotic.

I B : Ingrid Thulin stands for the most dangerous, the most irrational, the most instinctual in this bunch—the part most easily damaged, but also the most necesssary. Sebastian Fisher is the creative force, the executive element, the active, creative factor, the materialization, still held back by certain vestiges of social consideration, certain relics of human feeling and certain memories of what human relationships look like. He's the third person, the ordering, organizing, planning, in his whole behaviour a profoundly bourgeois factor— the anchor.

J S : He is also the figure who reminds us most naturally of certain figures in your later films. While Anders Ek is reminiscent of figures in your earlier ones.

I B : Yes. Mostly Anders Ek is reminiscent of that character in *The Face*; but no longer so strong and unified, terribly mixed up and gone to the dogs. He's the most run-down of them all, of course.

J S : You mean he's Vogler in *The Face*?

I B : Yes. But Vogler still had vitality, spiritual strength; while this fellow is almost a wreck.

T M : Yes, during his great explosion of hate Fisher lies on a sofa. It's all more like a psychiatrist's reception room than anything else. The signals in *The Rite* are such fun. We enjoyed them a lot. They're repeated in the bar, in that shop . . . and then he says: 'I'm an agent who does one thing and another abroad.' Is it United Artists you're thinking of, who look after certain contacts? There are lots of little signals of that sort in *The Rite*. Apparently quite irrational—as when Fisher comes in and says to the judge: 'I suppose you haven't anything else against me?' 'Yes, breaking the speed limit at Flensburg, in 1956 . . .' Is it you yourself who . . .?

IB: Yes, but not at Flensburg.

TM: Those odd places—Flensburg—those rather dull little German towns?

IB: And Grenoble! Then I've stolen a trick or two from Hjalmar Bergman, and put their income at two million dollars a year. Fantastic incomes.

JS: At one place there's another cue, where you say one loses the intimate touch as soon as a tape recorder's switched on. Now, I wonder where you can have got that from . . .

IB: Well, after sitting here together for 3,333 half-hours or however much it is, we know each other rather well—or do we?

JS: You enjoyed making that film. Didn't you also feel a personal satisfaction in making this anthology of so much in your earlier production? You take up theme after theme, and associate, wittily and clearly. Among all these loose ends one has no difficulty in finding one's way!

IB: It's a game, like everything else. As for one's intentions, one formulates them afterwards. It's a charge of dynamite I blow off into the air.

JS: How can you keep your aggressions so alive?

IB: If I didn't I'd commit suicide. There's always a tension in me between my urge to destroy and my will to live. It's one of my most elementary tensions, both in the way I create and in my material existence. Every morning I wake up with a new wrath, a new suspiciousness, a new desire to live.

JS: There's a key scene in a bar; scene eight. Sebastian Fisher has wanted all the time to pack in the tour, has even threatened to do so. But then this situation comes along which more or less forces him to stay with them and go on.

IB: For economic reasons.

JS: It's a form of blackmail. I understand an artist can feel himself in such a situation. You've spoken of it before.

IB: Well, the point is, Sebastian Fisher has been living far beyond his resources. In a friendly way Winkelman takes his revenge. The whole bar scene is a single compressed act of revenge on Winkelman's part.

TM: Of which both of them are certainly aware. One feels they're both enjoying it.

The Rite: the artiste confronted by his judge: Erik Hell with Ingrid Thulin and . . .

IB : All the persons in the play must be assumed to be living on a rather high level of consciousness.

JS : The scene also has something gay about it.

IB : Yes, it's comedy. Altogether, one can see *The Rite* as black comedy.

TM : A propos the rite itself, for me it's the definitive theatrical performance that puts paid to the audience. In it the limits between art and reality, and between life and death, are utterly blurred.

IB : When the interpreter kills the viewer, we can say we've reached the acme of committed theatre. The rite isn't just what they do at the end. It's a sort of papiermaché game, with markers and things, all sorts of hocus pocus. The rite is the game the artist plays with his audience, between the artist and society—all this hodge-podge of mutual humiliation and mutual need for one another. That's the ritual element.

JS : I see the end of the film, too, as the dream of the impossible, the ultimate in art—to make a ball stand still in the air. At that point their number becomes extremely mysterious. It has a real touch of heathen ritual about it.

IB : It's taken from the cult of Dionysius—to drive away the face of the god. You can find it in the Catholic mass. Curious, how things work. In the

... with Anders Ek and Gunnar Björnstrand

Catholic mass there's something called the elevation. At a particular moment the priest raises the chalice. That's something he doesn't do in the Lutheran Communion Service. In fact it's forbidden. The Catholic ritual of the elevation is a relic from the cult of Dionysius, whose priest held up the bowl of blood above his head to mirror the face of the god behind his back and so drive the god away.

J S : Which of the figures in this film do you feel most sympathy for?

I B : What am I to say to that?

J S : The one the audience is sorry for—the one I feel for myself most strongly—is the judge.

I B : I suppose I've taken the judge's side a little; much more than I originally intended.

J S : He's so exposed, he's trying to talk about himself all the time. And he wants to break off the performance.

I B : Then suddenly, when the knife comes out, he realizes he's walked into a trap. But the judge has done one stupid thing, and that was when Hans Winkelman, who really talks his language, asked him, implored him, not to interview Thea. We see the judge's face, filled with sadistic delight, as he says:

'I can only follow my instructions, so unfortunately we must have this interview.' Winkelman knows it'll go to the devil.

JS: Winkelman also humiliates the judge, partly by trying to talk him into cancelling the interview, partly by a straight bribe.

IB: Yes, that's *his* mistake. The judge has humiliated him by coming two hours too late to their appointment. Under a cloak of legalistic procedure, he puts him a lot of insolent and humiliating questions. For these three artistes the crucial thing is to let him have it all back. From the moment when the judge damaged Thea, he has become unforgivably involved.

JS: How do you think a TV audience will experience such a piece of personal perspiration?

IB: Frankly, it's more than I dare think about.

TM: Film critics like ourselves, who are an exclusive audience, and who are interested in Ingmar Bergman and his films—we're a different world altogether from the TV viewer in his sitting room. He's another race of human being.

IB: I've written a foreword to be broadcast the same evening . . . I say they've just got time to get to the nine o'clock performance at the cinema, that they can read a good book, or some magazine.

JS: I think Torsten's right. The public are going to see this film as a circus. Yet it's enormously suggestive. To understand Ingmar Bergman is not so important.

IB: It's not important at all.

JS: Formally speaking, you've built up this film almost throughout with close-ups and extreme mid-shots. There are almost no long shots. As a director it's your habit to switch incessantly between long shots or extreme mid-shots and close-ups.

IB: TV, as a medium, has quite another rhythm from the film, I feel. So I felt the camera needed to be loaded with more close-ups than usual, precisely because eyes are so important—faces, eyes, voices, hands.

JS: This poem about birds, which Claudia reads out to Fisher. Is it your own?

IB: Yes, it's just fun, just a game. It's written in some queer Strindbergian metre.

JS: Why have you put yourself into the confessional box, like a priest?

IB: To make the film cheaper.

TM: Here's a cross-reference to *The Seventh Seal*.

Bergman as the priest in *The Rite*—the 'figure of Death'

IB : Of course.

TM : And the figure of Death——

JS : How much did you get paid—the same as an extra?

IB : Hell no! I got paid for a speaking part—I've my lines, haven't I?

JS : They've nothing to do with the picture!

IB : Even so——

243

Råsunda Film Studios,
24 February 1969

TORSTEN MANNS: This time we've agreed to discuss some general motifs, not one particular film, but motifs which recur in many of them. Among other things, we've agreed on the child-motif, sex, and censorship. How about taking the child-motif first? The fact is, we've one little film left; and that's *Daniel*—a little scrap of film from *Stimulantia*, 1966.

So I've arranged the child-motif in four types. First, as a catalyst for subconscious phobias, the trauma and the archetypes—here *The Hour of the Wolf* is a good example: the little boy there goes straight back to the old man in the cupboard who appeared in that play, 'the little folk'.

The second is the child as an object of violence: *The Devil's Wanton*, where a baby is murdered, *The Virgin Spring* where the raped girl is herself almost a child, *The Shame*—this little dead girl found by Liv and also the dream of children, where it's smashed to pieces—and even the boy in *Frenzy* who arrives too late at the beginning and is told off by Gunnar Björnstrand (of all people)—he too is a little exposed fellow.

The third—in dreams of continuation, of togetherness, as the rescuer of relationships—a patent solution, one might say, not peculiar to yourself, but implicit in the whole of this *To Joy–Eva–Journey Into Autumn* complex, where the woman begs to have a child with Ulf Palme, and he says: 'I don't want to have some poor little chap somewhere I can't reach.' In *The Silence* it's less clear; but there the boy is definitely a means of communication

The child-motif in *Persona*: Elisabeth (Liv Ullmann) with image of son

between the two women. In *So Close to Life* the motif is completely patent—it's virtually a clinical film about children; about the three women's attributes to childbirth.

Finally the fourth, dwarf-motif—we've pretty well exhausted that. In *The Rite*, Hans speaks of his children, but no child is actually seen. I should very much like to know what your attitude to children is, from every point of view.

INGMAR BERGMAN: My first reaction to all you're saying is a dreadful feeling of oppression. Not specially aimed at myself, but a feeling of power-lessness. I can't explain it. A feeling that it's all so dull, that it will get duller, and what I've made, suddenly, is all dull and uninteresting too. I can't explain it. I don't know why it is, but as I sit here listening to you I feel furious—don't misunderstand this, Torsten. I've nothing against you personally. That's just how it is.

When someone pulls out a thread like this and says: 'Yes, well, surely it's this way? Aren't things like this? It's like this and it's like that,' I feel completely paralysed. I can't utter a word. Well, it's possible, things may be that way, I don't know. I'm not being cagey. It's simply that with me things don't work that way.

I can't discuss any leitmotif running through my films. Obviously I could hold a lecture on the humiliation motif—I even fancy we've gone through it rather thoroughly. But all this about children . . . I've eight children myself, so I've had a certain amount of experience of children and react according to certain patterns which have changed over the years. But I don't think it's of any consequence, nor do I feel it has any place in this document.

STIG BJÖRKMAN: Isn't this the fact of the matter: You feel what you're doing is always in a state of change: that you yourself change and make new films, which you load with new ideas? Then you realize that obviously in these works, stretching over a very long period of time, certain motifs, certain opinions recur and pursue you. They disturb your view of yourself and what you are expressing as being in a ceaseless state of flux. And this is why you adopt a negative attitude to all such summarizings?

IB: It's simply that one shuffles the cards in various ways—not to lead an observer astray, but simply because the content of one's mind at the time when one conceives one's work is different from what it was the time before, or the time before that.

This search for motifs, this form of analysis is something we've inherited from the study of literature, where it's reached the lunatic stage. They fit any work into its historical context, until in the end every piece of the puzzle fits so perfectly there's nothing to be added for the chap who's actually created the work. Here we have an unbridgeable gulf—at least between me and the people who write commentaries on my films. I can't correspond with such people. And this is no reflection at all on Torsten, for whom I've the warmest feelings.

I think I can explain it chiefly like this. For me, a film can never be something theoretical. What I've been trying to tell you all the time is that behind each production there has lain a practical, tangible reality. It has never been 'invented' or 'made up'. Sooner or later, whenever I've 'made something up' or 'intended something consciously' I've had to reject it as bad.

JONAS SIMA: I think this is a good way of seeing the matter, not least because it gives us a chance to raise a question of definition in connection with what Torsten has asked you.

TM: This sort of thing makes our work difficult. We're walking on glass. One never knows what one's going to tread on. But you're perfectly within your rights to tell us off and say 'What you're raising now is something I don't want to touch on . . .'

IB: Because I can't.

TM: Can't or won't—it makes no odds. It's you who decide!

IB: I really don't know what it is you want to get out of me. You've given me a lecture. Give me a concrete question!

JS: The three of us here, who've been interviewing you, represent three different ways of approaching your work—correct me if you think I'm wrong. I, for my part, have chiefly been trying to see your work in its social context. Stig has concentrated on questions of form. And Torsten is the analyst—which is perhaps hardest of all. Since your films are so personal and so autobiographical, the methodical approach presents a critical difficulty. Formal analysis, structural analysis, so-called, isn't enough. One is forced to use the genetic method, too. One must go from the work to the man behind it. This critical dilemma, which is our dilemma as interviewers, raises both practical and theoretical problems . . .

IB: And the instrument is rather blunt, you might say. A wound needn't necessarily find symbolic expression. It can also lead to a formal drive. Which is why everything floats in and out of everything else all the time.

JS: In a recent interview with a journalist, for example, you were asked about your relationship with your actresses. At once you asked him to switch off his tape recorder, and said it was beside the point. The journalist switched off his tape recorder—but wrote: 'It isn't beside the point!'—We're in the same dilemma.

TM: Your attitude is that if you've taken things from your own life, as you've always done—in various dimensions—you've said enough. You don't want the person who's come to see your film to get any further, because none of the rest concerns him.

IB: If I don't know what to say and feel embarrassed, it's because I don't understand what it is you're trying to get out of me. Suddenly I don't see clearly—every time you've put concrete questions to me I've tried to express myself in my own way and give you an answer. But when Torsten delivers a little lecture—however interesting I find it in itself—and then leaves me a wide field to expatiate on, I feel depressed, because it isn't a concrete question. For me my work, or whatever you like to call it—these thirty films—are something solid, something I've made. So I must have concrete questions if I'm to give you concrete answers.

JS: Surely you're not saying now that we're to get your sanction for the models we use for our analysis?

IB: No, I don't mean that.

TM: Why not?

SB: If someone had put the same question to me, I'd just have answered 'Yes'—and that would be that. Isn't it so that when one feels spontaneously 'Now we're coming to a field where I've lots to say', then it makes no odds how a question is formulated. For example, sometimes we've just said: 'Today we thought we'd talk about, say, *Journey Into Autumn.*' And you've just told us about it.

247

Bergman

Anyway, if we now ask you about *Daniel*—rather an unusual part of your output, after all—then I'd like to put you a purely concrete question about that film. Besides your full-length films, you make your own home movies. *Daniel* is one of them. But if you chose to film your son Daniel, you must have felt it had some significance at the time. Why did you elect to tell a larger circle of people about Daniel?

IB: My *Stimulantia* idea was actually an answer to *Mondo Cane*. The whole thing was planned from the beginning to be extremely modest, more of a game than what it turned into. And it ran completely off the rails, as it always does when several people try to make something together.

For my part I hardly knew what I should make. Then it occurred to me to make a cinetract, something as simple as could be, completely foursquare and straightforward. What was there, then, I was very fond of? I had several thousand metres of 16-mm film of Daniel. So I sat down and went through this material and picked out bits which I felt were good. I wanted to give Daniel a present on his second birthday—a testament, something he could have when he grew up.

It was all those words—guilt, conscience, prison, prisoner, punishment. All that sort of thing was to be banned. All those things I've been more or less damaged by myself—both as a child and an adult.

When I made the film I thought it worked well. But the reaction to it was completely negative. So obviously something was wrong somewhere.

SB: Are there any other subjects which you've thought of filming, or might think of filming, in that way?

IB: When I get back to Fårö I'm going to make a film about sheep-rearing. The idea has gradually grown on me to document Fårö, in short films lasting a couple of minutes or so. No large-scale profundities; just ten, fifteen, twenty short films.

JS: You've not only played a creative artistic rôle in Sweden's cultural life. You've also played a political one. You've been head of several theatres, artistic consultant at SF, inspector for the Film School, etc. Undeniably you've had great opportunities of playing an active part in cultural policy.

IB: I've given all that up now.

JS: Why?

IB: I've discovered I haven't the talent for the sort of strategy needed to carry through reforms in cultural policy. Nowadays I work on a more modest level, through my theatrical productions. There I can make such reforms as I think are needed, in collaboration with the management.

JS: It seems to me your attitude to the new film used to be rather dogmatic. When the Film School started up here in Sweden—1964, wasn't it?—I remember you saying the pupils could be chosen quite simply. The applicants could be given Strindberg's *A Sheet of Paper* to film, and you offered to give your opinion whether they had a gift for cinema or not. I wonder if you'd offer such a personal selection instrument today?

IB: I don't recall putting it that way. It's possible I did, but if so I must have repressed it. My belief is that anyone who has anything to say just gets going and makes something. I don't believe in education in a film school at all, except in the strictly technical matters.

JS: In spite of your tremendous hegemony over the Swedish cinema, which has lasted for so many years, very very few of the so-called Swedish new wave—if you'll allow the expression—can be regarded as Bergman disciples.

IB: None at all.

JS: Vilgot Sjöman, perhaps?

IB: He really has gone his own way!

JS: But young Swedish film-makers, for example Jonas Cornell, have asked you to play the pedagogue. People feel they need your experience, and you've always taken an interest in educational matters, though chiefly in the theatre.

IB: Film isn't so difficult. Theatre is much harder. A film is a once-and-for-all product. Theatre's a repetitive art, and there I'm deeply interested in pedagogic questions which tend to be neglected in favour of pseudo-phenomena.

JS: Do you mean mostly actors, or producers?

IB: Well, producers have their technical troubles too, and their difficulties are much greater in the theatre than in films.

JS: But since young film-makers want to share your experience—this whole interview could almost be regarded as a compendium for aspiring young film-directors—you're still willing?

IB: I don't force myself on anyone, and I can only discuss things in a strictly professional way, strictly between colleagues; as an older colleague to a younger. I've had certain practical experiences, common to everyone; and these I can tell them about. Nothing more.

JS: All this talk about 'Bergman the demon-director', one doesn't hear so much of it nowadays . . .

IB: No, I've become such a nice kind chap!

JS: In his diary from *Winter Light*, Vilgot Sjöman mentions an incident—he wasn't present at it himself—but there was some explosion on your part, someone burst into tears, and Vilgot writes that he was unpleasantly affected by it.

IB: Yes, it was a make-up girl.

JS: You've told us you carry on like Jehu, here at Råsunda, to get everything to function properly . . .

IB: Used to! Nowadays my reign of terror is of the milder sort.

JS: In the studio, during the actual filming, have you been allowed to carry on like that toward your actors and closest technical colleagues?

IB: Yes, I used to. Maybe it's not noticeable, but I'm always in a rage. It's one of my life-problems. I'm always angry. Are you too?

JS: Obviously!

TM: I am, always!

IB: I think Stig is too, really. Yes, he carries a great wrath inside him. But I've no inhibitions for my aggressions. Rather the opposite, I'd say. I've no threshold at all. I'm always lighting the fuse. Before I can say knife I'm swept away by a fit of rage, so I have to keep an eye on myself. I realize that any sort of emotional outbreak, every outburst of rage which isn't under control and which isn't, as they say, pedagogic, harms both myself and the other person. On the other hand, I don't think there's any harm in people knowing a great rage is going on somewhere. One must just never let it come out in an uncontrolled manner. Hasty words can't be caught on the wing. Bawl someone out, use a nasty vocabulary, and he'll never forget it.

And that's why I don't think anyone has heard me say an unkind word to an actor these last fifteen years. My results will only be so much the worse, I know that. Well, I've shouted at Liv a few times. But that's been more on the private level. She's said herself how I chased her into the fire in *The Shame*. She was tickled to death by it.

JS: All actors seem to want a part with you!

IB: Yes, actors like working with me and it's easy to explain. As a professional I've devoted all my time to learning how an actor functions, how to get the best results out of him. Since the actor is my chief instrument I have to learn how to collaborate one hundred percent, and that's something I've gradually figured out. They know they'll get all the service, the stimulation, and technical assistance they need.

JS: This reign of directors, which has prevailed for so long now in Swedish theatre and films, but which has been broken thanks to various collective productions and new possibilities of exerting influence in our theatres, etc.— how has it influenced your relationships with your actors?

IB: Don't forget it was I who first created those possibilities—it was I who started actors' councils. That's to say, it wasn't I who started it: it was Molière. It was I who thought actors should be a power unto themselves. You said something about the reign of directors?

JS: Yes, the hierarchy at the top, the despotic influence. Undeniably it has always existed. If one is a director, then one is a despot. It's obligatory. So says Bo Widerberg, for example. Maybe I'm attacking Stig here, but I too believe it's impossible to work collectively unless it has been decided in advance what everyone is to do.

IB: All I think is, someone must decide the route to be taken. Then one must try to agree on it, and then it's up to the director to see we follow that route together; that the agreements we've made are kept to. If everyone's in agreement, they'll try to keep to the pattern, make a common effort to preserve it intact. But you can't force them to.

TM: Such ideas are frequent, not only with you, but in the theatre as a whole. Ideas which collapse; and then theatrical criticism becomes an almost impossible task. But in criticizing films one is always assessing a single product.

IB: The greater the amateurism, the greater the collapse.

JS: What do you mean by that?

IB: An important component in an actor's education and equipment is his ability to repeat himself. No one requires him to be in the same emotional state night after night. But technically speaking he must. Every night he must give the audience exactly the same impression. No one can be expected to be in the same emotional state two days running; but he must, unconditionally, have the technique which enables him to give that impression. Otherwise the performance falls to pieces.

JS: You've no use at all then for the inspiration theory?

IB: The rehearsals are the creative period. Performances are a re-creation.

SB: Do you make a habit of attending performances of your own productions?

IB: The devil I do! That's something you can be sure of.

JS: Have you worked with any particular acting method?

IB: My own!

TM: Stanislavski and Strasberg?

IB: They represent other theatrical systems, other ways of rehearsing. We've built up our system on a certain economic basis. We know we can rehearse for between eight and ten weeks, and the length of the rehearsal period tends to clinch the technique used.

JS: What is the most important thing today, in your opinion, for a director, both in stage and films?

IB: He can be anyhow he likes, but if he has something to offer, something will come of it. If he hasn't, then he ought to be doing something else. Don't you think so, too?

252

The Royal Dramatic Theatre, 27 April 1970

STIG BJÖRKMAN: *A Passion* links up with *The Shame*. The second film is a continuation of the first. In *A Passion* there's a scene which begins where *The Shame* leaves off. This is the first time you've ever directly commented on, or followed up, one of your earlier films. Why did you do it now?

INGMAR BERGMAN: The relationships in *A Passion* grew out of the setting of *The Shame*, and for me this had a curious meaning. The war which was going on in *The Shame* now manifested itself for me in the same milieu but in a more surreptitious way. In the cry of the animals. In the tormented animals, the lambs stabbed to death, the burning horse, and the bird which flies against the windscreen. Meanwhile the real war—the war I can find no formulation for—has moved over to the TV set. Yes, I know it's a very simple metaphor. Max and Liv, a bit terrified and distrait, are watching the war on the TV; if they adopt the hanged puppy, it's because that's something they can understand.

It was the same actress, too, Liv Ullmann. I found the idea of Anna Fromm's experiences having a sort of secret background in the war in *The Shame* stimulating. If she can dream about it, it's because after all it's I who am giving her her dreams. The war in *The Shame*, *A Passion*'s background of violence, was in my mind all the time.

Before writing *A Passion* I'd written quite a different script, about entirely different matters. All I kept of it was the main characters' names, Anna,

A Passion: Bibi Andersson and Max von Sydow: the relationship link with *Shame*

Andreas, Elis, and Eva. By the time I'd written *A Passion*, the actors had already been signed on for the other film.

S B : So they were to play the same rôles, corresponding to the names of the rôles in *A Passion*?

I B : Yes, that's right. I thought: I'll make the same film, really, just change it about a little. But then it turned into quite a different story—it flew off at a tangent.

JONAS SIMA : That other script, did it vanish completely?

I B : It vanished completely. There was one idea in it I couldn't manage. After it had lain fallow awhile, I realized where the fault lay in the other script, so I re-wrote it; and it became *The Lie**.

TORSTEN MANNS : I think the first and last scenes in *A Passion* somehow hang together. These three suns we see at the beginning, they're a portent, aren't they? I've tried to find out what sort of an omen the sun is, but I haven't succeeded. Is it a *mene-mene-tekel* sign, pointing to the last scene, where Andreas burns up, or rather his picture is burned up?

* Title of the BBC version of *Reservatet*, 1970.

IB: There's nothing specially remarkable about all this. Parhelions—that's what the phenomenon of several apparent suns is called technically—have actually occurred. A painting in Riddarholm Church, in Stockholm, shows seven such suns, I think, which foreboded the Thirty Years War. Such celestial phenomena have been omens of violent events or catastrophes of various sorts. For me it's an old familiar sign.

TM: There's one in the Book of Revelations. The seventh seal . . .

IB: Something is foreboded, there's something menacing in the air. And then that nasty bucket which comes tumbling down from the roof, and won't stand up properly.

TM: *A Passion* is a film about catastrophe. That's how I experience it. It's a parabola, so to speak, from those suns to the final scene.

IB: What happens to Andreas? He dissolves. That man hasn't a chance of existing in the material world. He's on the way to dissolution. Whether one sees it in the film or not I don't know. He walks to and fro on the road and finally lies down—just before the image dissolves altogether.

TM: Isn't it because of the way his personality has developed, or rather not developed: with violence always coming to the surface, always breaking through? He's broken down, and the whole film breaks down as a result of it——

IB: It was fun seeing just how far I could go with the material, too. It was fascinating to see how the optical printer behaved when it overstrained itself. I've never seen a piece of equipment behave like that, like a nervy prima donna on the verge of a coloratura aria. The left side of the image was only half lit. And then to bring it into focus and hit the bullseye—oh, yes, there was much weeping and gnashing of teeth!

JS: What does the title, *A Passion*, mean? It can mean both passion and suffering; two sides of the same thing.

IB: In America someone has used the title *A Passion* already, so the film's going to be released under the title *The Passion of Anna*. Anna's passion. The Anna-passion, Anna's sufferings . . . a clearer definition of what it's all about.

SB: When I reviewed the film, I stressed Anna's passion. Anna, I felt, was the heart of the film, its emotional core. To some extent I felt, and still feel, her passion as something positive. She's the film's most consistent personality, and morally speaking the strongest. But her strength also contains extremely negative traits; the rigid demands she places on herself and everyone around her. There's something relentless about her nature, which paralyses those who are closest to her.

How do you see Anna? Do you experience her strength as something negative?

255

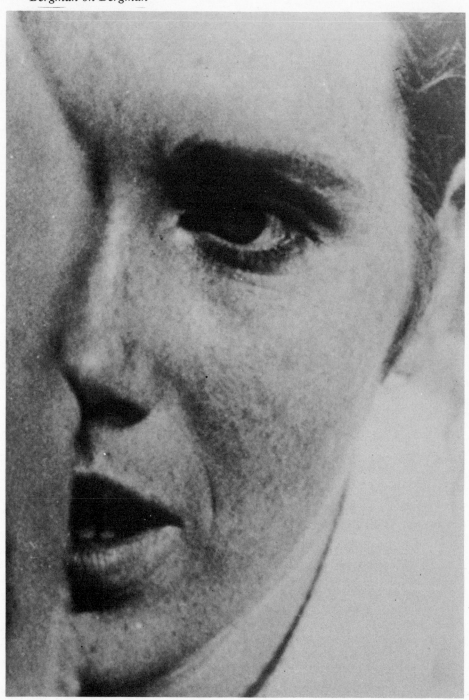

A Passion: Liv Ullmann as Anna Fromm

IB: She's always influencing others, a sort of moral force of nature. Sometimes she has had a negative effect, sometimes she can have a positive one—that depends on circumstances. Personally I feel she's terrifying. I'm scared stiff of moralists—I've been one myself. You would have had to look far to find a more moralistic moralist than me.

TM: But she's a more meaningful personality than Eva, with all her compromises?

IB: But Eva's always human, altogether like a human being; while Anna has something of the monster in her, something frightfully dangerous.

TM: No one can manage her?

IB: No. And she can't manage herself, either. There's something dreadfully destructive about her moralism, her incessant demands. This inability to accept herself, to accept the outside world, is about the most dangerous thing of all. I believe that before one can start to do anything, one must first accept oneself.

TM: This monstrous quality, which you say Anna has, is visible in two scenes. Among other things we've another little vampire scene. It's rather amusing. Such scenes crop up in your films now and again, probably unintentionally. They're just there. In *A Passion* there's a shot where Anna draws Andreas to herself; she puts her arms round his neck and is about to kiss him, but as she does so, she draws back the corner of her mouth, and one sees a sharp canine ...

IB: Yes, she has an impulse to strangle him. I hadn't thought about the tooth.

TM: You've a tooth like that yourself, I see!

IB: Yes, I have ...

TM: I'd like to ask you about that fantastic scene where Anna tells Andreas about the car accident. All one sees is Liv Ullmann's face, changing from hopeful joy to bottomless despair. Her face seems to change colour completely and her eyes become red as she talks. Is there some technical manipulation behind that shot? Her face is in close-up and you haven't moved the camera or changed the lighting. Did you use a heat-lamp or something of that sort?

IB: No, it's just an actress doing her job—which isn't bad. It's not often one sees that sort of thing. We snapped it up in the first take. We only rehearsed that scene from the technical point of view; ran through it a few times, and then shot it. That shot was made almost six months after the rest of the film was ready.

SB: The whole film is matched, isn't it? This scene too?

IB: No, you can hear a faint camera buzz in the background. It's not matched.

JS: Why do you match the soundtracks of your films nowadays?

IB: To get the close-up sound absolutely clear, so that the sound shall come off the lips. I'm so tired of the poor sound in Swedish films. Often it's due to poor recording conditions and fellows who can't hold a microphone—in spite of all the time they take getting the mikes into position!

  A Passion was shot in forty-five days. We prepared the camerawork, set up the camera, and the recording engineers took up a supporting soundtrack. Then we did all the sound afterwards. These actors are virtuosos at it.

JS: Eva seems a trifle simple-minded to me. In the supper table scene she suddenly gapes; as she sits there, her jaw drops. That's a marvellous bit of acting by Bibi Andersson.

IB: She's unsure of herself, torpedoed by her dominating husband whom she loves and lives with. Actually, I suppose she's no more or less sharp-witted than anyone else. Hers is a sort of exposed femininity, which prevents her from defending herself. Everything gets the better of her.

JS: But she's no match for her husband's intellectual virtuosity.

IB: She's intuitively sensitive, though. Doesn't she say to Andreas—'You must look out for Anna'?

SB: How was the supper scene in *A Passion* done? How much of the conversation is yours and how have the actors improvised? Is this scene matched, too?

IB: No, it isn't. The whole thing was perfectly simple. The script told them more or less what they were to talk about—the devil knows whether they did, though! The evening before, we met and went through what each of them should talk about. I explained the scene plan and the situation. They were to sit round a table, such or such food was to be served, such or such a red wine. Each actor had a clear idea of where he or she stood in the film. Then the camera was turned, first on one, then on the second, then on the third, then on the fourth, and the conversation was allowed to take whatever course it liked.

SB: Was that scene shot at a late stage in the filming?

IB: Yes, it was one of the last. Otherwise we couldn't have done it. Liv has a remarkable bit, too, where she suddenly begins defending her marriage and her voice becomes somehow wild and shrill and strange. Really good actors —who know their parts inside out and have a pretty good idea of what it's all about—can make up their own words. It works fine. And it doesn't have to be nonsense, either.

SB: Vergérus, in *A Passion*, and Vergérus in *The Face*, have many traits in common.

IB: Yes, they come from the same family. Elis Vergérus is a great-grandson or something of that sort to the Medical Officer. They've much in common.

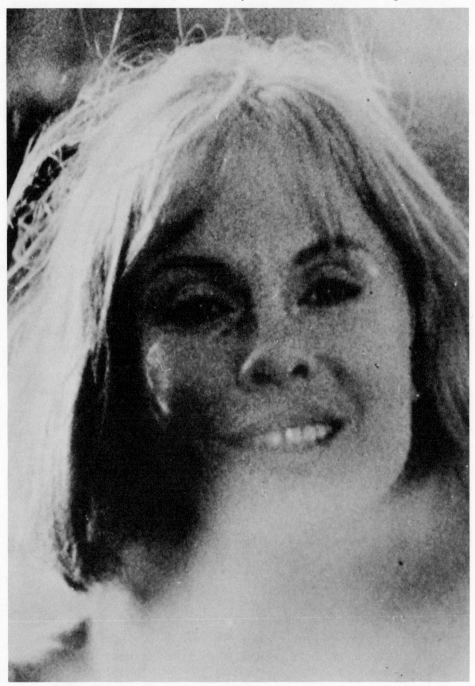

A Passion: Bibi Andersson as Eva Vergérus

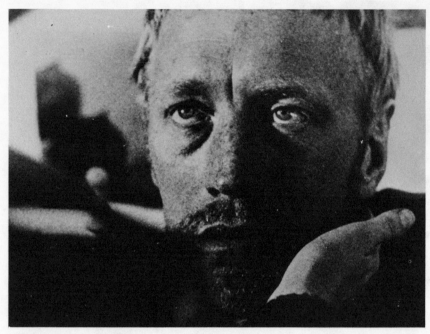

A Passion: Andreas Winkelman (Max von Sydow) and . . .

TM : Which of the two men in *A Passion* do you personally find the more agreeable, the more human—Andreas or Elis?

IB : I think they're both very human indeed. After Elis has gone completely astray, too. I'm thinking of all that hysterical image-talk. Besides which there's his unsureness of himself *vis-à-vis* his wife. He's anxious and jealous, always ringing up to find out where she's been. He tries to understand who she is, but has no insight into her nature.

TM : Hides behind cynical remarks.

IB : He's a man who's concealing an enormous sensitivity and sensibility behind a highly conscious outward attitude. When he says he doesn't lose any sleep over the political situation, that he doesn't lie awake at nights thinking of children in Biafra or anything of that sort, he's telling the simple truth. It's all quite conscious and thought out.

SB : We asked you just now which of the figures you find it easiest to sympathize with. Most of the people in *A Passion* have disagreeable traits, I think: or rather their characters have shortcomings which you don't hesitate to expose.

IB : In this film antipathies and sympathies are equally distributed. Actually, I like these people. I've nothing against them. They're finding life very difficult.

260

... Elis Vergérus (Erland Josephson)

From now on I don't think I'm going to deal with people of this sort. I regard them as belonging definitely to the past.

A Passion was troublesome to make, the worst schedule I've ever had. I'd arranged for everything to go pleasantly. Everyone liked being on Fårö, everyone had their own house, which should have made for a nice friendly atmosphere. But then, in some odd way, the film itself infected us; above all, of course, myself. And it all became dreadfully heavy-going. I haven't found it so heavy and difficult to shoot a film since *Winter Light*.

The script had been written straight off the cuff, it was more a catalogue of moods than a film script. Usually I solve most of the technical problems at the script stage; but here—both for lack of time and as a challenge to myself—I chose to cross my bridges as I came to them. This meant I had a lot to do all the time. I shot scenes, saw they were wrong, and had to remake them.

And then, too, it was almost the first time we'd worked in colour. The first time we'd used colour we'd made it entirely by the book. But with *A Passion* we'd got it into our heads we were going to make a *noch nie da gewesenes* colour film. And for the first time in many many years Sven and I clashed. I began to suffer from twinges of stomach ulcer, and Sven's giddiness came back. Two lunatics staggering about, looking at our takes, and hating.

Then again, there was a time-limit on the schedule. For economic reasons

The foreboding of catastrophe: *A Passion*: Anna (Liv Ullmann) and Andreas (Max von Sydow)

we had to do these re-shootings within a framework of forty-five days. Because we couldn't get it the way we wanted, we re-shot a great deal. The more sensitive sort of colour film wasn't available at that time, the sort which has double-x sensitivity. It was all terribly tough going.

JS: Was that partly why you didn't want us to talk about *A Passion* before?

IB: It was all so horribly close. The editing, too, was a terrific job. I had very much more material than usual. The first cut took out about 3,400 metres, I think, and that had never happened to me before. Now it's about 2,750. Even that's an unusually long film to be me.

JS: Even so, every time you talked about the film, it was with a sort of secret gaiety, I recall. One hadn't the least feeling you were tired or irritated.

IB: It was a challenge. After all, it's always stimulating. And I knew that somewhere in this material, somewhere in the script, somewhere in what the actors had achieved, we'd gone beyond our limitations.

SB: Did you use the colour in any special way? There's really only one scene in the film where colour is used in such a way that it acquires a value of its own, and that's the scene where Andreas and Eva meet in the sunset.

IB: We tried to get the landscape to look as it really does. You know yourself what it's like to shoot in colour in sunlight; how the colour can take on a sort of musical-comedy effect. It was a hell of a job to get the sun to function as I wanted it to. For example, there's no blue in the entire film. It all goes in greys, browns, and greens. And then, this red scene.

JS: *Fårö Document* arose out of your idea of making a film about sheep-breeding. How did it come about that it turned into a film about Fårö itself, and the people there?

IB: It was quite simple. Sven Nykvist and I thought we'd make this film about sheep-breeding. And immediately after the first night of *Wozzeck*, in mid-March, we went over to Fårö. Then my sheep-breeders got busy. I talked to a sheep-owner, Werner Larsson—the man who is interviewed in a bus. We began talking about the slaughterhouse, how though the slaughterhouse commands high prices it yields less to the producers than slaughterhouses on the mainland do. We felt there must be something tricky about that.

Gradually studying things on Fårö and the Fårö peoples' problems became more and more fascinating. I thought to myself: we must look into this slaughterhouse business; and the ferry traffic; and the bus traffic; and road policy. In many respects the island has been allowed to fall damnably behind the times. So I began looking into things and chatting with people, and one thing led to another. And then there was a wild tussle going on between the clergyman and the parish clerk!

JS: Did you work continuously on the film?

IB: As a matter of fact we did. It must have taken about forty-five days to shoot. We began on 15 March and were ready in early May 1969.

JS: One could call *Fårö Document* your first documentary. Or do you regard *Daniel* as a documentary too? You've already told us you've documented your own production with your 16- and 8-mm cameras——

IB: They don't count. *Fårö Document* is made from the outset as a film to be shown publicly. It is properly conceived, planned, and composed.

SB: The final conception of the film, your commentary at the end: is that something you wrote while editing it? Or did you have some sort of a script, in which you tried to direct the interviews and opinions you'd collected towards the final summing-up?

IB: I had stuck up a huge sheet of paper on the wall, written up various main rubrics and subtitles showing what I wanted to document, and crossed them off as we took them. The final message was written quite early on. It seems very unjust to me that all the people in Sweden who belong to organizations and pressure-groups should be able to obtain advantages for themselves, while those who aren't organized, or only badly, can't assert their rights at all.

JS: So your political attitude to your material was clear from the outset?

264

Bergman on the island of Fårö

IB: Whether it was political I couldn't say. After I'd been working on the film a few weeks, it just crystallized of its own accord. I felt they were living under humiliating conditions.

JS: You've bought an Arriflex camera and a Nagra tape recorder. Do you intend to go on making documentaries?

IB: Yes, I want to try my hand at it. I shall try to train myself. I want to learn how to handle the equipment and how to master it technically. Then I can be my own eye, my own hand, my own ear. After all, Sven isn't always available.

SB: Is *Fårö Document* going to affect your feature film production, do you think?

IB: No, I don't think so. Documentaries and feature films each go their own—quite different—ways. In feature films one is on a staircase or a road. Stone is laid on stone. In documentary I feel I'm an utter novice.

JS: Do you regard the documentary as not being a medium for film artists or filmic art?

IB: Of course it is! I learned a tremendous amount when making *Fårö Document*. But if this was all I could do—if someone in a 'State Film Office' in

265

Stockholm came along and said 'Bergman's made a good documentary; he has an obvious talent for documentary, we've seen enough of his feature films, so he must stop making feature films and go on with documentaries'—I'd stop altogether!

JS: You see a lot of films. Do you look at documentaries, too? Is there any particular documentary film-maker who particularly interests you?

IB: Schoendorffer's *The Anderson Platoon* is a good example of a documentary film. It was good.

JS: You also watch TV a lot. You see the documentary programmes?

IB: Of course.

I made *The Rite*, and it went on TV. In some way I thought it a shame that people on Fårö should have to see *The Rite*. In front of these friends of mine it embarrassed me no little. Perhaps you don't see what I mean. It seemed silly, in some way. I said to myself 'Now they're sitting down in their cottages to see Bergman's film.' And of course they were dreadfully disappointed. Obviously. Afterwards, when I made the Fårö film, I had a thought. And that was: this must be a film people will like. I've dedicated the film to the people of Fårö, and it isn't just an empty phrase. I made it for them, so that they could make themselves heard. And to know that the film has had a good three million viewers is rather fun.

JS: It's not only about people and personal relations. It's also about a landscape, about people's feelings for their own origins, out there on the island. Why have you settled on Fårö?

IB: Originally it was a romantic idea—the sense of being on an island, of the sea. One of these stupid notions one gets if one has never lived by the sea. After all, I come from Dalarna. But over the years Fårö has come to be indispensable for me. Out there everything assumes its proper proportions. One lives in spontaneous natural contact with an element—the sea. So do the people there. So do I. Which gives one perspective on one's own idea of one's own importance. It's restful to have a clear and realistic idea of one's own importance, or lack of it.

If I suddenly let out a shriek, here in Stockholm, or come to the theatre in a bad temper, then it spreads all over the bloody house, and very likely I get the idea that there's something remarkable about me being in a bad temper. Or if I change women, and it's commented on in the press; or make a public statement, or a film, I can get the idea into my head it's all very important and remarkable in some way. But if I let out a yell on Fårö—which it would never occur to me to do—at most a crow might fly up! And that's its precise, proper degree of importance. And this gives me a feeling of security.

JS: You've intimated to us that you have settled accounts with your own earlier films; that you're acquiring another view of the film, a new sort of

Bergman on location for *Fårö-dokument*

orientation. Is that true? And if so, is it based on your experience while working on *Fårö Document*?

IB: No, it's based on a complete change in my way of life. This hysterical attitude to work—this business of always, at all costs, having to be busy doing something—all that has left me. *Now I only do what I like, and what I feel I want to.* Nothing more! To begin learning how to use my Nagra and Arriflex will be exciting—I've never had the time before. I've a notion I'll be able to go on with it. What will come of it I've no idea. We'll see.

The Rite: 'star line-up' with Ingrid Thulin, Anders Ek and Gunnar Björnstrand

Filmography

Hets—Frenzy, Torment (1944)

Production Company	Svensk Filmindustri
Director	Alf Sjöberg
Assistant Director	Ingmar Bergman
Script	Ingmar Bergman
Director of Photography	Martin Bodin
Editor	Oscar Rosander
Set Designer	Arne Åkermark
Music	Hilding Rosenberg

Stig Järrel (*Caligula*), Alf Kjellin (*Jan-Erik Widgren*), Mai Zetterling (*Bertha Olsson*), Olaf Winnerstrand (*school principal*), Gösta Cederlund (*Pippi*), Stig Olin (*Sandman*), Jan Molander (*Pettersson*), Olav Riego (*Widgren*), Märta Arbiin (*Mrs Widgren*), Hugo Björne (*doctor*), Gunnar Björnstrand (*teacher*), Curt Edgard, Anders Nyström, Birger Malmsten.
Swedish première: 2 October 1944. Running time: 101 min.

Kris—Crisis (1945)

Production Company	Svensk Filmindustri
Production Manager	Lars-Eric Kjellgren
Director	Ingmar Bergman
Script	Ingmar Bergman. From the play '*Moderdyret*' by Leck Fisher

Director of Photography   Gösta Roosling
Editor   Oscar Rosander
Set Designer   Arne Åkermark
Music   Erland von Koch

Dagny Lind (*Ingeborg*), Inga Landgré (*Nelly*), Stig Olin (*Jack*), Marianne Löfgren (*Jenny*), Allan Bohlin (*Ulf*), Ernst Eklund (*Uncle Edvard*), Signe Wirff (*Aunt Jessie*), Svea Holst (*Malin*), Arne Lindblad (*the mayor*), Hjördis Pettersson. Swedish première: 25 February 1945. Running time: 93 min.

Det Regnar På Vår Kärlek—It Rains on Our Love (1946)

Production Company   Sveriges Folkbiografer
Producer   Lorens Marmstedt
Director   Ingmar Bergman
Script   Ingmar Bergman, Herbert Grevenius. From the
                        play '*Bra mennesker*' by Oskar Braathen
Photography   Hilding Bladh, Göran Strindberg
Editor   Tage Holmberg
Set Designer   P. A. Lundgren
Music   Erland von Koch

Barbro Kollberg (*Maggi*), Birger Malmsten (*David*), Gösta Cederlund (*man with umbrella*), Ludde Gentzel (*Håkansson*), Douglas Håge (*Andersson*), Hjördis Pettersson (*Mrs Andersson*), Julia Caesar (*Hanna Ledin*), Gunnar Björnstrand (*Purman*), Magnus Kesster (*bicycle mechanic*), Sif Ruud (*his wife*), Åke Fridell (*the pastor*), Bengt-Åke Bengtsson (*the Prosecutor*), Erik Rosén (*the Judge*), Sture Ericsson (*Kängsnöret*), Ulf Johansson (*Stålvispen*). Swedish première: 9 November 1946. Running time: 95 min.

Kvinna Utan Ansikte—Woman Without a Face (1947)

Production Company   Svensk Filmindustri
Director   Gustaf Molander
Script   Ingmar Bergman
Director of Photography   Åke Dahlqvist
Editor   Oscar Rosander
Set Designer   Arne Åkermark
Music   Erik Nordgren

Alf Kjellin (*Martin Grandé*), Gunn Wållgren (*Rut Köhler*), Anita Björk (*Frida Grandé*), Stig Olin (*Ragnar Ekberg*), Olof Winnerstrand (*Director Grandé*), Marianne Löfgren (*Charlotte*), Georg Funkquist (*Victor*), Åke Grönberg (*Sam Svensson*), Linnea Hillberg (*Mrs Grandé*), Calle Reinholdz, Sif Ruud, Ella Lindblom, Artur Rolén, Björn Montin. Swedish première: 16 September 1947. Running time: 100 min.

Skepp till Indialand—A Ship to India, The Land of Desire (1947)

Production Company	Sveriges Folkbiografer
Producer	Lorens Marmstedt
Director	Ingmar Bergman
Script	Ingmar Bergman. From the play '*Skepp till Indialand*' by Martin Söderhjelm
Director of Photography	Göran Strindberg
Editor	Tage Holmberg
Set Designer	P. A. Lundgren
Music	Erland von Koch

Holger Löwenadler (*Captain Alexander Blom*), Birger Malmsten (*Johannes Blom*), Gertrud Fridh (*Sally*), Anna Lindahl (*Alice Blom*), Lasse Krantz (*Hans*), Jan Molander (*Bertil*), Erik Hell (*Pekka, a member of the crew*), Naemi Briese (*Selma*), Hjördis Pettersson (*Sofie*), Åke Fridell (*manager of music hall*), Peter Lindgren (*foreign crewman*).
Swedish première: 22 September 1947. Running time: 102 min.

Musik i Mörker—Night is My Future, Music in Darkness (1947)

Production Company	Terrafilm
Producer	Lorens Marmstedt
Production Manager	Allan Ekelund
Director	Ingmar Bergman
Script	Dagmar Edqvist. From her own novel.
Director of Photography	Göran Strindberg
Editor	Lennart Wallén
Set Designer	P. A. Lundgren
Music	Erland von Koch

Mai Zetterling (*Ingrid Olofsdotter*), Birger Malmsten (*Bengt Vildeke*), Bengt Eklund (*Ebbe*), Olof Winnerstrand (*the Pastor*), Naima Wifstrand (*Mrs Schroder*), Bibi Skoglund (*Agneta*), Hilda Bergstrom (*Louisa*), Douglas Hage (*Kruge*), Gunnar Björnstrand (*Klaesson*), Åke Claesson, John Elfstrom, Sven Lindberg, Bengt Logardt, Marianne Gyllenhammar, Barbro Flodquist, Ulle and Rune Andreasson.
Swedish première: 17 January 1948. Running time: 85 min.

Hamnstad—Port of Call (1948)

Production Company	Svensk Filmindustri
Director	Ingmar Bergman
Script	Ingmar Bergman. From a story by Olle Länsberg
Director of Photography	Gunnar Fischer
Editor	Oscar Rosander
Set Designer	Nils Svenwall
Music	Erland von Koch

Nine-Christine Jönsson (*Berit*), Bengt Eklund (*Gösta*), Mimi Nelson (*Gertrud*), Berta Hall (*Berit's mother*), Birgitta Valberg (*Welfare worker*), Erik Hell (*Berit's father*), Nils Dahlgren (*Gertrud's father*), Stig Olin (*Thomas*), Sif Ruud (*Mrs Krona*), Hans Strååt (*Mr Vilander*), Harry Ahlin (*Skåningen*), Nils Hallberg (*Gustav*), Sven-Eric Gamble.
Swedish première: 18 October 1948. Running time: 99 min.

Eva (1948)
Production Company	Svensk Filmindustri
Director	Gustaf Molander
Script	Gustaf Molander, Ingmar Bergman. From a synopsis by Bergman
Director of Photography	Åke Dahlqvist
Editor	Oscar Rosander
Set Designer	Nils Svenwall
Music	Erik Nordgren

Birger Malmsten (*Bo*), Eva Stiberg (*Eva*), Eva Dahlbeck (*Susanne*), Stig Olin (*Göran*), Åke Claesson (*Fredriksson*), Wanda Rothgardt (*Mrs Fredriksson*), Inga Landgré (*Frida*), Hilda Borgström (*Maria*), Axel Hogel (*fisherman*), Lasse Sarri (*Bo at twelve*).
Swedish première: 26 December 1948. Running time: 97 min.

Fängelse—Prison, The Devil's Wanton (1948/49)
Production Company	Terrafilm
Producer	Lorens Marmstedt
Director	Ingmar Bergman
Director of Photography	Göran Strindberg
Editor	Lennart Wallén
Set Designer	P. A. Lundgren

Doris Svedlund (*Birgitta Carolina*), Birger Malmsten (*Tomas*), Eva Henning (*Sofi*), Hasse Ekman (*Martin Grandé, film director*), Stig Olin (*Peter*), Irma Christenson (*Linnea*), Anders Henrikson (*Paul*), Marianne Löfgren (*Mrs Bohlin*), Carl-Henrik Fant (*Arne*), Inger Juel (*Greta*), Curt Masreliez (*Alf*), Åke Fridell (*Magnus*), Bibi Lindquist (*Anna*), Arne Ragneborn (*her lover*).
Swedish première: 19 March 1949. Running time: 80 min.

Törst—Thirst, Three Strange Loves (1949)
Production Company	Svensk Filmindustri
Production Manager	Helge Hagerman
Director	Ingmar Bergman
Script	Herbert Grevenius. From the short story *Törst* by Birgit Tengroth
Director of Photography	Gunnar Fischer

Editor	Oscar Rosander
Set Designer	Nils Svenwall
Music	Erik Nordgren
Choreography	Ellen Bergman

Eva Henning (*Rut*), Birger Malmsten (*Bertil*), Birgit Tengroth (*Viola*), Hasse Ekman (*Doctor Rosengren*), Mimi Nelson (*Valborg*), Bengt Eklund (*Raoul*), Gaby Stenberg (*Astrid, his wife*), Naima Wifstrand (*Miss Henriksson, dancing teacher*), Sven-Erik Gamble (*the workman*), Gunnar Nielsen (*male nurse*), Estrid Hesse (*patient*), Helge Hagerman (*Swedish priest*), Calle Flygare (*Danish priest*), Else-Merete Heiberg (*woman on train*), Monika Weinzierl (*her little girl*), Herman Greid (*guard*), a glimpse of Bergman himself, just before the scene with the priests.
Swedish première: 17 October 1949. Running time: 88 min.

Till Glädje—To Joy (1949)

Production Company	Svensk Filmindustri
Production Manager	Allan Ekelund
Director	Ingmar Bergman
Script	Ingmar Bergman
Director of Photography	Gunnar Fischer
Editor	Oscar Rosander
Set Designer	Nils Svenwall
Music	From Mozart, Mendelssohn, Smetana, Beethoven (Egmont overture, First and Ninth Symphonies)

Maj-Britt Nilsson (*Martha*), Stig Olin (*Stig Eriksson*), Victor Sjöström (*Sönderby*), Birger Malmsten (*Marcel*), John Ekman (*Mikael Bro*), Margit Carlquist (*Nelly, his wife*), Sif Ruud (*Stina*), Rune Stylander (*Persson*), Erland Josephson (*Bertil*), Georg Skarstedt (*Anker*), Berit Holmstrom (*Lisa*), Björn Montin (*Lasse*), Carin Swenson, Svea Holm (*two women*), Svea Holst, Agda Helin (*nurses*), Maud Hyttenberg (*salesgirl*).
Swedish première: 20 February 1950. Running time: 98 min.

Medan Standen Sover—While the City Sleeps (1950)

Production Company	Svensk Filmindustri
Director	Lars-Eric Kjellgren
Script	Lars-Eric Kjellgren. From a story by P. A. Fogelstrom based on a synopsis by Ingmar Bergman
Director of Photography	Martin Bodin
Editor	Oscar Rosander
Set Designer	Nils Svenwall

Sven-Erik Gamble (*Jompa*), Inga Landgré (*Iris*), Adolf Jahr (*Iris's father*), Elof Ahrle (*Basen*), Ulf Palme (*Kalle Lund*), Hilding Gavle (*Hälaren*), John Elfström (*Jompa's father*), Barbro Hiort af Ornäs (*Rut*), Carl Strom (*Portis*), Märta Dorff (*Iris's*

mother), Ilse-Nore Tromm, Arne Ragneborn, Hans Sundberg, Lennart Lundh, Hans Dalberg, Ulla Smidje, Mona Geijer-Falkner, Harriet Andersson.
Swedish première: 8 September 1950. Running time: 101 min.

Sånt Händer Inte Här—This Can't Happen Here, High Tension (1950)

Production Company	Svensk Filmindustri
Production Manager	Helge Hagerman
Director	Ingmar Bergman
Script	Herbert Grevenius
Director of Photography	Gunnar Fischer
Editor	Lennart Wallén
Set Designer	Nils Svenwall
Music	Erik Nordgren

Signe Hasso (*Vera*), Alf Kjellin (*Almkvist*), Ulf Palme (*Atkä Natas*), Gösta Cederlund (*the doctor*), Yngve Nordvall (*Lindell*), Stig Olin (*the young man*), Ragnar Klange (*Filip Rundblom*), Hanno Kompus (*the pastor*), Sylvia Tael (*Vanja*), Els Vaarman (*woman in the cinema*), Edmar Kuus (*Leino*), Rudolf Lipp ('*The Shadow*').
Swedish première: 23 October 1950. Running time: 84 min.

Sommarlek—Summer Interlude, Illicit Interlude (1950)

Production Company	Svensk Filmindustri
Production Manager	Allan Ekelund
Director	Ingmar Bergman
Script	Ingmar Bergman, Herbert Grevenius. From a story by Bergman
Director of Photography	Gunnar Fischer
Editor	Oscar Rosander
Set Designer	Nils Svenwall
Music	Erik Nordgren

Maj-Britt Nilsson (*Marie*), Birger Malmsten (*Henrik*), Alf Kjellin (*David*), Georg Funkquist (*Uncle Erland*), Renée Björling (*Aunt Elisabeth*), Mimi Pollak (*Henrik's aunt*), Annalisa Ericson (*Kaj, ballerina*), Stig Olin (*ballet master*), Gunnar Olsson (*pastor*), John Botvid (*Karl*), Douglas Hage (*Nisse*), Julia Caesar (*Maja, dresser*), Carl Ström (*Sandell*), Torsten Lilliecrona (*lighting man*), Marianne Schuler (*Kerstin*), Ernst Brunman (*Captain*), Olav Riego (*doctor*), Fylgia Zadig (*nurse*), Sten Mattsson, Carl Axel Elfving, Gösta Ström and the ballet of the Royal Opera, Stockholm.
Swedish première: 1 October 1951. Running time: 96 min.

Frånskild—Divorced (1951)

Production Company	Svensk Filmindustri
Director	Gustaf Molander
Script	Ingmar Bergman, Herbert Grevenius. From a synopsis by Bergman
Director of Photography	Åke Dahlqvist

Editor	Oscar Rosander
Set Designer	Nils Svenwall
Music	Erik Nordgren

Inga Tidblad (*Gertrud Holmgren*), Alf Kjellin (*Dr Bertil Nordelius*), Doris Svedlund (*Marianne Berg*), Hjördis Pettersson (*Mrs Nordelius*), Håkan Westergren (*Manager P. A. Beckman*), Irma Christensen (*Dr Cecilia Lindeman*), Holger Löwenadler (*Engineer Tore Holmgren*), Marianne Löfgren (*Ingeborg*), Stig Olin (*Hans*), Elsa Prawitz, Birgitta Valberg, Sif Ruud, Carl Ström, Ingrid Borthen, Yvonne Lombard, Einar Axelsson, Ragnar Arvedson, Rune Halvarson, Rudolf Wenbladh, Guje Lagerwall.
Swedish première: 26 December 1951. Running time: 103 min.

Kvinnors Vantan—Waiting Women, Secrets of Women (1952)

Production Company	Svensk Filmindustri
Director	Ingmar Bergman
Script	Ingmar Bergman
Director of Photography	Gunnar Fischer
Editor	Oscar Rosander
Set Designer	Nils Svenwall
Music	Erik Nordgren

Anita Björk (*Rakel*), Maj-Britt Nilsson (*Marta*), Eva Dahlbeck (*Karin*), Gunnar Björnstrand (*Fredrik Lobelius*), Birger Malmsten (*Martin Lobelius*), Jarl Kulle (*Kaj*), Karl-Arne Holmsten (*Eugen Lobelius*), Gerd Andersson (*Maj*), Björn Bjelvenstam (*Henrik*), Aino Taube (*Anita*), Håkan Westergren (*Paul*), Marta Arbiin, Kjell Nordenskold, Carl Ström; brief appearance by Bergman, who looks interestedly at Maj-Britt Nilsson during the middle episode.
Swedish première: 3 November 1952. Running time: 107 min.

Sommaren Med Monika—Summer With Monika, Monika (1952)

Production Company	Svensk Filmindustri
Production Manager	Allan Ekelund
Director	Ingmar Bergman
Script	Ingmar Bergman, P. A. Fogelström. From a novel by Fogelström
Director of Photography	Gunnar Fischer
Editors	Tage Holmberg, Gösta Lewin
Set Designers	P. A. Lundgren, Nils Svenwall
Music	Erik Nordgren; waltz 'Karlekens Hamn' by Filip Olsson, played by Orno

Harriet Andersson (*Monika*), Lars Ekborg (*Harry*), John Harryson (*Lelle*), Georg Skarstedt (*Harry's father*), Dagmar Ebbeson (*Harry's aunt*), Naemi Briese (*Monika's mother*), Åke Fridell (*Monika's father*); *In glass shop:* Gösta Eriksson (*manager*), Gösta Gustafsson, Sigge Furst, Gösta Prüzelius (*employees*); *In wholesale green-grocery:* Arthur Fischer (*chief*), Torsten Lilliecrona (*driver*), Bengt Eklund (*first*

man), Gustaf Färingborg (*second man*); Ivar Wahlgren (*villager*), Renée Björling (*his wife*), Catrin Westerlund (*his daughter*), Harry Ahlin (*other villager*), Wiktor Andersson-Kulorten and Birger Sahlberg (*two men in street*), Hanny Schedin (*Mrs Bohman*), Åke Grönberg (*foreman*), Magnus Kessler and Carl-Axel Elfving (*workmen*), Anders Andglius, Gordon Löwenadler, Bengt Brunskog.
Swedish première: 9 February 1953. Running time: 96 min.

Gycklarnas Afton—Sawdust and Tinsel, The Naked Night (1953)

Production Company	Sandrews
Producer	Rune Waldekranz
Director	Ingmar Bergman
Script	Ingmar Bergman
Photography	Hilding Bladh, Göran Strindberg, Sven Nykvist
Editor	Carl-Olov Skeppstedt
Set Designer	Bibi Lindström
Music	Karl-Birger Blomdahl
Costumes	Mago

Harriet Andersson (*Anne*), Åke Grönberg (*Albert Johansson*), Hasse Ekman (*Frans*), Anders Ek (*Frost*), Gudrun Brost (*Alma*), Annika Tretow (*Agda, Albert's wife*), Gunnar Björnstrand (*Mr Sjuberg*), Erik Strandmark (*Jens*), Kiki (*the dwarf*), Åke Fridell (*the officer*), Majken Torkeli (*Mrs Ekberg*), Vanjek Hedberg (*Ekberg's son*), Curt Löwgren (*Blom*).
Swedish première: 14 September 1953. Running time: 92 min.

En Lektion i Kärlek—A Lesson in Love (1954)

Production Company	Svensk Filmindustri
Production Manager	Allan Ekelund
Director	Ingmar Bergman
Director of Photography	Martin Bodin
Editor	Oscar Rosander
Set Designer	P. A. Lundgren
Music	Dag Wirén

Eva Dahlbeck (*Marianne Erneman*), Gunnar Björnstrand (*Dr David Erneman*), Yvonne Lombard (*Suzanne*), Harriet Andersson (*Nix*), Åke Grönberg (*Carl Adam*), Olof Winnerstrand (*Professor Henrik Erneman*), Renée Björling (*Svea Erneman*), Birgitte Reimar (*Lise*), John Elfström (*Sam*), Dagmar Ebbeson (*nurse*), Helge Hagerman (*travelling salesman*), Sigge Furst (*priest*), Gösta Prüzelius (*train guard*), Carl Ström (*Uncle Axel*), Arne Lindblad (*hotel manager*), Torsten Lilliecrona (*porter*), Yvonne Brosset (*ballerina*).
Swedish première: 4 October 1954. Running time: 95 min.

Kvinnodröm—Journey Into Autumn, Dreams (1955)

Production Company	Sandrews
Production Manager	Rune Waldekranz
Director	Ingmar Bergman
Script	Ingmar Bergman
Director of Photography	Hilding Bladh
Editor	Carl-Olov Skeppstedt
Set Designer	Gittan Gustafsson

Eva Dahlbeck (*Susanne*), Harriet Andersson (*Doris*), Gunnar Björnstrand (*consul, Sonderby*), Ulf Palme (*Henrik Lobelius*), Inga Landgré (*Mrs Lobelius*), Sven Lindberg (*Palle*), Naima Wifstrand (*Mrs Aren*), Bengt-Åke Bengtsson (*director, Magnus*), Git Gay (*lady in the studio*), Ludde Gentzel (*photographer, Sundstrom*), Kerstin Hedeby (*Marianne*), Jessie Flaws, Marianne Nielsen, Siv Ericks, Bengt Schött, Axel Düberg; Bergman glimpsed in a train corridor.
Swedish première: 22 August 1955. Running time: 86 min.

Sommarnattens Leende—Smiles of a Summer Night (1955)

Production Company	Svensk Filmindustri
Production Manager	Allan Ekelund
Director	Ingmar Bergman
Assistant Director	Lennart Olsson
Script	Ingmar Bergman
Director of Photography	Gunnar Fischer
Editor	Oscar Rosander
Set Designer	P. A. Lundgren
Music	Erik Nordgren
Costumes	Mago

Eva Dahlbeck (*Desirée Armfeldt*), Ulla Jacobsson (*Anne Egerman*), Harriet Andersson (*Petra*), Margit Carlqvist (*Charlotte Malcolm*), Gunnar Björnstrand (*Fredrik Egerman*), Jarl Kulle (*Count Carl-Magnus Malcolm*), Åke Fridell (*Frid*), Björn Bjelvenstam (*Henrik Egerman*), Naima Wifstrand (*Madame Armfeldt*), Jullan Kindahl (*the cook*), Gull Natorp (*Mall, Desirée's maid*), Birgitta Valberg, Bibi Andersson (*actresses*), Anders Wulff (*Desirée's son*), Gunnar Nielsen (*Niklas*), Gösta Prüzelius, Svea Holst, Hans Strååt, Lisa Lundholm, Sigge Fürst, Lena Söderblom, Mona Malm, Joseph Norrman, John Melin, Sten Gester.
Swedish première: 26 December 1955. Running time: 108 min. (104 min., G.B.)

Sista Paret Ut—The Last Couple Out (1956)

Production Company	Svensk Filmindustri
Director	Alf Sjöberg
Script	Ingmar Bergman, Alf Sjöberg. From a story by Bergman
Director of Photography	Martin Bodin

Editor   Oscar Rosander
Set Designer   Harald Garmland
Music   Erik Nordgren, Charles Redland, Bengt
                          Hallberg

Olof Widgren (*Lawyer Hans Dahlin*), Björn Bjelvenstam (*Bo Dahlin*), Johnny
Johansson (*Sven Dahlin at eight*), Märta Arbiin (*Grandmother*), Jullan Kindahl
(*Alma, Dahlins' maid*), Jarl Kulle (*Dr Farell*), Nancy Dalunde (*Mrs Farell*), Bibi
Andersson (*Anita*), Aino Taube (*Kerstin's mother*), Jan-Olof Strandberg (*Claes
Berg*), Hugo Björne (*Lecturer*), Göran Lundqvist (*small boy*).
Swedish première: 12 November 1956. Running time: 104 min.

Det Sjunde Inseglet—The Seventh Seal (1956)
Production Company   Svensk Filmindustri
Production Manager   Allan Ekelund
Director   Ingmar Bergman
Assistant Director   Lennart Olsson
Script   Ingmar Bergman. From his play *Trämålning*
Director of Photography   Gunnar Fischer
Editor   Lennart Wallén
Set Designer   P. A. Lundgren
Music   Erik Nordgren
Choreography   Else Fischer
Costumes   Manne Lindholm

Max von Sydow (*Knight*), Gunnar Björnstrand (*Squire*), Bengt Ekerot (*Death*), Nils
Poppe (*Jof, strolling player*), Bibi Andersson (*Mia, his wife*), Åke Fridell (*Blacksmith,
Plog*), Inga Gill (*Lisa, Plog's wife*), Maud Hansson (*witch*), Inga Landgré (*Knight's
wife*), Gunnel Lindblom (*the girl*), Bertil Anderberg (*Raval*), Anders Ek (*the monk*),
Gunnar Olsson (*painter*), Erik Strandmark (*Skat*), Bengt-Åke Bengtsson (*merchant*),
Ulf Johansson (*leader of the soldiers*), Lars Lind (*the young monk*), Gudrun Brost
(*woman in the tavern*).
Swedish première: 16 February 1957. Running time: 95 min.

Smultronstället—Wild Strawberries (1957)
Production Company   Svensk Filmindustri
Production Manager   Allan Ekelund
Director   Ingmar Bergman
Assistant Director   Gösta Ekman
Script   Ingmar Bergman
Director of Photography   Gunnar Fischer
Editor   Oscar Rosander
Set Designer   Gittan Gustafsson
Costumes   Millie Strom

Victor Sjöström (*Professor Isak Borg*), Bibi Andersson (*Sara*), Ingrid Thulin
(*Marianne*), Gunnar Björnstrand (*Evald*), Folke Sundquist (*Anders*), Björn
Bjelvenstam (*Viktor*), Naima Wifstrand (*Isak's mother*), Jullan Kindahl (*Agda,*

housekeeper), Gunnar Sjöberg (*Alman, an engineer*), Gunnel Broström (*Mrs Alman*), Gertrud Fridh (*Isak's wife*), Åke Fridell (*her lover*), Max von Sydow (*Åkerman*), Sif Ruud (*Aunt*), Yngve Nordwall (*Uncle Aron*), Per Sjöstrand (*Sigfrid*), Gio Petré (*Sigbritt*), Gunnel Lindblom (*Charlotta*), Maud Hansson (*Angelica*), Anne-Marie Wiman (*Mrs Åkerman*), Eva Norée (*Anna*), Lena Bergman, Monica Ehrling (*twins*), Per Skogsberg (*Hagbart*), Göran Lundquist (*Benjamin*), Prof. Sigge Wulff (*Rector, Lund University*), Gunnar Olsson (*Bishop*), Josef Norman (*Professor Tiger*).
Swedish première: 26 December 1957. Running time: 90 min.

Nara Livet—So Close to Life, The Brink of Life (1957)

Production Company	Nordisk Tonefilm
Director	Ingmar Bergman
Script	Ingmar Bergman, Ulla Isaksson. From the short story 'Det vanliga vardiga' in her book *Dodens faster*
Director of Photography	Max Wilén
Editor	Carl-Olov Skeppstedt
Set Designer	Bibi Lindström
Medical Adviser	Dr Lars Engström

Eva Dahlbeck (*Stina Andersson*), Ingrid Thulin (*Cecilia Ellius*), Bibi Andersson (*Hjordis*), Barbro Hiort af Ornäs (*Sister Brita*), Erland Josephson (*Anders Ellius*), Max von Sydow (*Harry Andersson*), Gunnar Sjöberg (*Dr Nordlander*), Anne-Marie Gyllenspetz (*Welfare worker*), Sissie Kaiser (*Sister Marit*), Margareta Krook (*Dr Larsson*), Lars Lind (*Dr Thylenius*), Monica Ekberg (*Hjordis' friend*), Gun Jönsson (*night nurse*), Inga Gill (*woman*), Gunnar Neilsen (*a doctor*), Maud Elfsiö, Kristina Adolphson.
Swedish première: 31 March 1958. Running time: 84 min.

Ansiktet—The Face, The Magician (1958)

Production Company	Svensk Filmindustri
Production Manager	Allan Ekelund
Director	Ingmar Bergman
Assistant Director	Gösta Ekman
Script	Ingmar Bergman
Director of Photography	Gunnar Fischer
Editor	Oscar Rosander
Set Designer	P. A. Lundgren
Music	Erik Nordgren
Costumes	Manne Lindholm, Greta Johansson

Max von Sydow (*Albert Emanuel Vogler, mesmerist*), Ingrid Thulin (*Mander Vogler*), Åke Fridell (*Tubal, Vogler's assistant*), Naima Wifstrand (*Vogler's grandmother, a sorceress*), Gunnar Björnstrand (*Dr Vergérus, medical officer*), Bengt Ekerot (*Spegel, an actor*), Bibi Andersson (*Sara Lindqvist*), Gertrud Fridh (*Ottilia Egerman*), Lars Ekborg (*Simson, Vogler's coachman*), Toivo Pawlo (*Starbeck*), Ulla Sjöblom (*Henrietta*), Axel Duberg (*Rustan, butler*), Birgitta Pettersson (*Sanna, maid*).
Swedish première: 26 December 1958. Running time: 100 min.

Jungfrukällan—The Virgin Spring (1959)

Production Company	Svensk Filmindustri
Production Manager	Allan Ekelund
Director	Ingmar Bergman
Assistant Director	Lenn Hjortzberg
Script	Ulla Isaksson. From 14th-century ballad *Tores dotter i Vänge*
Director of Photography	Sven Nykvist
Editor	Oscar Rosander
Set Designer	P. A. Lundgren
Music	Erik Nordgren

Max von Sydow (*Herr Töre*), Birgitta Valberg (*Fru Märeta*), Gunnel Lindblom (*Ingeri*), Birgitta Pettersson (*Karin*), Axel Düberg (*thin herdsman*), Tor Isedal (*mute herdsman*), Allan Edwall (*beggar*), Ove Porath (*boy*), Axel Slangus (*old man*), Gudrun Brost (*Frida*), Oscar Ljung (*Simon*), Tor Borong, Leif Forstenberg (*farm labourers*).
Swedish première: 8 February 1960. Running time: 88 min.

Djävulens Öga—The Devil's Eye (1960)

Production Company	Svensk Filmindustri
Production Manager	Allan Ekelund
Director	Ingmar Bergman
Assistant Director	Lenn Hjortzberg, Ingmar Bergman. Freely adapted from Danish radio play
Director of Photography	Gunnar Fischer
Editor	Oscar Rosander
Set Designer	P. A. Lundgren
Music	From Scarlatti

Jarl Kulle (*Don Juan*), Bibi Andersson (*Britt-Marie*), Axel Düberg (*her fiancé*), Nils Poppe (*the pastor, her father*), Gertrud Fridh (*Renata, the pastor's wife*), Sture Lagerwall (*Pablo*), Stig Järrel (*Satan*), Gunnar Björnstrand (*the actor*), Georg Funkquist (*Count Armand de Rochefoucauld*), Gunnar Sjöberg (*Marquis Guiseppe de Maccopazza*), Torsten Winge (*old man*), Allan Edwall, Kristina Adolphson, Ragnar Arvedson, Börje Lundh, Lenn Hjortzberg.
Swedish première: 17 October 1960. Running time: 86 min.

Såsom i en Spegel—Through a Glass Darkly (1961)

Production Company	Svensk Filmindustri
Production Manager	Allan Ekelund
Director	Ingmar Bergman
Assistant Director	Lenn Hjortzberg
Script	Ingmar Bergman
Director of Photography	Sven Nykvist

280

Editor   Ulla Ryghe
Set Designer   P. A. Lundgren
Music   From J. S. Bach, Suite No. 2, D minor, for
                          'cello

Harriet Andersson (*Karin*), Max von Sydow (*Martin, her husband*), Gunnar Björnstrand (*her father*), Lars Passgård (*Minus, her brother*).
Swedish première: 16 October 1961. Running time: 89 min.

Lustgården—The Pleasure Garden (1961)
Production Company   Svensk Filmindustri
Director   Alf Kjellin
Script   Buntel Eriksson (joint pseudonym of Ingmar
                          Bergman and Erland Josephson)
Director of Photography   Gunnar Fischer (Eastmancolor)
Editor   Ulla Ryghe
Set Designer   P. A. Lundgren
Music   Erik Nordgren

Gunnar Björnstrand (*David*), Sickan Carlsson (*Fanny*), Bibi Andersson (*Anna*), Per Myrberg (*a young pastor*), Kristina Adolphson (*Astrid*), Stig Järrel (*Lundberg*), Gösta Cederlund, Torsten Winge, Hjördis Pettersson.
Swedish première: 26 December 1961. Running time: 93 min.

Nattvardsgästerna—Winter Light (1962)
Production Company   Svensk Filmindustri
Production Manager   Allan Ekelund
Director   Ingmar Bergman
Assistant Director   Lenn Hjortzberg
Script   Ingmar Bergman
Director of Photography   Sven Nykvist
Editor   Ulla Ryghe
Set Designer   P. A. Lundgren

Gunnar Björnstrand (*Thomas Ericsson*), Ingrid Thulin (*Märta Lundberg*), Max von Sydow (*Jonas Persson*), Gunnel Lindblom (*Karin Persson*), Allan Edwall (*Algot Frövik*), Olof Thunberg (*Fredrik Blom*), Elsa Ebbeson (*old woman*), Kolbjörn Knudsen (*Sixten Aronsson*).
Swedish première: 11 December 1962. Running time: 80 min.

Tystnaden—The Silence (1963)
Production Company   Svensk Filmindustri
Producer   Allan Ekelund
Director   Ingmar Bergman
Assistant Directors   Lars-Erik Liedholm, Lenn Hjortzberg

281

Script	Ingmar Bergman
Director of Photography	Sven Nykvist
Editor	Ulla Ryghe
Set Designer	P. A. Lundgren
Music	From J. S. Bach, the Goldberg Variations
Costumes	Mark Vos-Lundh

Ingrid Thulin (*Ester*), Gunnel Lindblom (*Anna*), Jörgen Lindström (*Johan*), Håkan Jahnberg (*maître d'hôtel*), Birger Malmsten (*barman*), the Eduardini (*seven dwarfs*), Eduardo Gutierrez (*manager of the dwarfs*), Lissi Alandh (*woman in cinema*), Leif Forstenberg (*man in cinema*), Birger Lensander (*cinema doorman*), Nils Waldt (*cinema cashier*), Eskil Kalling, K. A. Bergman, Olof Widgren, Kristina Olansson (*double* for Gunnel Lindblom).
Swedish première: 23 September 1963. Running time: 95 min.

För Att Inte Tala Om Alla Dessa Kvinnor—Now About These Women (1964)

Production Company	Svensk Filmindustri
Production Manager	Allan Ekelund
Director	Ingmar Bergman
Script	Ingmar Bergman, Erland Josephsson under pseudonym, Buntel Eriksson
Director of Photography	Sven Nykvist (Eastmancolor)
Editor	Ulla Ryghe
Set Designer	P. A. Lundgren
Music	Erik Nordgren

Jarl Kulle (*Cornelius*), Eva Dahlbeck (*Adelaide*), Bibi Andersson (*Humlan—Bumble Bee*), Harriet Andersson (*Isolde*), Gertrud Fridh (*Traviata*), Mona Malm (*Cecilia*), Barbro Hiort af Ornäs (*Beatrice*), Karin Kavli (*Mme Tussaud*), Georg Funkquist (*Tristan*), Allan Edwall (*Jillker*), Gösta Prüzelius, Jan-Olof Strandberg, Göran Graffman, Jan Blomberg, Axel Düberg, Ulf Johansson, Lars-Erik Liedholm, Lars-Owe Carlberg, Carl Billquist, Yvonne Igell, Doris Funcke.
Swedish première: 15 June 1964. Running time: 80 min.

Persona (1966)

Production Company	Svensk Filmindustri
Production Manager	Lars-Owe Carlberg
Director	Ingmar Bergman
Assistant Director	Lenn Hjortzberg
Script	Ingmar Bergman
Director of Photography	Sven Nykvist
Editor	Ulla Ryghe
Set Designer	Bibi Lindström
Music	Lars-Johan Werle
Costumes	Mago

Bibi Andersson (*Alma*), Liv Ullmann (*Elisabeth Vogler*), Margaretha Krook (*the

doctor), Gunnar Björnstrand (*Herr Vogler*), Jörgen Lindström (*the boy*).
Swedish première: 18 October 1966. Running time: 84 min.

Stimulantia (1967)
Production Company   Svensk Filmindustri

Episode: *Daniel* (1965/66) directed and photographed by Ingmar Bergman, with
music played by Käbi Bergman. (Swedish première: 28 March 1967.)
Other episodes directed by Hans Abramson, Lars Gorling, Arne Arnbom, Jörn
Donner, Tage Danielsson and Hans Alfredson, Gustaf Molander, Vilgot Sjöman.

Vargtimmen—Hour of the Wolf (1966)
Production Company   Svensk Filmindustri
Production Manager   Lars-Owe Carlberg
Director   Ingmar Bergman
Assistant Director   Lenn Hjortzberg
Director of Photography   Sven Nykvist
Editor   Ulla Ryghe
Set Designer   Marik Vos-Lundh
Music   Lars-Johan Werle
Costumes   Mago
Special Effects   Evald Anderson

Liv Ullmann (*Alma*), Max von Sydow (*Johan Borg*), Erland Josephson (*Baron von
Merkens*), Gertrud Fridh (*Corinne von Merkens*), Bertil Anderberg (*Ernst von
Merkens*), Georg Rydeberg (*Archivist Lindhorst*), Ulf Johanson (*Curator
Heerbrand*), Naima Wifstrand (*old lady*), Ingrid Thulin (*Veronica Vogler*), Lenn
Hjortzberg (*Kreisler*), Agda Helin (*maid*), Mikael Rundqvist (*boy*), Mona Seilitz
(*woman in mortuary*), Folke Sundquist.
Swedish première: 19 February 1968. Running time: 89 min.

Skammen—Shame, The Shame (1967)
Production Company   Svensk Filmindustri
Production Manager   Lars-Owe Carlberg
Director   Ingmar Bergman
Script   Ingmar Bergman
Director of Photography   Sven Nykvist
Editor   Ulla Ryghe
Set Designer   P. A. Lundgren
Costumes   Mago
Military Adviser   Stig Lindberg

Liv Ullmann (*Eva Rosenberg*), Max von Sydow (*Jan Rosenberg*), Gunnar Björnstrand (*Colonel Jacobi*), Sigge Fürst (*Filip*), Barbro Hiort af Ornäs (*Mrs Jacobi*),

Håkan Jahnberg (*Lobelius*), Ingvar Kjellson (*Oswald*), Willy Peters (*elder officer*), Ulf Johansson (*the doctor*), Axel Dahlberg (*the pilot*), Borje Ahlstedt (*interviewer*). Simultaneous premières in Sorrento, Stockholm: 29 September 1968. Running time: 102 min.

Riten—The Rite (1968)

Production	Svensk Filmindustri/Sveriges TV/Cinematograph
Director	Ingmar Bergman
Assistant Director	Christer Dahl
Script	Ingmar Bergman
Director of Photography	Sven Nykvist
Editor	Siv Kanälv
Costumes	Mago
Sound	Olle Jacobssen

Ingrid Thulin (*Thea Winkelman*), Anders Ek (*Albert Emmanuel Sebastian Fischer*), Gunnar Björnstrand (*Hans Winkelman*), Erik Hell (*Judge Abramsson*). Swedish première: 25 March 1969 (TV). Running time: 74 min.

En Passion—A Passion, Passion of Anna (1969)

Production Company	Svensk Filmindustri/Cinematograph
Producer	Lars-Owe Carlberg
Production Manager	Brian Wikström
Director	Ingmar Bergman
Script	Ingmar Bergman
Director of Photography	Sven Nykvist (Eastmancolor)
Editor	Siv Kanälv
Script Supervisor	Katinka Farago
Production Designer	P. A. Lundgren
Sound	Lennart Engholm

Liv Ullmann (*Anna Fromm*), Bibi Andersson (*Eva Vergérus*), Max von Sydow (*Andreas Winkelman*), Erland Josephson (*Elis Vergérus*), Erik Hell (*Johan Andersson*), Sigge Fürst (*Verner*), Svea Holst (*Verner's wife*). Swedish première: 10 November 1969. Running time: 101 min.

Fårö-dokument (Faaroedokument)—Faro Document (1969)

Production Company	Cinematograph
Director and Reporter	Ingmar Bergman
Camera	Sven Nykvist

Swedish première: 1 January 1970. Running time: 78 min.

284

The Touch (1970)

Production	Co-production: Cinematograph/ABC Pictures Corporation (New York)
Production Manager	Lars-Owe Carlberg
Director	Ingmar Bergman
Director of Photography	Sven Nykvist
Editor	Siv Lundgren
Music	Jan Johansson
Sound	Lennart Engholm, Harry Engholm
Costumes	Mago

Bibi Andersson (*Karin, Mrs Andreas Vergerus*), Barbro Hiort af Ornäs (*her mother*), Åke Lindstrom (*a doctor*), Mimmi Wahlander (*a nurse*), Elsa Ebbeson (*the matron of the hospital*), Elliott Gould (*David Kovac*), Staffan Hallerstam (*Anders Vergerus*), Maria Nolgard (*Agnes Vergerus*), Max von Sydow (*Dr Andreas Vergerus*), Anna von Rosen and Karin Nilsson (*Vergerus family neighbours*), Erik Nyhlen (*an archaeologist*), Margaretha Bystrom (*Secretary to Dr Vergerus*), Alan Simon (*the museum curator*), Per Sjostrand (*another curator*), Aino Taube (*the woman at the staircase*), Ann-Christin Lobraten (*a museum worker*), Carol Zavis (*the BEA air hostess*), Dennis Gotobed (*the British immigration officer*), Bengt Ottekil (*a London bellboy*), Sheila Reid (*Sara, sister of David Kovac*).
Running time: 113 min.

Viskningar och Rop—Cries and Whispers (1972)

Production Company	Cinematograph. In co-operation with Svenska Filminstitutet
Producer	Ingmar Bergman
Production Manager	Lars-Owe Carlberg
Assistant Director	Marik Vos
Script	Ingmar Bergman
Director of Photography	Sven Nykvist (Eastmancolor)
Editor	Siv Lundgren
Music	Chopin's Mazurka in A minor (Op. 17, no. 4) played by Käbi Laretei; Saraband from Bach's Suite No. 5 in E minor played by Pierre Fournier
Sound	Owe Svensson

Harriet Andersson (*Agnes*), Ingrid Thulin (*Karin*), Liv Ullmann (*Maria*), Kari Sylwan (*Anna*), Erland Josephson (*Doctor*), Georg Arlin (*Fredrik*), Henning Moritzen (*Joakin*), Anders Ek (*Isak*), Inga Gill (*Aunt Olga*).
Swedish première: December 1972. Running time: 91 min.

Index